T0325372

Bodhichitta

Bodhichitta

PRACTICE FOR
A MEANINGFUL LIFE

Lama Zopa Rinpoche

Compiled and edited by Gordon McDougall

Wisdom Publications
199 Elm Street
Somerville, MA 02144 USA
wisdompubs.org

Library of Congress Cataloging-in-Publication Data
Names: Thubten Zopa, Rinpoche, 1945– author. | McDougall, Gordon, 1948– editor.
Title: Bodhichitta: practice for a meaningful life / Lama Zopa Rinpoche; edited by
    Gordon McDougall.
Description: Somerville, MA: Wisdom Publications, [2019] | Includes bibliographi-
    cal references and index. | Description based on print version record and CIP data
    provided by publisher; resource not viewed.
Identifiers: LCCN 2018039799 (print) | LCCN 2018055041 (ebook) | ISBN
    9781614296034 (e-book) | ISBN 9781614295792 (hard cover: alk. paper) | ISBN
    9781614296034 (ebook)
Subjects: LCSH: Bodhicitta (Buddhism)
Classification: LCC BQ4398.5 (ebook) | LCC BQ4398.5 .T57 2019 (print) | DDC
    294.3/422—dc23
LC record available at https://lccn.loc.gov/2018039799

ISBN 978-1-61429-579-2   ebook ISBN 978-1-61429-603-4

22 21 20 19 19
5 4 3 2 1

Cover photo by Ven. Roger Kunsang. Cover design by MTWDesign.
Interior design by Gopa & Ted2, Inc. Set in Adobe Garamond Pro 11.25/15.3.

Wisdom Publications' books are printed on acid-free paper and meet the guidelines
for permanence and durability of the Production Guidelines for Book Longevity of
the Council on Library Resources.

♻ This book was produced with environmental mindfulness. For more information,
please visit wisdompubs.org/wisdom-environment.

Printed in the United States of America.

CONTENTS

Appendices: Bodhichitta Meditations

EDITOR'S PREFACE

Tᴏ ᴄᴏᴍᴘʟᴇᴛᴇʟʏ and spontaneously wish to become omniscient in order to benefit every single living being—that is the mind of enlightenment, *bodhichitta*. When I first heard that definition I was awestruck and a little terrified. This is what I'm supposed to be aiming for! It is a very daunting task, but when led by Lama Zopa Rinpoche we are in the very best of hands. There are few who can bring the subject of bodhichitta to life like Rinpoche.

It has been my privilege to have worked on Rinpoche's teachings since 2008 when I started with the Lama Yeshe Wisdom Archive (LYWA), where I collected and edited Rinpoche's teachings on the topics of the *lamrim* (the graduated path to enlightenment). The archive is huge, with transcripts of almost all the teachings Rinpoche has given over the last forty years, and so the task was not a small one.

Anybody who has sat in front of Rinpoche will know that he rarely teaches in a straight line. A discourse on emptiness can morph into one on impermanence, suffering, karma, or any other subject, but underlying it all is bodhichitta. And so, to compile this book I have had to trawl the archive, finding and arranging the subjects within the teachings on bodhichitta in the order used by most of the great Tibetan masters, specifically Pabongka Dechen Nyingpo in *Liberation in the Palm of Your Hand* and Lama Tsongkhapa in *Lamrim Chenmo* (*The Great Treatise on the Stages of the Path to Enlightenment*).

In general, quotes in this book have been taken from published texts such as Shantideva's *A Guide to the Bodhisattva's Way of Life* and have been cited accordingly, but some are Rinpoche's own translations, which I've taken from the transcripts. As Rinpoche very often investigates the words within a verse thoroughly, what I have often ended up with is more a paraphrase.

I can't begin to thank all those who have worked so hard to make this book a reality. Not just Laura Cunningham at Wisdom, who has been a joy to work with, but the many volunteers and workers, those who painstakingly recorded Rinpoche, those who transcribed and checked the audio files, and the team at LYWA who have archived and managed the files and transcripts. Most of all, however, I want to thank Rinpoche for creating such a wealth of Dharma gold to inspire us. Sometimes when I'm trawling the archive looking for a particular topic and I work through many hundreds of files of Rinpoche's courses, I feel I'm swimming in an ocean of his holy words. It is a wonderful feeling.

I apologize for any errors found in this book; they are 100 percent mine. May this book inspire people to turn away from self-interest and develop the altruistic wish for enlightenment. May whatever merits gained from the creation of this book be dedicated to peace in this troubled world, to the long life, well-being, and fulfillment of the wishes of all our holy teachers, especially His Holiness the Dalai Lama and Lama Zopa Rinpoche, and to the flourishing of the Foundation for the Preservation of the Mahayana Tradition and of the Dharma throughout the world.

Gordon McDougall
Bath, England

INTRODUCTION

....

W<small>E ALWAYS WANT</small> the best. When we go shopping we always look for the best quality. We know the shops that sell the best fruit, the best pizza, the best ice cream; we make sure we buy food with the best flavor, the most delicious taste. If we know where to get the very best, we make sure we do. Those who accept inferior things do it because they either can't afford the best or don't know about it, not because they don't want the best there is.

In the same way, all sentient beings are looking for the best happiness. According to the Mahayana Buddhist tradition, the very best happiness is enlightenment, and the only way to attain enlightenment is through the incredible mind of bodhichitta. If people knew about this they would definitely try to achieve this mind, but because very few know about it, very few take the path to enlightenment.

Just as many of us can't buy top-quality things because of our limited budgets, sentient beings don't all embrace the Dharma because of their limited understanding. Everybody wants the best-quality happiness, but most people seem to think this is a mundane sense pleasure; they don't realize this is in fact a form of suffering. Similarly, nobody wants any suffering at all, but most people see suffering as only being gross sufferings such as relationship problems, unemployment, hunger, or illness. Their understanding of suffering is very limited. Because they have no idea about the entire suffering of samsara, they have no wish to be free from it.

Suffering, in this context, refers to the suffering and the origin of suffering that are the first two of the four noble truths, the first teaching the Buddha gave after he became enlightened. Without fully understanding these, sentient beings cannot understand that there can be an end to all suffering and that there is a definite path that leads to that end: the truth of cessation and the truth of the path, the second two of the four noble truths. Everybody wants happiness and to avoid suffering, but without these vital understandings they mistake their goal, seeking only a temporary alleviation of some of their suffering rather than the complete elimination of it.

Therefore the greatest benefit we can offer sentient beings is to be able to show them what true happiness is and to be able to lead them to that true happiness, to full enlightenment. But there is no way we can do this if we ourselves don't realize bodhichitta, which is the mind that wishes to achieve enlightenment in order to lead all other sentient beings into that same state. This is why listening, reflecting, and meditating on the entire path to enlightenment, on all the preliminary subjects that lead to bodhichitta and to the subjects within the teachings on bodhichitta itself, are of utmost importance.

In *A Guide to the Bodhisattva's Way of Life*, the great eighth-century Indian master Shantideva said,

> Since the limitless mind of the Sole Guide of the World
> has upon thorough investigation seen its preciousness,
> all beings wishing to be free from worldly abodes
> should firmly take hold of this precious Awakening Mind.[1]

The Sole Guide of the World is, of course, an epithet for Guru Shakyamuni Buddha,[2] the perfect leader, the one to lead all sentient beings from suffering to full enlightenment. The Buddha is omniscient; he has the ability to faultlessly perceive infinite objects of knowledge simultaneously. He sees every single existence of all three times: past, present, and future. There is no way we can comprehend the scope of his understanding. If we tried to explain all the qualities of the Buddha's mind, we would never be finished; this is something we cannot know until we ourselves attain enlightenment.

With his infallible wisdom, through thorough investigation, the Buddha has checked and seen how precious bodhichitta is. He has seen that bodhichitta is the source of happiness of *all* beings: worldly beings, those who have transcended worldly existence, and even fully awakened beings. There is no happiness that does not arise from bodhichitta. Every single pleasure we worldly beings have ever experienced, even a gentle breeze on a hot day, has arisen from bodhichitta. This is not talking about transcendental happiness, which comes once we have achieved one of the great Mahayana paths and which requires bodhichitta; this is simply talking about ordinary worldly happiness.

We can see this quite simply when we consider karma. All happiness comes from virtuous actions; it is impossible to experience happiness from nonvirtue. How are virtuous actions created? Only by practicing the Dharma, which means following the guidance of enlightened beings, the buddhas. Where do buddhas come from? From bodhisattvas, and bodhisattvas are born from the wonderful mind of bodhichitta.

As the only source of all happiness, we should strive to attain bodhichitta, and when we have it we should firmly take hold of it, never letting it degenerate in the slightest. Nothing on earth can compare to the mind of bodhichitta—no phenomenon, no experience, no pleasure. There is no material object, no jewel, no achievement that compares. Everything else is utterly worthless in comparison.

We need to begin to develop this mind right now, this very moment. We simply don't know how long we have before we leave this body and take another. And unless we can take the mind of bodhichitta with us into the next life, we have no way of knowing when we can ever even try to develop it again—let alone attain it.

What Is Bodhichitta?

Bodhichitta is such an incredible mind. It is the thought to benefit every single sentient being, without exception, without excluding one single hell being, one single hungry ghost, one single animal, one single human being, one single demigod, one single god.[3] It is the thought to benefit every being on the ground, in the ground, in the sea, in the air—every ant on every mountain, every fish in every ocean, every bird and insect in every field, every single sentient being in all the six realms.

Bodhichitta is a Sanskrit word that means the mind of enlightenment or the awakening mind: *bodhi*, meaning "awakened" or "awakening," and *citta*, meaning "mind." The Tibetan for *bodhichitta* is *jangchup sem*: *jang*, meaning the "elimination," as in the destruction of all gross and subtle obstacles; *chup*, meaning "development," as in fully developing or perfecting all the mind's positive qualities or realizations; and *sem*, meaning "mind." This mind that strives for enlightenment completely, spontaneously, continuously works at nothing other than benefiting all living beings. A person who possesses such a priceless mind is called a bodhisattva.

Before we reach that spontaneous altruistic mind, we must consciously think of reasons to induce this state, and so that type of bodhichitta is called *effortful bodhichitta* or *contrived bodhichitta*. When the uncontrived and spontaneous wish for enlightenment always manifests, then it is *effortless bodhichitta*.

Effortful bodhichitta relies on reasoning, using logic and quotes from the scriptures to reinforce our wish to benefit others. We logically understand all the arguments, and in meditation we feel we must attain enlightenment for all other beings. But that state of mind is not integral yet, and so we slip out of it when we are not analyzing the reasons or meditating on it. Without relying on reasoning, we are still not able to transform our mind into a totally altruistic one. This is why effortful bodhichitta is also called *created bodhichitta*.

Effortless, uncontrived, or uncreated bodhichitta, on the other hand, does not rely on reasoning. We no longer have to dwell on how all sentient beings are suffering, how they are devoid of happiness and incapable of lifting themselves from this state, and how we alone are able to help them. Even without reasoning, that deep wish to help is naturally there.

Effortful bodhichitta is compared to licking sugarcane skin; by meditating on bodhichitta through reasoning, we might get a strong feeling for the suffering of sentient beings—the taste might be there—but after the meditation that feeling does not remain. On the other hand, the actual mind of bodhichitta that arises through continuous training is like licking the actual sugarcane pulp. Whereas the skin might have a little sweetness due to the pulp inside, the actual pulp is so sweet, so delicious. That is what we actually want to eat. This mind of effortless bodhichitta is so precious, so wonderful.

To understand just how powerful bodhichitta is, we must understand that it is not just a feeling, like love or compassion, but an actual main mind, one of the six principal consciousnesses. What does that mean?

I haven't read any Western psychology books completely, but many years back I was given what was supposed to be a very good book on the mind. Looking through it, however, I was unable to find a clear, concise definition of *mind*. It discussed things about the mind at great length, but there was very little on what the mind actually was. This is something we learn at a very young age in Tibetan monasteries. Everything we learn in a monastery is in order to lead us to liberation and enlightenment, and it is considered important that we know exactly what the mind is in order to transform it from its deluded state to a perfect one. Just as somebody must learn everything there is to know about a computer in order to be able to build and program it, we need to know everything about the mind.

We have body and mind. The body has color and form, whereas the mind is colorless and formless. The mind's nature is clear and perceiving. Like a mirror unobscured by dust, it has the power to reflect back an object of the senses. Within the mind there are many different minds, divided into the principal or main consciousnesses and the secondary mental factors. There are six principal consciousnesses: a direct perception for each of the five senses—seeing, hearing, smelling, tasting, and touching—and a mental direct perception. The principal consciousness perceives the object directly without any embroidery or overlay. It is like the boss. The mental factors, the minds that accompany each principal consciousness, are like the employees who work for the boss. Traditionally there are fifty-one mental factors divided into different types: positive minds such as love; delusions such as anger and pride; and changeable mental factors, minds that can be positive or negative, such as sleep.[4]

The mind called bodhichitta is made up of two aspirations—the wish to free all sentient beings from suffering and the wish to attain enlightenment in order to do that. But bodhichitta is not a mental factor; it is a principal consciousness accompanied by these two intentions. Thinking of the suffering of others and developing the wish to free them from it is all part of conceptual thinking, as is developing the wish to attain enlightenment to do that, but the actual mind of bodhichitta is spontaneous, a state of mind beyond reasoning, something we feel from our heart. This is effortless bodhichitta.

This is the mind we must aspire to. To practice the Dharma only on the meditation cushion doesn't work. In reality we don't spend so much time in meditation. Most of our day is spent in mundane activities such as eating, sleeping, and so forth, so if we only create virtue for the short time we are meditating, then we will make little progress. Therefore we need to integrate our Dharma practice into our daily life so that each second becomes most beneficial for all sentient beings. With bodhichitta there is never any confusion; we see what is most beneficial, and we naturally and spontaneously do it. Whatever we decide to do is only for the benefit of others, never for our own benefit. That wish is there, no matter what we are doing. Whatever activity we do, our heart constantly spontaneously wishes to achieve enlightenment for all other sentient beings. Moreover, we take on the *sole* responsibility for this.

This mind is compared to how a mother feels about her beloved only child when that child is sick. The mother loves the child so much, seeing them as the most precious thing in the world. When her child is sick, regardless of what else she is doing—washing, cooking, shopping, or whatever—she is always so concerned, wishing them to be free from that sickness.

Say a family at a picnic sees a young baby fall into a fire. While the other relatives are shocked—they cannot do anything to help the child—the mother, without a second's thought, plunges into the fire to save her baby. There is no hesitation, no thought of her own safety; she *has* to save her precious child. This is the attitude we hold for all sentient beings, this 100 percent determination to liberate them all and lead them to enlightenment.

This feeling for all sentient beings comes from first reflecting on how unbearable it is that we ourselves are trapped in the endless cycle of suffering called samsara, how cyclic existence is nothing but suffering. Finding it so disgusting, so terrifying, we want to be free from it immediately. But then we see how all other sentient beings are also suffering in this way and they too want to be free from it, and so we generate compassion for all of them. From this, the spontaneous sense of responsibility for them all arises, the special attitude that just precedes bodhichitta.

The Importance of Bodhichitta

The great masters such as Lama Tsongkhapa[5] explained that bodhichitta is the heart of Mahayana Buddhism. If we are living with loving-kindness, with compassion, with the precious thought of enlightenment, then we are practicing the essence of the Mahayana. The whole purpose of whatever we do within Mahayana Buddhism is to develop the good heart, and so whatever we do that helps bring this about helps us on the path to enlightenment. Then all temporary and ultimate happiness and all realizations come easily, with hardly any effort at all.

Because of that, whether sitting to meditate or doing an everyday action such as driving to work, it is so useful to begin every action with a bodhichitta motivation. We should check everything we do to see whether the action is worthwhile or harmful, and we should cultivate the former and abandon the latter. If we are about to do a negative action, no matter how small, we should think that it is of no benefit and will only bring suffering and so determine not to do it. Then we can transform our mind into the loving, compassionate thought of enlightenment. In that way, we can train our mind, ensuring that any action we do is free from self-cherishing, only benefiting others and bringing us closer to enlightenment.

For that, of course, we ourselves have to understand that only the top-quality happiness of enlightenment is good enough, and so we must renounce the whole of samsara, which we do by seeing that the nature of samsara is suffering. That involves having a firm understanding of all the elemental subjects of the path such as perfect human rebirth, karma, impermanence and death, and so forth.

Furthermore, the minds of loving-kindness and compassion are vital in bringing happiness to ourselves and to all other sentient beings. Developing compassion toward others, whether it is one sentient being or countless, is the path that leads us there. In fact, this is the heart of the entire Buddhadharma: of the Hinayana teachings, the Mahayana Paramitayana teachings, and the secret Vajrayana teachings.[6]

The Vinaya, the teachings on ethical discipline and vows, says that what differentiates Buddhism from other religions is the emphasis on compassion for all other sentient beings. And so compassion is at the heart of the entire Buddhadharma and without question at the heart of the Mahayana, because without compassion and loving-kindness there is no way to transform our mind into bodhichitta. And without bodhichitta we are unable to gain the higher realizations and to completely destroy both the disturbing-thought obscurations and the more subtle obscurations to knowledge that block us from full enlightenment.[7]

Therefore, feeling compassion for even a few seconds when we see two insects fighting is part of our path; it brings us a little bit closer to enlightenment. The stronger the compassion we generate, the more our mind is purified of negativities, and the easier and quicker it is to complete the work of accumulating merit.

If we think of the benefits, we realize this practice is unbelievably precious. The benefits are like the infinite sky, so vast we can never finish explaining them; they lead us all the way to enlightenment, causing us to achieve the infinite qualities of a buddha's holy body, holy speech, and holy mind. Then, even after that, we continue to benefit all sentient beings, and so the results of that moment of compassion are never finished.

Even before we attain bodhichitta and become a bodhisattva, by no longer working for the self, we stop harming others and instead only ever work for them. In that way we completely turn our life around. From beginningless lifetimes we have been continuously working solely for our own well-being, only to obtain happiness for ourselves alone. Now, developing our compassion and loving-kindness, we start working for others until we reach the stage where we no longer have the slightest thought for our own welfare, and every thought is purely to benefit others. Although there might be some possibility of falling back into self-concern when we have just attained bodhichitta, as we advance that possibility lessens until we can never act selfishly again. Our route to full enlightenment is ensured. This is the greatness of bodhichitta.

The Route to Bodhichitta

First we need to understand how vital it is to develop bodhichitta, and then we need the techniques to do that. This is what we will explore here.

When we understand that the selfish mind chasing samsaric pleasure is a mind of dissatisfaction, we can start to renounce it and work toward the happiness of future lives—and then the renunciation of the whole of samsara. This involves understanding the various topics of the *lamrim*, or graduated path to enlightenment, such as perfect human rebirth, death and impermanence, karma, and the various sufferings of samsara. These are all part of ripening our mind so that it is ready to develop bodhichitta.

For bodhichitta, we need to see that all other sentient beings are suffering in samsara too and that it is our responsibility to help them. We cannot do that while we are following the self-cherishing mind. Only by renouncing a selfish life can we recognize that all happiness comes from others, that everything in our life that brings us happiness has come from the kindness of other sentient beings.

Whether an action is virtuous or nonvirtuous depends on the motivation we have, on whether it is the result of a selfish mind or a selfless one. Aside from committing any of the ten nonvirtues,[8] even simple acts such as eating, walking, sleeping, or drinking coffee can be nonvirtuous if our motivation is selfish, if we are clinging to the happiness of this life. The more cups of coffee we drink, the more nonvirtue we create; the bigger the mug we use, the bigger the negative karma. Therefore we need to see how important the correct motivation is with every action we do. And the best motivation is the bodhichitta motivation, the wish to attain enlightenment for the sake of all other sentient beings. This stems from seeing the suffering of all other beings and developing first compassion and then great compassion for them all, even those who harm us.

There is no other way. To lead all sentient beings to peerless happiness, we must know all the levels of mind and what methods will best suit them—and that requires having an omniscient mind, perfect power, and fully developed compassion, so that we can work perfectly for all beings without the slightest mistake.

Developing this incredible mind brings many benefits for ourselves and others. Traditionally they are listed as ten, which we will look at, including entering the Mahayana and becoming a bodhisattva, accumulating unbelievable merit and purifying so much negative karma with everything we do, and finally completing the path and becoming enlightened.

Then, based on equanimity, we train in one of the two ways of attaining bodhichitta, or a combination of the two. The first is the seven points of cause and effect: (1) We see that all beings have been our mothers countless times, (2) we recall how kind they have been as our mothers, and (3) we determine to repay that kindness. From that we develop (4) loving-kindness, (5) compassion, and then (6) the special attitude that takes responsibility to free them from suffering. These six causes produce the one result, (7) bodhichitta.

The second way is equalizing and exchanging self and others, a more advanced technique where we see how we and all other sentient beings are equal and, recalling the disadvantages of harboring the self-cherishing mind and the advantages of cherishing others, we exchange ourselves with others. Of course, this does not mean physically exchanging our body for theirs but exchanging our selfish concern for cherishing them and doing whatever is needed to bring them from suffering into happiness. We do this through the wonderful mind-training practice of *tonglen*, taking and giving, where we take the suffering of others on ourselves in order to destroy the self-cherishing mind, and we give them all our happiness and merit.

This requires a lot of effort and understanding, and there are many meditations we can do to help us. Some are included here, such as meditations on equanimity, the seven points of cause and effect, and tonglen.

In *The Jewel Lamp*, Khunu Lama Rinpoche[9] said,

> The thought desiring to dispel
> every mistake from every sentient being
> and to bring every being to full knowledge is bodhichitta.
> Of all wonderful things, this is the most wonderful.[10]

In his book there are many verses that tell us how bodhichitta is the best, the supreme mind. Of course it is! It is the mind that wishes every single being to be completely free from all suffering. What greater mind can there be than that?

Among all the thoughts we can have, the most wonderful thought is bodhichitta. Why is that? Because it has incredible benefit for ourselves and for all others. It is the thought of wanting to free every sentient being from every delusion, from every suffering. Can there be anything superior to that? Of this Shantideva said,

> If even the thought to relieve
> living creatures of merely a headache
> is a beneficial intention
> endowed with infinite goodness,

then what need is there to mention
the wish to dispel their inconceivable misery,
wishing every single one of them
to realize boundless good qualities?[11]

The wish to free somebody else from a headache is a very beneficial mind, so the wish to free all beings from all headaches is a mind of incredible virtue. But if we extend that not just to one kind of temporary problem of all beings but to all the possible sufferings all beings can experience, gross and subtle, physical and mental, then that mind is unimaginable, incredible, the supreme among the supreme.

PART I
THE SUPREME MEDICINE

*By depending on the medicine of bodhicitta
all the diseases of the all-rising delusions are cured.
Therefore, there is no question at all
that there is no better medicine in samsara than bodhicitta.*

—KHUNU LAMA RINPOCHE,
THE JEWEL LAMP, VERSE 286

1 : BODHICHITTA IS THE GATEWAY TO THE MAHAYANA

WHEN WE EXPLORE the ways we have to help ourselves and others, we will see that nothing compares to bodhichitta. This is what Khunu Lama Rinpoche said in *The Jewel Lamp* and what Shantideva said in *A Guide to the Bodhisattva's Way of Life*. According to Shantideva,

> It is the supreme ambrosia
> that overcomes the sovereignty of death;
> it is the inexhaustible treasure
> that eliminates all the poverty of the world.
>
> It is the supreme medicine
> that quells the world's disease.
> It is the tree that shelters all beings
> wandering and tired on the path of conditioned existence.[12]

In the West, when a new medicine is discovered that cures a particular disease, long articles are written about it in scientific journals and television programs are made about it. Then commercial companies patent it, and it becomes a big commodity that everybody talks about. That is only for one medicine that can cure one disease for a few people. Bodhichitta can cure every disease, both mental and physical, for all beings. This is what Guru Shakyamuni Buddha and the other thousand buddhas of this fortunate eon, with their unfathomable concern for the welfare of all beings, have seen. So why don't we have endless television programs telling people how beneficial bodhichitta is? Shantideva also said this,

> All the buddhas who have contemplated for many eons
> have seen it to be beneficial;
> for by it the limitless masses of beings
> will quickly attain the supreme state of bliss.[13]

Of the many realizations we can develop in order to progress on the path to enlightenment, such as equanimity, the wisdom of how things exist, an understanding of karma, and so forth, the greatest realization we can strive for is the peerless mind called bodhichitta.

Generating bodhichitta means systematically cultivating the mind that increasingly cares for all sentient beings, that is, developing the will to benefit others. This is what Maitreya explained in his *Ornament for Clear Realizations*,[14] the philosophical text that shows the whole path to enlightenment. At first, when we are consumed with self-concern, even thinking about such an attitude is difficult. But the more we see the advantages of such a mind, the stronger our determination to have it becomes, thus increasing our capacity to benefit others.

For countless rebirths until now, we have only ever done things for our own happiness, often at the expense of others. With bodhichitta we put self-interest aside and work solely for others. The "happiness" our self-cherishing mind has sought for us has, in fact, been a fantasy. We can see when we study subjects such as the four noble truths that any mental state poisoned with attachment to sense pleasures—what we would normally consider worldly happiness—is suffering in that there is an underlying dissatisfaction, one that will lead to future grosser suffering.

On the other hand, when we put that selfish mind aside and start working for others, as a byproduct we effortlessly attain a real sense of happiness that will not let us down. Not only that—we are developing our mind toward its ultimate potential, the fully awakened mind of enlightenment. As I often say, real happiness begins when we start cherishing others.

Everything we do in our daily life is for happiness, whether for our own happiness or for the happiness of others. The definition of Dharma is that which keeps us from suffering and hence leads us to happiness, particularly the happiness of liberation and full enlightenment. The very essence of the Dharma taught by the kind, compassionate Guru Shakyamuni Buddha is bodhichitta. This altruistic thought to achieve enlightenment for all other sentient beings lies at the heart of everything he taught.

BODHICHITTA AND THE WHOLE BUDDHIST PATH

The Buddha said in the *Sutra of Individual Liberation* (*Pratimoksha Sutra*),

> Do not commit any nonvirtuous actions,
> perform only perfect virtuous actions,
> subdue your mind thoroughly—
> this is the teaching of the Buddha.

The Kadampa *geshes*[15] explained that the whole Buddhist path comes down to this advice—to not harm others and to benefit others, and in order to do those, to pacify the mind.

The compassion toward all beings that is the essence of Buddhism entails not harming them, which means not committing nonvirtuous actions. This encompasses all beings, even those who have harmed us. For that, we need to develop equanimity, to see all beings as equal in deserving our nonharm, not partially seeing one as deserving help and another as deserving harm. Even for somebody who has harmed us or who hates us, even for strangers or nonhumans, our fundamental Buddhist practice is nonharm.

Additionally, in Mahayana Buddhism the emphasis is not only on not harming but also on helping in any way we can. We subdue our mind and train it in order to be able to offer perfect service to other sentient beings, without mistake. That means leading them away from all suffering and its causes and toward the peerless happiness of full enlightenment. To be able to do that, we ourselves have to be fully qualified, which means having attained full omniscience. Then, with perfect power we can reveal whatever method suits every sentient being according to their level of mind, their karma.

Developing bodhichitta comes into the teachings on the graduated path of the higher capable being. In the forty years from his enlightenment to his parinirvana, the Buddha gave 84,000 teachings, all of which are included in the Tripitaka, the three collections, or baskets, of the teachings: the Vinaya basket on morality and discipline, the Abhidharma basket on philosophy, and the Sutra basket, the other teachings of the Buddha.

In Tibetan Buddhism, and particularly the Geluk tradition, all these teachings are incorporated into the lamrim, the path to enlightenment that entails the graduated path of the lower capable being, the graduated path of the middle capable being, and the graduated path of the higher capable being.

The graduated path of the lower capable being is the path of a being trying to attain a fortunate rebirth. It includes subjects such as the perfect human rebirth (its usefulness, how difficult it is to find again, and so forth); impermanence and death; the sufferings of the lower realms; refuge; and then karma. The entire graduated path of the lower capable being is contained in the first piece of advice in the verse above, to not harm others.

The graduated path of the middle capable being is the path of a being trying to gain not just a fortunate rebirth but also liberation from the whole of samsara. The meditations here are on the general sufferings of samsara and the twelve links of dependent origination,[16] which show why we circle in samsara. It also includes the shortcomings of delusions, practicing the antidotes to all that, and the three higher trainings of morality, concentration, and wisdom. The graduated path of the middle capable being is also included in the first piece of advice, to not harm others.

The third level of the path, the graduated path of the higher capable being, includes all the Mahayana teachings, including all the Vajrayana, or tantric, teachings. The graduated path of the higher capable being is included in the second piece of advice, to benefit others.

So within these two pieces of advice, to not harm others and to benefit others, is the entire Buddhadharma. This is what is taught in the great Tibetan Buddhist monasteries such as Sera, Ganden, and Drepung, the Geluk monasteries of Lama Tsongkhapa's lineage, which study the vast Nalanda tradition developed by the great pandits such as Nagarjuna, Atisha, and so forth.

From a very young age, Tibetan monks and nuns study the extensive philosophical subjects within the Buddhadharma, in both the sutras— the Buddha's own words—and the commentaries written by the great pandits such as Lama Tsongkhapa. They not only learn these texts but also put them into practice, integrating everything within the lamrim into their lives.

If we too do this, if we live our life with this attitude, then we will work only to benefit others, without sectarianism, without discrimination, whether a sentient being seems beautiful or ugly, whether they help us or harm us. We work to free *everybody* from the oceans of samsaric suffering and bring them to full enlightenment.

If we have this goal, if this is the main purpose of everything we do, then so many problems disappear. The selfish mind is the major obstacle to developing compassion and causes all our problems. On the other hand, cherishing others is the source of all happiness, for ourselves and all others, and so working for all other beings is the fastest route to destroy all our problems. This life's parents gave us this life's body and nurtured us, fed us, protected us, and educated us; therefore we can easily see how we need to show love and compassion to them. But, as we will see when we discuss the seven points of cause and effect, *all* beings have been our kind mothers and so we need to show the same concern for all of them.

The Four Ways of Clinging

In the Sakya tradition, there are four things that block us from attaining the three paths of lower, middle, and higher capable beings. They are the *four desires* or the *four clingings*:

1. If you cling to this life, you are not a Dharma practitioner.
2. If you cling to future lives' samsara, your mind is not in renunciation.
3. If you cling to cherishing the I, that is not bodhichitta.
4. If you cling to the I, that is not the right view.[17]

The Nyingma and Kagyü traditions have *the four aspects of the trans-formed mind*, which refers to much the same thing. The "transformed mind" of their teaching is the mind that has firstly renounced this life, then renounced all samsaric perfections and happinesses, then totally renounced self-cherishing and so cherishes others with bodhichitta, and finally renounced the wrong view that holds the I and phenomena as inherently existing. This corresponds to the three principal aspects of the path in the Geluk tradition, where renunciation of this life and of the whole of samsara are combined. We will look at that later.

Clinging to this life, we are trapped in the thought of the eight worldly dharmas[18]—being happy when having material possessions and unhappy when not having them, wanting happiness and comfort and not wanting unhappiness and discomfort, wanting praise and not wanting criticism, wanting a good reputation and not wanting a bad reputation—and so nothing we do can become the Dharma. It is impossible for any action to be both a worldly action and a Dharma action, so while we are wrapped up in the affairs of this life, we cannot be a Dharma practitioner.

Overcoming the eight worldly dharmas corresponds to the graduated path of the lower capable being. When we have renounced this life and no longer work for the unsatisfactory happinesses of this life, we can call ourselves a Dharma practitioner because our life and our Dharma prac-tice are equal. This pure mind of letting go of attachment is a peaceful, free, happy mind. Letting go of clinging to this life is the fundamental practice, the most basic level of Dharma practice.

In retreat or in our daily life, we need to watch our mind carefully all the time to see that attachment to the eight worldly dharmas does not creep in. If we see a mind such as attachment to comfort or reputation or aversion to criticism arising, we need to destroy it, to apply whatever remedy is appropriate, such as meditating on impermanence and death or on love.

Until now we have given freedom to our desire, allowing the thought of the eight worldly dharmas to flourish, causing us all our problems, but now we give freedom to ourselves. We break our slavery to the eight worldly dharmas that have constantly abused us, bringing us one problem after another, one suffering after another. Now, always watching our mind, always destroying the mind of attachment when it arises, we have incredible freedom and happiness. Having renounced this life, we have relinquished the first clinging, and we can consider ourselves a Dharma practitioner.

After we have renounced this life, the next level of practice is when we can renounce the whole of samsara. This is the second clinging. As long as we cling to samsaric happiness, to samsaric perfections, there is no way we can generate a mind renouncing samsara and so no way we can attain liberation. The door to the path to liberation is through seeing the whole of samsara as suffering and therefore renouncing it. We need this next step for liberation.

The third of the four clingings is clinging to the self-cherishing mind. As long as we cherish ourselves, there is no space to cherish others, no way to develop bodhichitta, and no way to attain enlightenment. Just as renouncing samsara is the door to liberation, attaining bodhichitta is the door to enlightenment. Whether a normal daily action or one we consider a Dharma activity such as reciting mantras or doing retreats, whatever we do actually becomes an obstacle to achieving enlightenment if we are still clinging to the self.

The last of the four clingings is clinging to wrong view. As long as we don't renounce the wrong view that sees all things as inherently existing, there is no way we can realize the absolute nature, the right view that sees the emptiness of the inherent existence of all things. Most importantly, there is no way we can realize the absolute nature of the self.

Perhaps we have a good intellectual understanding of emptiness, but as long as we cling to an instinctive sense that the I is truly existent, that it exists from its own side, then we cannot say we are holding the right view of emptiness. We perceive emptiness directly when we have reached the path of seeing, the third of the five paths, and only then do we stop creating new negative karma that produces future samsara. This is a very advanced mind. All other minds can help us toward this realization, but it is only here that we are totally free from the entire suffering of samsara; then we have everlasting happiness, liberation.

The Five Paths and Tantra

Both the Hinayana and the Mahayana traditions talk about the five paths through which we must progress to attain our goal:

1. the path of merit
2. the path of preparation
3. the path of seeing
4. the path of meditation
5. the path of no more learning

There is a slight difference in how the paths are described within the Hinayana and the Mahayana, and the goal is slightly different: individual liberation and enlightenment, respectively. In the Mahayana tradition, the first path, the *path of merit*, refers to the period in which we accumulate merit by listening to the Dharma, reflecting on its meaning, meditating, and so forth, in order to fully realize the teachings within our mindstream in the future.

With the *path of preparation* we gain a penetrative insight on emptiness, one in which the conceptual understanding of emptiness is conjoined with a very deep meditative experience. But we have yet to realize it directly, so we are still an ordinary being.

Then, through continual meditation on emptiness, we enter the *path of seeing*. Before, our understanding of emptiness was mixed with conceptualizations, but now it is a direct realization. We become an *arya* being. Having attained this path we have a spiritual body—as opposed to our worldly body—that is different from the body of the arya being of the Hinayana path. Because we no longer have to go through death, we don't have to experience rebirth, old age, sickness, and yet another death.

With the *path of meditation*, our direct realization of emptiness becomes stabilized and continuous. Even on the fourth path, there are still very subtle residual defilements, and so during that time we work on slowly destroying even these.

From the time of realizing emptiness directly on the third path until the last path, we progress through stages called the ten *bhumis*, or grounds. The first bhumi is on the path of seeing, the second to seventh bhumis are during the path of meditation, and the eighth to tenth are during the path of no more learning. It is when we achieve the tenth bhumi, while on the fifth path, the *path of no more learning*, that we attain enlightenment.

In the Hinayana tradition, when we have completed all five paths, we achieve the cessation of the whole of samsara and attain the sorrowless state called nirvana or liberation. From a Mahayana perspective, although such a state is amazing, it is not sufficient. Even if we can free ourselves completely from all suffering, our journey is not complete without continuing on to try to free all sentient beings. We need to enter the Mahayana path and actualize bodhichitta. Then, as a bodhisattva, we go on to practice the bodhisattva's activities, the six perfections, or *paramitas*—the perfections of patience, morality, generosity, enthusiastic perseverance, concentration, and wisdom—and the four means of drawing disciples to the Dharma—giving, speaking kind words, teaching to the level of the student, and practicing what we teach. Then, having worked through the five paths and attained the path of no more learning—enlightenment—we can work perfectly for the welfare of all sentient beings.

This is the path according to the Paramitayana, the nontantric aspect of the Mahayana. But it is also possible to attain enlightenment extremely quickly by entering the Vajrayana, or tantric path, once we have actualized the common path of renouncing samsara, attaining bodhichitta, and realizing emptiness.

There are four levels of Vajrayana: *kriya*, or action tantra; *charya*, or performance tantra; yoga tantra; and highest yoga tantra. Only with highest yoga tantra can we attain enlightenment within one brief lifetime of this degenerate time. Having received an initiation from a qualified vajra master, the mind is ripened and we can practice the generation stage and the completion stage. When we attain the final part of the completion stage, called the union of clear light and illusory body, we achieve the unification of no more learning, the fully enlightened state.

BODHICHITTA WITHIN THE THREE PRINCIPAL ASPECTS OF THE PATH

In *The Foundation of All Good Qualities*, Lama Tsongkhapa said,

> Having become a pure vessel by training in the
>   general path,
> please bless me to enter
> the holy gateway of the fortunate ones:
> the supreme vajra vehicle.[19]

The tantric path is entered through attaining the general path, meaning the three principal aspects of the path: renunciation, bodhichitta, and the realization of emptiness. This makes it very clear that we need these three realizations *before* we can enter the Vajrayana, otherwise any tantric practice we do will not even be the cause for liberation. Without renunciation we can never free ourselves from attachment; without emptiness we can never eliminate the root of samsara; without bodhichitta we can never develop the cause of enlightenment. The three principal aspects of the path are indispensable for the Vajrayana; they are what make it a special shortcut to enlightenment.

His Holiness the Dalai Lama explains that just as the special holiday food made of butter and cheese that Tibetans love exists due to the kindness of the cheese—I suppose we would say our beloved ice cream exists due to the kindness of the milk—so the Vajrayana being a shortcut to enlightenment is due to the kindness of the three principal aspects of the path. We could practice tantra for eons without them, and we would still be unable to attain enlightenment.

Therefore whatever we do should be imbued with renunciation, bodhichitta, and emptiness. Even just saying a *mala*[20] of a mantra should have this special quality. Just knowing is not enough. Especially if we do a daily *sadhana*,[21] we must meditate on the deity based on renunciation, bodhichitta, and emptiness. It is vital not to miss this, otherwise there is little flavor to our practice. With the three principal aspects of the path, on the other hand, whatever we do will have great taste; it will have very deep meaning, and every moment of our life will be oneness with the path, oneness with the deity.

Pabongka Dechen Nyingpo, the author of *Liberation in the Palm of Your Hand*, was the root guru of two of His Holiness the Dalai Lama's tutors: His Holiness Ling Rinpoche and His Holiness Trijang Rinpoche. He said that people can spend their whole lives concentrating on watching the mind, but without renunciation, bodhichitta, and emptiness, all their efforts have little meaning. Even the strongest concentration can only lead to different, more subtle levels of existence, such as in the form or formless realm.[22]

We might have great concentration but will still be in samsara. We need to understand how this is not enough. The Hindu and other traditions in India, for instance, have incredible concentration practices, but while they do have single-pointed concentration (*samadhi*), they do not have penetrative insight (*vipashyana*) that realizes the absolute true nature. They have their own explanations of ultimate nature that are actually the opposite of reality, presenting impermanent things as permanent.

In the lamrim texts, calm abiding and special insight come after bodhichitta. Meditating on emptiness through great calm abiding based on bodhichitta can *never* become the cause of samsara. On the contrary, it becomes the cause that eliminates the very root of samsara and leads to enlightenment.

The most important of the three principal aspects of the path is bodhichitta. Without bodhichitta, even if we have fully renounced samsara and realized emptiness, we can enter the Hinayana path and attain nirvana, but we will still be unable to attain enlightenment. Maybe after having stayed in great bliss for many, many eons we will be awoken from our concentration and will move toward enlightenment, but that is such a long way away. We should aim to attain enlightenment now, in everything we do, and for that we need bodhichitta. That is what makes life highly meaningful.

Even if we are unable to attain bodhichitta before we die, there is nothing to be upset about. Our life will have still been highly meaningful, because we have spent it trying to develop bodhichitta. Each time we meditate on bodhichitta, by making our life the cause of happiness for all sentient beings, we purify our mind so much that we get closer and closer to enlightenment. This is why, among the hundreds of practices we can do, such as Vajrayana deity practice or meditating on emptiness, the principal practice should always be bodhichitta. When we keep bodhichitta as our main practice, we can be assured we are obtaining the most meaning from our life. To do extensive purification, to accumulate extensive merit, the best way, the infallible method, is to train in bodhichitta.

While we are trapped in self-cherishing, there is no way to realize emptiness, and bodhichitta is the mind that frees us from self-cherishing. With the self-cherishing mind there is no renunciation, and so again developing bodhichitta is the key. But specifically, even though we might be able to develop incredible concentration and possibly realize emptiness without bodhichitta, without it there can never be enlightenment.

Somebody with bodhichitta is considered the most fortunate of the fortunate. Even a new bodhisattva who has yet to realize emptiness is more fortunate than an *arhat*—those transcendental beings on the Hinayana path who have completely removed all disturbing negative thoughts, have a full realization of emptiness, and are totally free from suffering and its causes. Therefore, of the three principal aspects of the path, bodhichitta is considered the most important.

Attaining Bodhichitta Is Impossible without Renunciation

To train in bodhichitta we need to have renounced samsara. Some people think that it is possible to actualize bodhichitta without this, that we can be kind to others but still hold on to attachment to this life. Of course, being kind to others is wonderful, but if we want more than that, if we want the peerless mind of bodhichitta, we need to turn our back on worldly concerns. To think that bodhichitta is attainable without renouncing samsara is to misunderstand what bodhichitta is, thinking it is a light and easy practice. We need a mind that has fully renounced the trivial pleasures of this life, and that can only be obtained through thoroughly understanding our own suffering in all its levels of subtlety. Then we can see how all other beings are also suffering.

In *The Foundation of All Good Qualities*, Lama Tsongkhapa said,

> Just as I have fallen into the sea of samsara,
> so have all mother migratory beings.
> Please bless me to see this, train in supreme bodhichitta,
> and bear the responsibility of freeing all migratory beings.[23]

This is a request to the merit field, the guru-buddhas, to grant blessings so that we are able to see that, just like us, all other sentient beings are suffering in samsara in many different ways. Seeing that, we make the request that we can train in bodhichitta in order to be able to bear the burden of freeing them from all suffering and leading them to enlightenment.

This verse shows clearly how in order to generate great compassion and develop bodhichitta, we must relate our understanding of suffering to all beings, seeing how they have been friend, enemy, stranger, father, mother, brother, sister, wife, husband, child—every possible relationship. This requires thinking about past lives, seeing the continuity of the mind and how it has continued from one life to the next and how all the karmic imprints travel with the mind, bringing all the different types of suffering.

The sufferings of this life are many, but we can summarize them as birth, old age, sickness, and death. The suffering of birth is behind us, the sufferings of old age and sickness are with us now (or will be soon), and we have death waiting for us in the future. We are helpless not to experience these.

Furthermore, because we are controlled by karma and delusion, whenever our senses encounter any sense object, various disturbing thoughts arise: attachment to an attractive object, aversion to an unpleasant object, and so forth. Every day, every hour, hundreds and hundreds of karmic imprints are placed on our mental continuum due to disturbing thoughts, each creating the conditions for future lives in samsara. Unless we apply the meditations that are antidotes to our attachment, anger, and ignorance, this process will go on forever, each day bringing hundreds of thousands of samsaras with these suffering aggregates.[24] This is terrifying.

Seeing this, we can develop deep renunciation for the whole of samsara, and feeling our own samsara to be unbearable, we look at all others and see they are in the same tragic situation, trapped in samsara. We then naturally feel that their suffering is also unbearable. With this thought strong compassion arises and then strong bodhichitta grows. The stronger the bodhichitta, the quicker we achieve realizations and attain enlightenment. We are then able to become the perfect guide to quickly lead all sentient beings to enlightenment.

A bodhisattva has a stronger renunciation of samsara than an individual-liberation practitioner. Without completely turning our back on self-interest, how can we hope to cherish all other sentient beings? This essential renunciation, which will lead to strong compassion and loving-kindness, the causes of bodhichitta, will not come from reading a few books about the Mahayana and having a nice feeling for bodhichitta. That does not automatically make us a Mahayanist practicing bodhichitta.

Another common misconception is that because bodhisattvas choose to remain in samsara to best help sentient beings, bodhisattvas have not given up samsara, that they have not been released from it. In the sutra texts there are many references to bodhisattvas wishing to be born in the lower realms in order to suffer for the sake of other sentient beings. This shows the great courage of the bodhisattva, not the wish to enjoy samsara. To think that we can hang on to the attachment to sense pleasures and attain bodhichitta at the same time is a total misunderstanding.

Bodhisattvas fully comprehend that the nature of samsara is total suffering. To us it seems a pleasure grove, but to them it is like standing in the middle of a raging fire. Because of their great love for all sentient beings, in order to release all sentient beings from that suffering, they are willing to remain in samsara. However, that does not mean they are in their own samsara; they have totally renounced all attachment, and so although they live in the samsaric world, they are not in samsara. Without renouncing samsara, how could a bodhisattva help others extensively? Even with a lot of love and compassion, with limited wisdom the help they could give others would be limited.

Buddhism talks about two bodhichittas, *conventional bodhichitta* and *ultimate bodhichitta*. As we will see, conventional bodhichitta is the mind wishing to become enlightened in order to benefit all sentient beings, and ultimate bodhichitta is the wisdom that realizes emptiness in the mind of a superior bodhisattva. Both are needed for enlightenment, and neither is possible without renunciation. So renunciation, wisdom, and bodhichitta are all needed.

Each of the Three Aspects Reinforces the Others

Each of the three principal aspects of the path reinforces the other two. There is a practice you can do where you focus on one of the aspects for a certain period—say, a day—and then move to the next.

Let's start with *renunciation*. You determine that for the whole of that day you will make your project renunciation. You still do what you would normally do—go to work, go shopping, or whatever—but instead of the usual motivation of gaining the maximum pleasure for yourself, try to see that the nature of everything is suffering, which it is. So, when you go to a shop, don't buy things in order to increase your attachment and dissatisfaction but to see how involved you are with the affairs of this world. Do the same with your work or watching a movie.

Look around you at all the activities going on in your city, how busy everybody is and how, really, almost all of it is about attachment and ignorance and so has the nature of suffering. Specifically, it all has the three types of suffering: the suffering of suffering, the suffering of change, and pervasive compounding suffering. Look at those on the streets who are obviously suffering. This is the first of the three types of suffering, the suffering of suffering. But also look at those who think they are enjoying themselves shopping, eating, drinking, having a good time. They are experiencing the suffering of change, the second type of suffering, which we would normally regard as pleasure. Because of its transitory nature, it is bound to let us down and so is also a form of suffering. On top of that, everybody is experiencing pervasive compounding suffering, the third of the three types of suffering. Because our five aggregates are controlled by karma and delusion, their nature is suffering.

No matter where you look, you see all three types of suffering. There is not one tiny part of the city that is free from suffering. No matter who you see—the very rich, the very poor, whatever lifestyle, whatever job—they are still continuously suffering. Whether they are experiencing pleasure, pain, or indifference, they are still suffering.

This is what you should look out for, looking below the surface of all the busy activities. Just hanging around on a street corner can be a whole lamrim teaching. If you watch the people and animals around you with this lamrim awareness, then everything becomes advice to you and becomes the cause to strongly generate the thought of the renunciation of samsara, the first of the three aspects of the path. It causes you to renounce the causes of suffering, the very things that the other people are chasing. Furthermore, you see how all these things are in fact empty of existing independently, and you develop deep compassion for those around you, which leads to bodhichitta.

On another occasion, do the same thing but this time focus on practicing bodhichitta, the second aspect. Use everything you see to generate bodhichitta within your mind. Rather than seeing the different types of suffering that others around you are experiencing as a means of generating the thought to renounce samsara, see how all these things tie these beings into suffering, creating the cause to circle in samsara, and so develop great compassion for all of them. Whoever you see, use that person to develop compassion: a blind person, a poor mother with many children, a busy executive, a police officer, a criminal. They are each suffering in their own way, each experiencing the results of the previous negative karma they have created, and so each is deserving of compassion. And because you rely on them to develop compassion, they are offering you a great kindness, so remember their kindness and do tonglen for them, the practice of taking all their suffering and offering them all your positive qualities. Doing this, everything becomes a lesson in bodhichitta.

Finally, you can do the same with an understanding of emptiness, the third of the three aspects of the path. Leave your house determined that everything you do and see that day will be done with the motivation of seeing everything as an illusion or as an example of dependent arising, arising in dependence on causes and conditions. Whatever you see— every shop, every car, every person, every dog, every tree—be aware that to your senses it appears as existing from its own side, but that is completely untrue. In fact, everything is completely empty of existing from its own side.

Using the three principal aspects of the path like this, you can use every experience in your normal day to lead you further toward enlightenment.

2 : BODHICHITTA IS THE REAL MEANING OF LIFE

THERE IS NO samsaric happiness that we have never experienced. In fact, we have experienced every samsaric pleasure countless times. The reason we seem to be encountering new pleasures or new problems is simply because we cannot remember our past lives. When we can realize that we have already undergone whatever pleasure or problem we are currently experiencing innumerable times before, we will see that striving for samsaric perfection is fruitless; we are always doomed to dissatisfaction. Therefore we must determine to break the never-ending cycle of suffering.

However, even if we could overcome suffering completely, the real meaning of life would still elude us. It is not enough to practice the Dharma solely for our own happiness. Even animals work toward their own happiness, day and night. A cow finds grass and is happy; a horse finds water and drinks it, thinking, "May I be happy." If they are happy, it is good; if they are suffering, it is bad. If that's our attitude, are we any better than the animals and insects?

Living in a beautiful house, eating delicious food, is that any better than the animal living in the forest eating grass? Of course, the level of enjoyment might be much greater, but is it any more meaningful? A life filled with riches—the most magnificent house, the most wonderful clothes, the most delicious food—is as worthless as the poorest life if it is lived just for selfish pleasure. We have this particular body and we call ourselves "human," but are we any different from the animals? Each of us is really just an animal with a human body.

Even among animals some show compassion. I heard about a cat that lived very happily with its mouse neighbor. The mouse was there right in front of the cat, but they lived very peacefully together. Animals can help each other. So in that way they are better than we humans who only work for our own happiness.

So much money and effort—by ourselves and our parents—have gone into having this life we now have. We have worked so hard to learn the alphabet, to learn the subjects at primary and high school, to gain our degree at university. We have put so much time and effort into finding the right, well-paid job and we are still working incredibly hard to get what we want. We work so many hours a week to pay for our house to give us comfort and shelter, for our clothes and food, and for our enjoyments; we spend so much money on medicine, health care, and insurance. When we get sick it costs so much to have an operation or some expensive treatment.

We spend so much energy trying to stay healthy, going to the gym, listening to the advice people give us about health, knowing what food is yin and what food is yang, spending hours jogging in the mountains. We think that living our life in this way, taking such good care of our-selves and seeking out the best enjoyments, is what gives it meaning. Unless we can see that living our life for others is really what gives life meaning, what else can we think?

In fact, this busy life of chasing health and enjoyment is a very empty life. There is no meaning at all, no purpose in living like this. All our effort totally fails to give meaning to our life. All the knowledge we have collected is just like data in a computer. We could become the richest person in the world, somebody who is featured all the time on television and in magazines. We could be a household name, known to every person young and old, with the biggest reputation in the world. However, our life is completely empty.

We each lead a selfish life, not recognizing that all happiness comes from others. We see others as a means to our happiness rather than see-ing that by serving them we attain true happiness. Everything in our life that bring us enjoyment has been received from other sentient beings; nothing we have ever owned exists without their effort. The clothes we wear, the food we eat, the house we live in all come from the kindness of so many sentient beings. Countless beings have died or experienced great pain to give us these things. Many have created negative karma to ensure we have what we want. But while we are enjoying all these things, we don't give a single thought to benefit others. Our only concern is our own happiness, always wondering what will make *me* happy.

Here's an analogy: We buy a house after many, many years of incredibly hard work, saving every penny we can, enduring great physical hardship, day and night. Then we let somebody stay in our house and we feed them, thinking they can help out by working for us. However, instead of helping us, they steal our money, our possessions, and so forth. When we realize this we are furious, wanting to find them and scream at them. Thinking of how they used us, sleeping in our big bed under our warm, soft blanket, never giving even one thought to all the hard work we had done to bring this all about, we go crazy with anger. If we could find them, and if we had a bomb, they would no longer exist!

If this seems an extreme example, this is really how we are with all other sentient beings all the time: taking the results of their hard work and never thinking once of the suffering they have had to go through to give us our pleasure.

The Bodhichitta Motivation

Until we renounce the selfish mind, there will be little benefit in anything we do. Even if we work for others in some way, the mind is up and down and there are always problems, misunderstandings, and personal conflicts. We might be in a profession that is very beneficial for others, such as medicine or education, but with a self-centered motivation we are blocked from feeling any sense of fulfillment. On the surface, someone who has taken ordination should be so happy because he or she is of great benefit to others, but unless the motivation is altruistic, this is not so. The problem is not the job but the motivation for doing it. What should cause enormous joy and satisfaction only causes frustration and dissatisfaction because of the ego.

Even if we logically know that working for others is the route to happiness, unless we can overcome the selfish mind, there will be little benefit. It will all just feel like an incredible burden, like a mountain pushing down on our head.

We can be doing all the "right" things, but if we are not doing anything to transform our basic selfishness, we block whatever we do from being beneficial for ourselves or for others. Many people study the Dharma for a long time and then give it up, saying it is flawed or not relevant or something. The reason the Dharma has failed to help them is because, although they might have studied it, they have never really practiced it; they have never brought the Dharma into their lives, and so nothing they have done has become the Dharma—it is not the teachings of the Buddha that are at fault but their way of thinking. That's why checking our motivation is so important. We must do everything for the right reasons; otherwise, nothing will be of any benefit.

In our life, the habit of selfish concern is so strong and the habit of selflessness is so weak. This is what Shantideva said in *A Guide to the Bodhisattva's Way of Life*:

> How incredibly powerful the unceasing negativities are,
> whereas virtuous thoughts are so weak.
> What other merit besides bodhichitta
> can overcome them?[25]

Even when a positive action is done, compared to the negative actions we habitually do, it has very little power. We are so overwhelmed by nonvirtue that it becomes very hard to create any virtue at all. Until we overcome our selfishness through developing bodhichitta, the self-centered attitude will color everything we do. If we want to quickly purify all the negative imprints that are on our mindstream and have been there since beginningless time, the most skillful, wisest method is to cultivate this pure thought that leads all sentient beings to enlightenment.

As I often say, the purpose of our life is not just to obtain happiness for ourselves, not just to solve our own problems; the purpose of our life is to be useful for others, to be beneficial for others, to free numberless other living beings from all their sufferings and to lead them to happiness. *This* is the purpose of our life.

Therefore, the purpose of our life, the meaning of our own life, is limitless like the sky. We have the responsibility to bring happiness to numberless other living beings. If we have compassion, then, rather than receiving harm from us, the numberless beings receive peace and happiness. Being alive as a human being—for an hour, a minute, or even a second—in order to achieve enlightenment so we can enlighten all sentient beings brings meaning to our life.

Whereas cherishing the I opens the door to all problems, the minute we cherish others we open the door not only to our own happiness and enlightenment but also to the happiness of all other living beings. Why? Because when just one person generates bodhichitta, that attitude will lead to numberless beings being liberated from all their sufferings and to achieving every happiness. Our bodhichitta will cause the numberless hell beings to be free from suffering and achieve all happiness, including enlightenment. Our bodhichitta will cause the numberless hungry ghosts to be free from suffering and achieve all happiness, including enlightenment. Our bodhichitta will cause the numberless animals to be free from suffering and achieve all happiness, including enlightenment. Our bodhichitta will cause the numberless human beings to be free from suffering and achieve all happiness, including enlightenment. Our bodhichitta will cause the numberless gods and demigods to be free from suffering and achieve all happiness, including enlightenment. Our bodhichitta will cause the numberless intermediate-state beings[26] to be free from suffering and achieve all happiness, including enlightenment.

The situation is urgent. It's unbearable for us to delay generating bodhichitta for a day, for an hour, or for even a minute. It's unbearable for us not to have this realization. Because other sentient beings are suffering so much, and they need happiness so much, they need us to change our attitude from cherishing the I to cherishing others. This can't wait. The need for our bodhichitta is a million times more urgent than a heart attack victim's need for emergency treatment in a hospital. The need for our bodhichitta is a million, billion, trillion times more urgent. We *must* change our attitude from cherishing the I into cherishing others.

In our life there is nobody to work for except other sentient beings. There is no purpose in living our life except to work for sentient beings. Any work other than for sentient beings is meaningless.

Even if we have achieved the state of an arhat and have been released from samsara by having purified all the gross obscurations, our work is still not finished. We need to purify even the subtle obscurations to knowledge and attain enlightenment in order to do perfect work for sentient beings. Without this perfect power it's like an armless mother trying to save her child who has been taken by the river. She has the wish and the compassion but not the ability to save that child. We need the perfect power, the perfect understanding, the perfect compassion of a buddha.

All the effort we put into staying alive—everything we buy, all the clothes, all the food, all the medicines, all the items for our body from our hair to our toes—is only worthwhile if our life is to serve others. Trying to have a long and healthy life is only worthwhile because of this. Having a major illness, even dying, should be experienced for the benefit of others. The best way to experience death is on behalf of other living beings, in order to help them have happiness and be free from suffering. With this bodhichitta motivation we are able to keep our mind in a state of peace and tranquility as we die and so die with real happiness.

The purpose of life is not to live long and be healthy, nor is it to have money or power or reputation; it is just to be useful to others. With such an attitude, no matter what happens—good or bad, success or failure—everything is transformed into the path to enlightenment. Then, even a life-threatening illness does not perturb us. Rather than making us drown in self-pity, it makes us generate more compassion, looking for the very best way to benefit the numberless sentient beings. Whatever occurs in our life, we are fulfilling our potential as much as we can and so our goal is being achieved.

Even if we aren't Buddhist, even if we don't think about enlightenment, even if we consider ourselves unreligious, we can still see that the purpose of our life is to cause happiness for other living beings, to free them from suffering. To generate the good heart is to give meaning to life.

Therefore, right after we wake up each morning, we should rejoice that we haven't died during the night and that today we are again in this precious human body with this perfect human rebirth and the opportunity to develop our good heart. Then we should see that our priority, our responsibility, is to serve others, to free them from suffering and lead them to happiness. That's our job. That's our duty. Starting each day like this, there is so much peace and happiness for ourselves and for others.

We Are Responsible for Others' Happiness

The bodhichitta attitude means we have the responsibility for the happiness of the numberless other living beings. What do I mean by responsibility? Whether or not sentient beings receive harm or peace and happiness from us depends entirely on whether we have compassion for them. Without compassion the self-centered mind remains, creating attachment, anger, and so forth, which directly or indirectly brings harm to numberless other sentient beings from life to life. With compassion this does not happen. Therefore it is entirely in our hands whether we harm or benefit sentient beings.

What does it mean to benefit others? It simply means causing them to have happiness, but just as there are many levels of happiness, there are many levels of benefit we can bring them.

The first level of benefit is, with a sincere heart, to cause others to have happiness and comfort in this life. Giving medicine to those who are sick, food to those who are starving, money to those who don't have a means of living, material aid to those in need—these are all very important benefits we can bring them. Helping others have a happier, more comfortable life is a great service we can offer them, and we should do it as much as possible, but this will not be the cause for them to be truly happy.

The next level of benefit is to cause others to have happiness in all their future lives—not just one or two future lives, but all their coming future lives while they are in samsara. Even though this is still temporary happiness, it is much more important than this life's happiness, which is very short term.

More important than this benefit is to bring the numberless sentient beings to ultimate, everlasting happiness—liberation from the whole of samsara, from the cycle of death and rebirth and all the problems that occur in between. By showing sentient beings how to completely eliminate karma and delusion, including the seed of the delusion, we help them completely cease samsara and all its suffering. If we are able to do that, it is far more important than bringing them to the temporary happiness of future lives.

Even more important is to help sentient beings completely cease even their subtle negative imprints and lead them to great liberation, to peerless full enlightenment. There is nothing beyond that to be developed. This is the most beneficial use of our life.

So there are many different levels of happiness we can lead others to, and of course, sentient beings need all these levels, but to bring them to enlightenment is the most important service we can offer. Because eliminating the root of suffering can only be achieved by practicing the Dharma, leading all sentient beings to the complete peace of nirvana and enlightenment by showing them the Dharma is the best motivation we can have. This is our universal responsibility.

The Refuge and Bodhichitta Prayer

Because attaining enlightenment in order to lead all other sentient beings to that same state is the greatest service we can offer others, it is vital that a bodhichitta motivation is behind whatever we do. This is why the refuge and bodhichitta prayer that many people do each morning is very important. Although it is only four lines long, it contains so much:

> I go for refuge until I am enlightened,
>   to the Buddha, the Dharma, and the Supreme
>   Assembly.

By my merit of giving and other perfections,
may I become a buddha to benefit all sentient beings.[27]

Buddhist prayers such as this might sound like Christian prayers, and if you developed an aversion to praying when you were young, you might have a similar aversion to them. But prayer is a meditation; each word has incredible, deep meaning, like the limitless sky. You need to meditate on each word; if you don't it just becomes a prayer.

What each word expresses is so powerful that it affects the mind, leaving an imprint on the mental continuum, even if we don't fully understand the meaning. Just like planting seeds in our garden can produce a crop that can feed everybody, this prayer plants a positive seed in our mental continuum. What grows is a bodhi tree, the mind of enlightenment.

There is a famous banyan tree in India that is so huge its branches can shade five hundred carriages, but it came from a tiny seed. Mental evolution is much bigger than this. A small banyan seed, which results in a huge tree, is nothing compared to saying this prayer, which results in full enlightenment. With the imprints planted by reciting this prayer, in our next lives we will meet the Dharma again and again, and understanding the meaning of these words will be so much easier because we heard them in a past life. Having planted the seed, it's so much easier to practice and actualize realizations, and then, by entering the Mahayana path and taking universal responsibility, ceasing even the subtle defilements.

After we become enlightened, the effects of the prayer don't stop there. We are then fully qualified to liberate numberless sentient beings from the oceans of samsaric sufferings and the cause of those sufferings, and to bring each and every single sentient being to full enlightenment.

This is the effect that happens to our mental continuum by saying this prayer. It contains the whole of the Buddhadharma: the *base*, the two truths, conventional and ultimate; the *path*, method and wisdom; and the *goal* to be achieved, the *rupakaya* and *dharmakaya*, the holy body and holy mind of a buddha.

When we take refuge, we do so for two reasons: out of fear of samsara and out of deep respect for the Three Rare Sublime Ones—the Buddha, the Dharma, and the Sangha. The Mahayana has a third element to refuge: compassion. By knowing that the nature of our own samsara is total suffering, we realize how all other beings are in exactly the same situation, caught up in samara and experiencing only suffering. On the basis of our own fear and the wish to be free from it, we wish all others likewise to be free from all suffering. Then we go a step further by taking on the responsibility to free them ourselves. Without this sense of responsibility we might have compassion but not the great compassion of Mahayana Buddhism.

This prayer not only combines taking refuge and generating bodhichitta but also the *causal refuge* and the *resultant refuge*. When we say, "I go for refuge until I am enlightened," this is the causal refuge, where we take refuge in the causal Buddha, Guru Shakyamuni Buddha; the causal Dharma, the teachings of the Buddha; and the causal Sangha, the spiritual community that helps us attain our goal. The last two lines of the prayer—"may I become a buddha . . ."—are the resultant refuge, where we take refuge in the absolute or resultant objects of refuge: our own eventual buddhahood, our own spiritual attainments, and the absolute Sangha.

Furthermore, Pabongka Dechen Nyingpo said that this prayer contains two types of bodhichitta: *aspirational* or *wishing bodhichitta* and *engaging bodhichitta*. The first part of the final line, "may I become a buddha," is the aspirational bodhichitta, the thought of seeking enlightenment; and "to benefit all sentient beings" is the engaging bodhichitta, the thought of seeking to work for others.

"By my merit of giving and other perfections" shows us not only the path we must take—attaining bodhichitta and practicing the six perfections—but also *why*: in order to benefit all sentient beings.

Although the Tibetan term *drowa* is translated here as "sentient beings," it seems to express so much more than this neutral term. I prefer *transmigratory beings* because that shows beings who are trapped in terrible suffering, very pitiful, with no freedom at all, totally overcome by karma and delusion. That term, *transmigratory being*, has a wealth of meaning; it encapsulates the whole of the teachings on the twelve links of dependent origination, the twelve interconnecting chains of cause and effect that are the mechanism that keeps us trapped in samsara. The first link, the fundamental ignorance that misunderstands reality, creates the second link, karma. That then leads to consciousness forming and contact with sense objects, which in turn leads to clinging and craving and that leads to birth, which inevitably leads to old age and death. Seeing how all beings are enslaved like this, great compassion can easily grow. Seeing what we must do to help all transmigratory beings forever circling in the suffering six realms of samsara, we understand how there is nothing more urgent than taking refuge.

This short prayer is extremely powerful. It could be the focus of months of meditation. Aspiring to full enlightenment and the bodhisattva's way, we are working for the benefit of not just some sentient beings but *all* sentient beings. We want to not only give food to the hungry and shelter to those without, not only freedom from oppression and illness, but complete enlightenment to each and every sentient being. This is a huge mind; this is the biggest mind, all contained in a few small words.

The Importance of Motivation

In his *Guide to the Bodhisattva's Way of Life*, Shantideva warned that we need to guard our mind and never commit nonvirtue. He said,

> Even those who wish to find happiness and overcome misery
> will wander with neither aim nor meaning
> if they do not comprehend the secret of the mind—
> the paramount significance of the Dharma.[28]

Here, "the secret of the mind" does not mean some high realization such as clear light or the illusory body; it is not talking about anything very complicated. We can interpret the secret of the mind as meaning the different levels of motivation we have for doing any action. This verse emphasizes the importance of watching and protecting our mind, of keeping it in virtue, because happiness and suffering are dependent upon our own mind, our own positive and negative thoughts. One way of thinking produces happiness; another way of thinking produces suffering and problems. Everything—from day-to-day problems and the sufferings of the six realms up to liberation and enlightenment—depends on our mind, our way of thinking.

Shantideva called this the secret of the mind because most of us are completely unaware that suffering and happiness come from our own mind and not from external objects. Without this secret we have no way of understanding the importance of always keeping a positive motivation.

If we look at just the human beings in this world—not even considering the animals, hell beings, and hungry ghosts—we will see that sentient beings do not know what needs to be abandoned and what needs to be practiced. Despite having great intelligence and having learned so many things, human beings do not know this one thing!

I heard about a couple who has spent fifteen years studying a few dolphins in the ocean. Every day they go on the boat and study the dolphins' lives. I think there are only three, four, or five dolphins—anyway, very few. This couple has spent fifteen years studying them! And there are many people who, after obtaining a degree in university, study just one insect! Their learning is unbelievable. They have so much knowledge, but not this one knowledge, not this vital thing.

The need for the correct motivation is illustrated by Pabongka Dechen Nyingpo's description of four people reciting the *Praises to the Twenty-One Taras* prayer with four different motivations. The first person recites the prayer with a bodhichitta motivation, with the wish to attain enlightenment in order to be of benefit to all sentient beings. Because of that motivation the recitation becomes the cause for enlightenment. The second person recites the prayer with the motivation to attain complete renunciation and hence attain liberation from all suffering. With such a motivation the recitation becomes the cause for that, but not to attain enlightenment. The third person recites the prayer with the motivation to achieve the happiness of future lives, and so the recitation becomes the cause for that, but not for liberation or enlightenment.

The fourth person recites the Tara prayer only with the motivation to obtain the happiness of this life: long life, good health, wealth, and so forth. This last person's recitation does not become the cause for a good rebirth, liberation, or enlightenment, and in fact, even though this person is reciting a Dharma prayer, the motivation is nonvirtuous, and therefore it only becomes the cause for future suffering.[29]

Because of the power of mantras and prayers, words can pacify obstacles and have some benefits, but that does not mean that the person's motivation is Dharma or that the action of reciting the prayer itself will be the cause for future happiness. Because the action is done with a worldly motivation, it is only worldly dharma and is the cause of suffering.

The secret of the mind is knowing what is and what is not Dharma, and these four different motivations are a clear indication of this. The first three are Dharma and the last one is not. That the real cause of happiness comes from having a virtuous motivation is something hidden from most people but not from somebody who practices the Dharma, watching the mind to ensure it is always virtuous and practicing renunciation, working sincerely toward complete liberation.

In the next verse, Shantideva said,

> This being so,
> I shall hold and guard my mind well.
> Without the discipline of guarding the mind,
> what use are many other disciplines?[30]

No matter how much Dharma we know, how long we meditate, or what sadhanas we do daily, if the motivation is not virtuous, the action is only ever non-Dharma and the cause of suffering. That is why we must guard our mind well. As Shantideva asked, what use are any practices, particularly taking the various vows not to commit nonvirtues, if we leave our mind unguarded and mindlessly commit whatever nonvirtue is our habit? The *actual* practice is left out, and so the practice can never be beneficial. The mouth is forming the Dharma words, but the mind is completely crazy, like an out-of-control elephant destroying everything in its path, or like a tsunami crashing over the land, washing away all positive aspects of our life. When that happens all sorts of problems come: mental problems, relationship problems, sickness, and so forth.

If we need mindfulness in our daily life—to avoid traffic accidents, to avoid getting fired, and so forth—we need it in our Dharma practice much more. Unless we guard our mind and use what we have learned from Buddhism to subdue our mind and solve our deep-rooted problems, our Buddhist education is a waste of time. If our Dharma knowledge does not become a method to achieve peace, what is the point?

There are many levels of vows we can take to protect our mind and make our life so fruitful, but without guarding our mind to ensure we keep those vows, what is the use of having so many vows and practices? We can change our external conduct and act as a pure and devoted Dharma practitioner, but it is our inner conduct we need to change. That is exactly why we have the vows and practices in Buddhism. Sitting rigid for hours, clicking the beads on a mala, shaving our head—none of these outer manifestations can dig out the root of suffering; they cannot remove the cause of samsara. Only protecting the mind can do that.

With incorrect motivation, the "religious" practices we do can well become the cause for our many problems rather than the cure. Instead of pacifying the mind, they can increase the ego, the attachment, the anger, and the other negative minds that they are designed to destroy. We could be puffed up with pride that we are such a well-known practitioner or be attached to our reputation or our Dharma texts. We can even become angry when others suggest we are not an earnest practitioner of patience!

For instance, all over the world people go to temples to pray, assuming the action itself—worshiping God or a deity—is a pure action. But somebody can go to a temple for a number of reasons—to enjoy the pleasant walk there, to impress others, and so forth—and be using the temple for selfish ends. People don't see that things such as dressing up and taking nice offerings, when done for selfish motivations, are impure and so the source of suffering.

Protecting our mind is something we should take very seriously, seeing how vulnerable and easily corrupted our mind is in its present state. Of this, in the next verse Shantideva said,

> Just as I would be attentive and careful of a wound
> when amidst a bustling, uncontrolled crowd,
> so I should always guard the wound of my mind
> when dwelling among harmful people.[31]

We protect the wound of our mind by watching our mind and our motivation in everyday life. Every moment of every day, objects appear to our sense faculties demanding attention, potentially pulling us away from our awareness and into attraction or aversion. This is like trying to move through a bustling market full of people while nursing a wounded arm—one touch and the wound would be incredibly painful. We must be utterly careful and vigilant. Like taking an aspirin as soon as a headache occurs, by applying the meditation techniques whenever we see our mind becoming negative, we can transform our mind from the cause of suffering into the cause of happiness.

That is why it is so vital to always guard our mind. This is said in the thought-transformation text *Eight Verses on Mind Training* by Langri Tangpa:

> During all my activities I will probe my mind,
> and as soon as affliction arises—
> since it endangers myself and others—
> I will diligently train myself to confront it directly
>   and avert it.[32]

The Tibetan for "diligently," *tsentap*, literally means "immediately and with effort." How do we avert any afflictions that arise in our mindstream as soon as we encounter them? By applying the paths of wisdom and method: by immediately meditating on emptiness to instantly dispel the wrong concept that the negative mind is based on, and by using what we have learned from studying the lamrim as antidotes to whatever negative mind has arisen.

It's important to prevent delusions from arising, but it's even more important to avert and destroy them if they have already arisen. It's best not to let the thief sneak into our house to steal our valuables, but if they do, we need a way to catch them and subdue them. If we don't, they may well creep up on us from behind and hit us over the head with a big hammer, meaning we not only lose our precious possessions, but we also end up in the hospital. In the same way, if we can't immediately recognize and avert our negative emotions, that can set up a whole chain reaction of a negative mind leading to a negative action creating another negative mind and so on and so forth. Soon, it won't just be a hammer the thief is hitting us with but a whole bomb!

Shantideva explained that one moment of anger destroys eons of merit. We always need to be vigilant and avert any negative mind the instant we notice it: anger, attachment, pride, spitefulness, or whatever. That way, we are always able to keep the mind virtuous and only create the causes for happiness.

If we don't have any delusions, any hallucinations, then of course we don't need to practice awareness because our mind will just naturally be aware. But until that time we will always need awareness, we will always need to watch the mind, to guard it from delusions arising. Because everything is impermanent, because everything is constantly changing, it is definitely possible to transform our current mind into a mind that is one with the Dharma, with the three principal aspects of the path. Our attachment can become nonattachment, or renunciation of the whole of samsara; our cherishing of self can become cherishing of others, or bodhichitta; our ignorance can become the wisdom of realizing emptiness. That is definitely possible. Just as the mind has been the creator of the problem-causing delusions we now have, it can also be the creator of our wisdom and bodhichitta.

The Essence of the Perfect Human Rebirth

The ultimate nature of our mind is the clear light: buddha nature. This is what gives us the potential to fully develop our mind, to transform it from as it is now into a mind completely purified of all stains and with all good qualities. Because our mind has buddha nature, we have this potential to cause all this happiness for all sentient beings. Because we have this potential, we have the responsibility to do it.

Furthermore, we not only have buddha nature, as do all sentient beings, but we also have the supremely good fortune to have received this perfect human rebirth, this life with its eight freedoms and ten richnesses,[33] which gives us the perfect tool to develop our mind to full enlightenment, something so few other sentient beings have.

It is almost impossible to understand how amazing and rare this opportunity is. We have met the perfect teachings and the perfect teachers, and we have all the tools at our disposal—our education, our intelligence, our interest, our freedom, and so forth—to destroy the root of our suffering, our self-cherishing mind, and fully develop the wonderful mind of bodhichitta. Even a quick look at the beings about us—those with the same social situation as we have, those higher and lower, all the animals that share our world with us—will show us the uniqueness of this situation we have found ourselves in. Of this Shantideva said,

> Just like a blind man
> discovering a jewel in a heap of rubbish,
> likewise by some coincidence
> an Awakening Mind has been born within me.[34]

Even a small diamond is worth so much money. If the world were covered in diamonds, we wouldn't think anything of it, but we value diamonds above all other jewels because of their rarity. If we found a huge one we would be so happy, realizing that our money worries were over. Likewise, this precious mind of bodhichitta is so rare and so valuable.

How incredible that we have even heard the word *bodhichitta*—let alone understood its value and been taught ways of developing this inestimable mind.

The one thing that is considered even more valuable than a diamond or even all the treasures of the god realms is the wish-granting jewel, a jewel that has the power to grant any wish. In previous times, on auspicious days such as the full-moon days, bodhisattvas who had created great merit could go under the ocean to get these most precious jewels. These wish-granting jewels were covered in mud, so they had to be cleaned three times, the final time with very fine cotton to remove the subtle stains. When they were placed on a banner on top of a house on a full-moon night, whatever material wishes the people might desire—money; a long, healthy life; and so forth—would be immediately obtained.

Imagine what we could do if we owned one wish-granting jewel. Imagine if we owned a thousand or a million or a zillion. However, that is still nothing compared to having this perfect human rebirth and the opportunity to develop bodhichitta. With a zillion wish-granting jewels we could have any material thing we wanted—all the wealth of the god realms, if we wished—but that could not buy us one atom of real happiness or liberation or enlightenment. With this perfect human rebirth and the compassionate attitude, we can progress on the path, freeing ourselves from all delusions and realizing all good qualities, bringing the peerless happiness of enlightenment and allowing us to benefit all sentient beings, so there is no comparison between the two.

Milarepa[35] didn't have one jewel, not even one *paise* (a hundredth of an Indian rupee), and yet he was so happy. Dedicating his life to the service of others, he went from great happiness to greater happiness, and he was able to attain full enlightenment in that lifetime, all because of bodhichitta. Therefore, we must not waste even a second of this incredible opportunity we have. As Shantideva said,

> This precious human body, qualified with its freedoms
>   and richnesses,
>   is extremely difficult to find again.

If I don't obtain the benefits with this body,
how can I hope to attain a precious body again
    in the future?[36]

There is no greater loss than wasting our precious human life, not training our mind in method and wisdom. We can generate this precious
thought of bodhichitta, this ultimate good heart, because we have
received the best possible body to be able to do this.

We can generate bodhichitta easily and strongly because we live in
the southern continent[37] where life is a mixture of happiness and suffering, and it is therefore easy to generate very strong renunciation of
samsara by realizing the nature of suffering. With that, developing compassion toward other sentient beings becomes easy, which in turn leads
to bodhichitta and to full enlightenment. This is not possible for beings
living in other continents.

We have received this body capable of generating bodhichitta, and we
have met the Mahayana teachings that show us how to develop bodhichitta and practice the six perfections. We have met the Mahayana
virtuous friend, the guru, and received teachings and taken vows from
him or her. This is all due to having this perfect human rebirth.

Being born here, we have a human body born from a womb and con-
stituted of the three white substances received from the father—sperm,
bone, and marrow—and the three red substances from the mother—
skin, blood, and flesh. Such a body is needed in order to practice tantra,
especially highest yoga tantra. Only in this body, only on this southern
continent, can we as beginners achieve enlightenment very quickly.

On top of this, we have been born in a world where there are the
twenty-four special holy places of Heruka Chakrasamvara, an aspect
of the Buddha. If we practice this tantric path, the *dakinis* of these
twenty-four holy places bless our body and chakras[38] as we are meditating. Because of this, we are very quickly able to open our chakras and
generate the very high tantric realization of clear light, giving us the
possibility of achieving enlightenment in this lifetime, quickly accomplishing the work for all kind mother sentient beings.

(I often use the term *kind mother sentient beings*. The term looks very short, but it contains the entire graduated path of the higher capable being. If we know this, whenever we hear the term it becomes incredibly powerful for us; it becomes a whole meditation in a glance. Just hearing the word *kind* we remember how all sentient beings have been so incredibly kind to us, how they are the source of all our happiness, and we see them in great beauty, without any discrimination, just like we see our mother or our best friend.)

We are working toward enlightenment, but enlightenment is just a tool to allow us to best benefit all other sentient beings. When we eat ice cream, the main thing is eating the ice cream. We need to open the tub, put the spoon in, and lift the ice cream to our mouth. But the reason for all this is to taste the ice cream, to get it into our mouth and into our stomach. None of the other things are our main goal. In the same way, there are many things we need to do to become enlightened, but the main motivation in everything we do should be to benefit others. If we are mainly concerned with others' welfare, then we have a mind that is close to bodhichitta.

Taking the Essence of This Life

If the most beneficial method to help others is to become a buddha, how can we do that? It's not like taking a picture—click, and the picture is taken. It's not like flicking a switch and a light comes on. We won't get there just thinking that enlightenment is a nice idea and it would be wonderful if we could help all sentient beings. Without undergoing many hardships and working very hard for a very long time, and without strong determination, we won't be able to purify the obscurations and accumulate the merit we need to attain full enlightenment. The only method to attain this great goal is by developing bodhichitta, and the only chance we have to do that is while we have this precious human body, qualified with the eight freedoms and the ten richnesses.

If our mind is enriched with bodhichitta, then whatever action of body, speech, or mind we do is unstained by the self-cherishing mind, and so every single action we do single-pointedly becomes a method to accumulate extensive merit and is highly beneficial for others.

We need this firm, clear motivation to only help others in everything we do. I remember once a music producer in Hong Kong asked me whether he should have a child or not. I met him after his mother had died, and he had produced an album of music by a famous Hong Kong singer for the Maitreya Project. I told him that before he decided, he must have a very clear goal, a clear direction for the child's life. If he wanted to bring a child into this world, he should aim for the child to be a source of peace and happiness for the whole world, to bring up the child with a good heart, with loving-kindness and compassion, and with a sense of universal responsibility for all sentient beings' happiness. This is the way any couple should bring up their child. With such a motivation, having a child is very worthwhile. Otherwise, we make so much sacrifice and use so much energy and time raising the child, educating them, feeding them, clothing them, and then they leave home and become only a source of suffering for others.

With bodhichitta everything we do is for every sentient being, and so we collect limitless skies of merit no matter what the action is. The only reason we are doing *any* action is to benefit all our kind mother sentient beings. If we are saying a mantra, we are saying it for all the people of the world, all those who are suffering terribly such as those in Africa dying of starvation or those refugees from the many wars, and all those who happen to have comfortable lives at the moment.

If there is a fly on the wall nearby, we are saying the mantra for that fly. We are saying it for the ants crawling along the floor, for the worms in the garden, for the birds, for the dogs, for the cats, for the foxes, for the horses, the sheep, and the cows. Every mantra is dedicated to every animal, insect, bird, fish, and human, as well as every hungry ghost, hell being, god, and intermediate-state being.

Perhaps, from where we are right now, we can see a few flies and birds, but most animal sentient beings are invisible to us. Beneath our feet are countless worms, ants, spiders, and other animals. We rarely think of their pitiful lives, of how worms are attacked by birds as soon as they come to the surface or taken by fishermen and pushed live onto hooks. There are billions and billions of sentient beings. We are terrified of some, such as spiders, sharks, or snakes, but we are saying that mantra for each sentient being, cute or terrifying. We are saying the mantra for all the carnivores, such as lions and tigers, and the poor herbivores that are eaten by the carnivores, such as deer and zebra.

I saw a documentary on television about a drought in Africa. The animals had to travel a great distance to drink any water at all. Monkeys and wildebeests came to a watering hole but there was just mud. The monkeys were very skinny from hunger and thirst, and they fought each other viciously. It was so sad.

With bodhichitta we are saying mantras for all those monkeys and wildebeest and all the other starving, thirsty animals. That is such an amazing thing. Walking to the shops, every step we cover benefits countless animals, big and small, those we can see and those we can't, those in our country and those in other countries, those that are well fed and those that are starving. Because we have bodhichitta, every step is done for the welfare of *all* living beings without missing one, and so we are helping all those animals. Thinking about details like these, we can see just how incredible this practice of bodhichitta is. It's really mind-blowing!

Even though we still haven't attained the actual realization of bodhichitta, by having the aspiration to attain it and by regularly saying the refuge and bodhichitta prayer, any action we then do with a bodhichitta motivation becomes so beneficial. Whether it is cooking for others, teaching others in school, working in a hospital, gardening, working on a production line producing goods for others to use, we are serving other sentient beings anyway—those sentient beings need these things for their happiness—but with a bodhichitta motivation we are also helping lead them and all sentient beings to enlightenment.

Think of all the ants in Africa, even just on one mountain; think of all the sentient beings in the oceans and in the air, living in forests and in the ground. Bodhichitta covers all sentient beings. It covers all the terrorists and all the leaders of all the countries. When we recite one mantra or do one sadhana, it includes all the armies of all the countries, all the soldiers who kill others and who are killed, the Americans, the British, the Iraqis, the Syrians, all the people who torture and are tortured.

I saw footage of people kept in a huge football stadium and how an executioner made some people lie down, knowing they were going to die, and then he made those people's families watch as he chopped off their heads with a long knife while the families were forced to clap. I couldn't bring myself to watch while he was beheading the people. This wasn't a movie, it wasn't make-believe with actors and fake blood; it was a real event. It was just unimaginable what the people suffered. But the prayer, the mantra, or the sadhana we recite with bodhichitta covers all sentient beings, the executioner and the victims and the victims' families. It includes everybody in every country—China, Tibet, India, Europe—every sentient being everywhere.

An action done with a bodhichitta motivation covers not only every sentient being in this world but also throughout the numberless universes. That includes the realms of the desire, form, and formless realm gods such as the Tushita god realm and the Heaven of Thirty-Three[39]— and the hungry ghost realm and the hell realm. We are doing that action for all those beings.

Instead of becoming nonvirtue, every single action we do becomes the most powerful virtue, whether it is shopping, cleaning the house, working for a Dharma center, or whatever. We are doing it for the benefit of all sentient beings, and so everything we buy, every step we take, everything we do creates limitless skies of merit. If we say 108 mantras of a deity practice, we create 108 causes for enlightenment. If we do any action with a bodhichitta motivation, it creates the cause for enlightenment, laying the foundation of the path that will take us all the way there. Then, attaining enlightenment, without a single mistake we are able to repay the great kindness of all those mother sentient beings who have helped us get there.

Only Now Can We Take This Opportunity

Now, at this time, we must do everything we can to transform our mind so we can not only cease harming others but also develop all our good qualities, in order to be able to help others in as vast a way as possible. If we could clearly see our own state of mind and see that we have nothing but virtuous thoughts, then we could afford to feel very happy, but probably if we really looked, we would be horrified. With all the self-cherishing clouding our mind, can we even expect another human existence after we die, let alone a perfect human rebirth with its eight freedoms and ten richnesses? Shantideva said,

> If when I have the chance to live a wholesome life
> my actions are not wholesome,
> then what shall I be able to do
> when confused by the misery of the lower realms?

> And if I commit no wholesome deeds [there],
> but readily amass much wrongdoing,
> then for a hundred million eons
> I shall not even hear the words "a happy life."

> For these very reasons, the Buddha has said
> that as difficult as it is for a turtle to insert its neck
> into a yoke adrift upon the vast ocean,
> it is more difficult to attain the human state.[40]

If we fail to attain another human body, we can be assured of a body that brings us nothing but untold suffering and, worse still, allows us no chance to develop any virtue at all, thus locking us into more and more suffering in the future. Even if we are somehow able to find a rebirth in the upper realms, we are still unable to create any virtue at all, thus ensuring nothing but misery in our consequent lives.

To show how difficult it is to obtain a human rebirth, the Buddha used the example of a blind turtle, swimming below the surface of a vast ocean and surfacing only once every hundred years. Floating randomly with the currents on the surface of the ocean is a golden ring or yoke. The chances of the turtle happening to rise to the surface in such a way that its neck slips through the ring is infinitesimal. Such are the chances of us attaining another human rebirth.[41]

Somehow, miraculously, we have this precious human body, and we have met the Mahayana teachings on bodhichitta and have the time and the inclination to study them and to meditate on them. How incredible that is! And how rare that is.

It is worth thinking of how few people, let alone animals and other sentient beings, have this opportunity. When we think about the billions of people on this planet, how many have the chance we have to develop on the path? We could have been born as a peasant or a migrant worker; we could have been born into a refugee family or in a war zone. There are so many terrible lives we could have had that would mean nothing but poverty, hardship, and misery, where there would be no freedom at all to do anything, where it would be just the most basic survival. The vast majority of beings have no choice; they must kill, steal, lie, or do any of the other nonvirtuous actions just to survive. A beggar has no choice, a soldier has no choice. Even a general in an army must order others to kill, creating terrible negative karma every day.

We are free of all these types of existence. At this moment we are living in a situation where we can avoid creating negative karma. But we have been even more fortunate than that. There are comparatively few people able to follow any spiritual path. And of those who do, how many have met the Buddhadharma? And how many of *those* have met the Mahayana? We can see that this is the one route not just to attain total freedom from suffering but also to gain full enlightenment.

From the buddhas' side, all they want is for all sentient beings to have limitless happiness and no suffering at all. The reason this has not happened is because of the delusions of sentient beings blocking them from receiving that help. Until now, we have been in that situation, but now, miraculously, we are in this unparalleled situation where we can lift ourselves out of the cycle of suffering. What greater madness could there be than having this opportunity and not using it?

If we don't know how to drive a car or our business suffers a loss, then others around us will laugh at us and think we are kind of foolish.

The most foolish one of all is whoever has this unique and rare chance to practice the Dharma and who fails to do so. We have untold freedom and enjoyment now thanks to the ripening of the karma from our previous virtuous acts, so if we complacently indulge in sense pleasures, thinking our good fortune will never end, and never do anything to provide for our future happiness, there is no greater deception than this.

Perhaps we have been playing the lottery all our life, buying tickets every week and watching as our numbers never come up. Then one day, there they are, and we are suddenly a multimillionaire. Think of the incredible odds, how so many millions of people play the lottery and how few win, and here we suddenly have so many millions of dollars. We will never have to work again; we can buy a huge house and go on a world cruise. There is nothing we can't now do. But on the way to receive our prize, we decide that our pocket is full of junk, and so we throw all the tissues and stuff into a bin—the winning lottery ticket along with the trash. Could there be anything more stupid?

Wasting this perfect human rebirth is much, much more stupid. If we are so careful with even a ten-dollar note, of course we would be a million times more careful with a winning lottery ticket. Why, then, are we not a billion billion times more careful with the wonderful human existence we have miraculously found ourselves in? If we could really see how precious this life is, we would value it like a mountain of winning lottery tickets, like a universe of wish-granting jewels. For countless eons we have lived lives with not one scrap of happiness or one opportunity to develop our good qualities; for countless eons in the future, unless we use this opportunity, we will only suffer again. Therefore, there is no greater foolishness than not using this unique opportunity. Of this Shantideva said,

> And if, having understood this,
> I still foolishly continue to be slothful,
> when the hour of my death arrives
> tremendous grief will rear its head.

Then if my body blazes for a long time
in the unbearable flames of hell,
inevitably my mind will be tormented
by the fires of unendurable remorse.[42]

Sitting back, becoming fat and complacent, without understanding the source or fragility of all our good fortune, we can waste our entire life. Then, at the time of our death we will see this, and incredible terror and grief will overwhelm us. We made no preparations for our future life at all while we had the freedom, and now, at the time of our death, it is too late. Faced with the horror of the hell realm, caused by our nonvirtuous, self-cherishing mind, we see the folly we have committed, and we are consumed by terrible remorse. We didn't do what we could have done so easily, and now we must endure the unendurable for an unimaginably long time.

To have this body of freedoms and richnesses and to waste it so completely is crazy. It is like we are overcome by some malevolent spirit, like we have been hypnotized. We must not let this happen. That is why it is so important to study the lamrim topics such as perfect human rebirth and impermanence and death. We must do everything possible to make our human existence meaningful and thus ensure another perfect human rebirth and another chance to further develop on the path to enlightenment. And the best way we can make it most meaningful is to train in bodhichitta.

The Buddha explained that if the number of beings in all the upper realms—humans, demigods, and gods—is comparable to the amount of dirt we collect under one fingernail when we scrape the earth, then the number of beings in the lower realms is equivalent to the amount of earth left behind: the whole planet. The number is unimaginable. Even the animals that we can see are innumerable. And if the number of beings in the upper realms is as small as the amount of dirt under one fingernail, then the number of human beings is far, far smaller. And, of course, the number of human beings experiencing a perfect human rebirth is far, far smaller than even that.

This is the rarest rebirth, the one that is most difficult to attain. Without looking at the difficulty of attaining the causes, without seeing the rarity of the existence of the Dharma, just considering numbers, this is so rare.

The Rarity of Bodhichitta

Virtue is extremely rare. In *A Guide to the Bodhisattva's Way of Life*, Shantideva said,

> Just as a flash of lightning on a dark, cloudy night
> for an instant brightly illuminates all,
> likewise, in this world, through the might of the Buddha,
> a wholesome thought rarely and briefly appears.[43]

Samsara is completely dark, only illuminated for the briefest moment by a flash of Dharma. This is how rare and precious it is that we have met the Dharma. From beginningless time until now we have lived blinded by the darkness of ignorance, without the light of Dharma. Because it has rarely happened that we have created the causes to have an existence such as the one we now have, we must use this precious time without wasting a second; like a lightning flash, it will soon be gone and we will be in darkness again. Therefore, like grabbing a precious jewel we have seen on the roadside in that flash of lightning, we must grab hold of this chance for liberation and enlightenment.

In another verse Shantideva said,

> With behavior such as this
> I shall not win a human body again,
> and if this human form is not attained
> there will be solely wrongdoing and no virtue.[44]

When Shantideva refers to "behavior such as this," he means our normal worldly behavior: clinging to this life's happiness. When we have such a mind, we can forget about enlightenment or even getting out of the bondage of samsara; with such behavior we cannot even hope for another human rebirth. And if that is so, then it is almost impossible to do anything but create nonvirtue in our lower realm body.

Imagine explaining to somebody trapped in great poverty how we need to think of the welfare of each and every sentient being. Such a vast mind would scare them, and for them, engaging in the practice would be far too difficult. For such a person it would seem a huge burden, like having to carry a great mountain. We need great merit to even start to develop bodhichitta. Of this, Shantideva said,

> Do even fathers and mothers
> have such a benevolent intention as this?
> Do the gods and sages?
> Does even Brahma have it?
>
> If those beings have never before
> even dreamed of such an attitude
> for their own sake,
> how would it ever arise for the sake of others?[45]

Those beings we consider as most concerned about our welfare—our parents, our teachers, even great gods such as Brahma—have never heard of such a vast mind, so of course normal people find it inconceivable. Even our parents, no matter how kind and caring they are to us, do not have bodhichitta.

Our parents and teachers and the samsaric gods all want freedom from suffering for themselves and for those in their care, but even in a dream they could not conceive of freedom from *all* suffering for themselves, meaning liberation and enlightenment, let alone for all other sentient beings. This is how rare bodhichitta is.

Even if we say the words "all sentient beings" with our mouth, still in the depth of our heart our own happiness is paramount; we hold this like a Mount Everest above all other things. This is because we have neither taken our understanding of our own suffering deep enough, to the level where we can see that all our suffering stems from self-cherishing, nor taken our understanding of others' suffering to the level where great compassion arises.

Without this understanding, no matter how much we long for bodhichitta, it just won't happen. Changing our attitude from self-centered to only thinking of others is a remarkable thing, an incredibly rare thing, like having a rainbow in our room. It is such an amazing thing that it might well seem impossible, but if we meditate strongly enough it will happen. Shantideva said the birth of this altruistic attitude is an unimaginable marvel.

We need to have so much merit to even hear the word *bodhichitta*, let alone to have the opportunity to study it or to meditate on it. So few people in this world have this opportunity. The majority of Buddhists are from countries such as Sri Lanka, Burma, and Thailand that practice the path of individual liberation, and although compassion plays a huge part in that philosophy, the term *bodhichitta* is not even used and there are certainly no teachings on it.

Christianity has many amazing teachings on compassion, but it doesn't offer the complete path to liberation and enlightenment. There is no mention of bodhichitta. Christian morality teaches compassion for other humans, for instance, but it doesn't mention compassion for animals; I have heard that many Christians believe that animals are a gift from God to humans as food. His Holiness the Dalai Lama tells of the great Christians who are revered for sacrificing their lives caring for others, such as those who serve lepers, not caring if they themselves catch the disease. Even that incredible compassion is not the great compassion for all sentient beings that leads to bodhichitta.

We are so fortunate that we have this rare opportunity. Even just reciting *om mani padme hum*, Chenrezig's mantra, reminds us of bodhichitta, and so does turning a *mani* wheel. We should analyze just how rare this chance is and how we have created such great merit in the past to have this opportunity, and then see how we must continue to create such merit to be able to continue developing in this way. Therefore everything we do should be done with a bodhichitta motivation. As Khunu Lama Rinpoche said in *The Jewel Lamp*,

> When you walk, walk with bodhichitta.
> When you sit, sit with bodhichitta.
> When you stand, stand with bodhichitta.
> When you sleep, sleep with bodhichitta.
>
> When you look, look with bodhichitta.
> When you eat, eat with bodhichitta.
> When you speak, speak with bodhichitta.
> When you think, think with bodhichitta.[46]

The reason we are alive is to eliminate every suffering of every kind mother sentient being. With this motivation, every second of our life becomes incredibly meaningful, not narrow but infinite like the limitless sky. We are all responsible for the happiness of all other sentient beings; it is in our hands.

This is so logical, but because so few people seem to be able to see the importance of compassion in our life, I thought it might be good to advertise compassion in order to inspire people. Compassion slogans could be printed on mugs to remind people when they have their coffee, or as bumper stickers to remind them when they drive. One way I did actually do this was by having some people produce bookmarks with these ideas on them. They became very popular. Modifying it from Khunu Lama Rinpoche's wonderful verses, the bookmark finally said,

> Live with compassion
> Work with compassion
> Die with compassion
> Meditate with compassion
> Enjoy with compassion
> When problems come, experience them with compassion

When I started living in the United States we needed a car. When we got one I decided to put some advertisements on it, so we stuck a sign along one side that said, "No anger, no enemy"; the other side had "The best way to achieve peace and happiness for all is by cherishing others" and His Holiness the Dalai Lama's saying, "My religion is kindness." There was a big spare wheel at the back of the car so I had *om mani padme hum* written there as well as "Anybody who sees or touches or remembers this car, may they be free from suffering and achieve enlightenment." And because so many insects could die by hitting the front of the car as we drove, I had mantras placed on the front windscreen, such as Medicine Buddha's mantra, *om mani padme hum*, and others. The back of the car had Green Tara, White Tara, the Thirty-Five Buddhas, Lama Tsongkhapa, and other buddhas.

People behind us read some messages, and as they came alongside us they read others, and as they passed us they could see even more in the front. I think quite a few people looked in the car to see who was driving. I saw a few people looking upset, maybe expecting a more extremist person at the wheel. Anyway, I'm sure many people realized this was a Buddhist car. One time somebody circumambulated the car. Quite a few people gave the thumbs-up sign as they drove past (and very occasionally a thumbs-down).

As His Holiness the Dalai Lama always says, "If you must be selfish, then be wisely selfish, not narrow-mindedly selfish."[47] Here, His Holiness is saying even if our motivation is for our own happiness, the way to achieve that is through caring for others. With intelligence we can see that by working only for others we neither harm them nor receive harm from them. If we have any understanding of karma we see that only happiness will result and therefore this is the "wisely selfish" thing to do.

Taking the Medicine

Bodhichitta is the medicine that can cure all illnesses and destroy all suffering. Of this Shantideva said,

If I need to comply with a doctor's advice
when frightened by a common illness,
then how much more so when perpetually diseased
by the manifold evils of desire and so forth.

And if the people dwelling on this earth
can be overcome by just one of these,
and if no other medicine to cure them
is to be found elsewhere in the universe,

then the intention not to act in accordance
with the advice of the All-knowing Physicians
that can uproot every misery,
is extremely bewildering and worthy of scorn.[48]

Shantideva compared knowing the Dharma but not bothering to practice it with not taking our doctor's advice. We can have a huge store-
room of medicine in our house, but if we don't take it we will never be
cured. Then we will die with a house full of medicine!

Just as we cannot simply carry around a bag of medicine without
taking it and expect to be cured, only having an intellectual understanding of Buddhism alone does not fulfill the purpose of our life. We
have to put that understanding into practice. We can be a great scholar
of Buddhism, with university degrees in all the Buddhist subjects; we
can have memorized both the Kangyur and the Tengyur—the entire
Buddhist canon—and be a world-famous lecturer earning thousands of
dollars for each appearance, and yet we can still suffer from all sorts of
emotional problems such as anger, jealousy, pride, depression, and the
like. In fact, all our knowledge can swell our pride and arrogance and
bring even more problems.

There is no contradiction in the Dharma. There is no Dharma medicine that works for one person and not for another. All the buddhas
work constantly for all sentient beings. A councilor works for their

town, a politician works for their country, but the buddhas work for all sentient beings equally, working in whatever way suits sentient beings' propensity, manifesting in whatever way best benefits them. The buddhas are like wise doctors knowing exactly what is needed to cure the patient. If we are still not cured until now it is not because the buddhas are partial and help some sentient beings but not others or that they lack the skill, but because we don't have the karma to be helped by them due to our past negative actions.

We have to follow a doctor's advice to cure something simple such as a headache, but even then headaches keep recurring. We should investigate and find out the reasons why such medicine doesn't stop us from getting sick in the future.

External medicines treat the manifestations of suffering, not the root cause. When we cut a tree down it will grow back unless we have also cut its roots. In the same way, we need to cut the root of our suffering, our fundamental ignorance, to stop the delusions that grow from that to bring suffering and illness. Therefore, in order to alleviate the suffering of the great delusion, just as we willingly follow a doctor's advice for a headache, why shouldn't we exactly follow the advice of the Buddha and practice the Dharma? That means transforming the mind, something we can do every second of our life, no matter where we are or what we are doing.

3 : THE TEN BENEFITS OF BODHICHITTA

ALTHOUGH THERE ARE countless benefits of attaining bodhichitta, in the sutra *Manjushri's Own Words*, *The Sutra of the Beautiful Tree*, and the lamrim texts such as *Lamrim Chenmo* and *Liberation in the Palm of Your Hand*, there are ten main benefits listed:

1. Bodhichitta is the sole gateway to the Mahayana.
2. We gain the name "child of the buddhas."
3. We outshine the arhats.
4. We become a supreme object of offering.
5. We accumulate enormous merit.
6. We rapidly purify negative karma.
7. We accomplish whatever we wish.
8. We are not bothered by hindrances.
9. We quickly complete the path.
10. We become a source of happiness for others.

Entering the Mahayana path is the only way to attain full enlightenment, and bodhichitta is the only way to enter the Mahayana. As soon as we do, even if it has just been a few minutes before, we immediately become a child of the buddhas and overshadow even the great arhats by our lineage, just as a prince with the potential to become a king overshadows the most powerful minister.

When we become a bodhisattva we become the supreme object of offering for all sentient beings. They accumulate incredible merit by making offerings to us, and we ourselves accumulate incredible merit. The higher the realizations we have, the more merit we create and the more merit others create by making offerings to us. Similarly, because of the great power of bodhichitta, we quickly and easily purify all our remaining negativities.

With bodhichitta we can easily accomplish whatever we wish without being bothered by internal or external hindrances. Because of this we can quickly complete the path and become fully enlightened. The final benefit is that we become the source of happiness for all sentient beings.

We will discuss these benefits in more detail below. The first four benefits of bodhichitta examine the remarkable qualities of this wonderful mind, whereas the next six look at what we accomplish when we have such a mind.

1. Bodhichitta Is the Sole Gateway to the Mahayana

The first benefit is that bodhichitta is the sole door into the Mahayana path. In the same way that we need to buy a ticket and enter through a gate to get into an exhibition of beautiful paintings, we need bodhichitta to enter the gateway into the supreme vehicle called the Mahayana.

Once we have attained bodhichitta we are not only a bodhisattva but also a Mahayanist. Just having rooms full of Mahayana texts and statues of tantric deities doesn't make us Mahayanist. Even wearing the red robes of a Tibetan Buddhist monk or nun doesn't mean we are a Mahayanist. Without bodhichitta, we're like artificial fruit that looks good but is completely inedible. This is important to know. Many of us study Mahayana topics and even take on a tantric commitment, but without bodhichitta it means little. There is no other way we can complete the path.

In *Hymns of Experience*, Lama Tsongkhapa said,

> Generating the mind [bodhichitta] is the central axle of
> the supreme vehicle path;
> It's the foundation and the support of all expansive deeds;
> To all instances of two accumulations it is like the elixir of gold;

It's the treasury of merits containing myriad collections
   of virtues.

Recognizing these truths the heroic bodhisattvas
Uphold the precious supreme mind as the heart of their
   practice.
I, a yogi, have practiced in this manner;
You, who aspire for liberation, too should do likewise.[49]

Lama Tsongkhapa compared bodhichitta to the central axle, around which all else revolves; we could also say it's like the trunk of a great tree, without which nothing else could grow. A great tree has hundreds of branches and thousands and thousands of leaves, producing masses of flowers and fruit, but this all comes from the main trunk.

Everything comes from bodhichitta. It's the foundation of all the bodhisattva's great deeds. Without bodhichitta there would be no chance to develop the perfections of a bodhisattva's activities, such as the perfections of generosity and patience, nor could we progress along the five paths of merit, preparation, seeing, meditation, and no more learning.

Lama Tsongkhapa also compared bodhichitta to the elixir that transforms iron into gold. Only through the power of bodhichitta can we quickly amass the two accumulations of method and wisdom, which become the cause of enlightenment. Every second we accumulate infinite merit; therefore, as Lama Tsongkhapa said, it's a treasury of merit. We can achieve whatever we wish, like being given a wish-granting jewel.

Worldly people who know nothing about karma use expressions such as "fortune" or "good luck," but they are really just talking about positive karma ripening. We win a lottery and we think it's nothing but good luck, but this "luck" is really being created all the time by the virtuous actions we create. When we understand this we suddenly have the choice to create our own luck by watching our mind, watching our karma. This is the treasury of merit we create.

In the next verse, Lama Tsongkhapa advised us to keep bodhichitta as our heart practice. No matter what other practices we have, this is the quickest way to purify all obscurations and accumulate all merit and thereby complete our work for ourselves and for others. Without bodhichitta, although our practice might be strong for a time, it will inevitably wane. With bodhichitta, on the other hand, seeing the tragic plight of all sentient beings, we will always be inspired to work as hard as we can to overcome all obstacles and complete the path to enlightenment.

We can spend a lifetime in a strict retreat and have absolutely stable concentration, but without bodhichitta there will still be self-cherishing and the chance of ending in the lower realms. There are many stories that exemplify this.

For instance, there is the story of the two long-term meditators doing a Yamantaka retreat in Pembo, near Lhasa. One died, but the other meditator continued the retreat, doing a nightly *sur* practice, which is offering burning *tsampa*[50] to all the sentient beings of all six realms, especially the spirits. One night a terrifying apparition appeared to him in the shape of Yamantaka, with many arms and heads and looking utterly fearful. Terrified, the meditator asked who the apparition was, and it replied that it had been that meditator's friend, now reborn as a hungry ghost, here to get some sustenance from the smell of the burning tsampa.

Although the late meditator had practiced Yamantaka in a highest yoga yantra deity practice for a long time, he had not combined this with the three principal aspects of the path—renunciation, bodhichitta, and right view (the realization of emptiness)—and so he was unable to transform his mind and rid it of the delusions that eventually led to his rebirth as a hungry ghost. This shows how vital the right motivation is in anything we do.

We can have unshakable concentration, not just for an hour or a few days but for eons, but we have still not entered the Mahayana. Even if we are advanced in the completion stage practice of highest yoga tantra, where we have control over the winds and can visualize ourselves as the deity perfectly for however long we want, without bodhichitta we're like a small child staring at paintings on a temple wall. Perhaps we are trying to practice *tummo*, the inner fire technique of the six yogas of Naropa.[51] This is such an advanced practice, but without bodhichitta it's like trying to stoke a fire with a bellows, nothing more. There is no benefit at all in doing it.

To break free from the whole of samsara, the vital practice is realizing emptiness, but this realization alone, without bodhichitta, will not allow us to enter the Mahayana. Arhats with their great practice have gained incredible powers and are completely free from suffering, but though they have attained nirvana they have still not entered the Mahayana. It is much better to enter the Mahayana from the start.

2. We Gain the Name "Child of the Buddhas"

The second benefit of bodhichitta is that we receive the name "child of the buddhas." Of this, Shantideva said,

> The moment an Awakened Mind arises
> in those fettered and weak in the jail of cyclic existence,
> they will be named a "child of the buddhas"
> and will be revered by both humans and gods of the world.[52]

At the very moment we attain bodhichitta, we become an object of prostration for worldly people and samsaric gods. We are a child of the buddhas because, just as a child is physically created by the union of the father and the mother, we have attained bodhichitta through taking refuge in the Three Rare Sublime Ones—the Buddha, Dharma, and Sangha—and we will become a buddha by depending on the buddhas, particularly Shakyamuni Buddha, his teachings, and his Sangha.

This name "child of the buddhas" is true of even a new bodhisattva who has yet to directly realize emptiness and so become an arya bodhisattva. The Tibetan translation for this level of bodhisattva is something like "ordinary" bodhisattva, but comparing the ordinary worldly being's mind and the "ordinary" mind of the new bodhisattva is like comparing the earth and the sky—the difference is huge. But this bodhisattva mind is ordinary in comparison to the higher bodhisattvas, those who have realized emptiness directly.

Shantideva showed us that even though we are still trapped by delusion in samsara, "fettered and weak in the jail of cyclic existence," the very second we attain the mind of bodhichitta, we become a holy being to be revered by all. All other human beings and higher samsaric gods will prostrate to us and admire us, no matter what our external appearance might be.

Bodhichitta is the best beauty. No matter how ugly or poor we are by worldly standards, we become the object of reverence because of our amazing altruistic mind. A bodhisattva might be a penniless, filthy beggar, with torn rags for clothes and dirty matted hair; they might be a hippie, skinny and dirty, shunned by everybody, looking and acting completely crazy; they might have leprosy and be a despised outcast. But the very second that person generates bodhichitta, they are considered a holy being, an object of veneration, surpassing even an arhat who has realized emptiness and removed all gross delusions. In *The Jewel Lamp*, Khunu Lama Rinpoche said,

> Bodhichitta beautifies the whole appearance of the face.
> Bodhichitta lends beauty to the wideness of the eyes.
> Bodhichitta gives beauty to the sound of the voice.
> Bodhichitta makes behavior beautiful.[53]

With the power to lead all of us out of the sufferings of samsara, the bodhisattva's mind has the power to shake samsara. It is said that when a being first attains bodhichitta, that act has such power that not only does the physical world really shake but also even the thrones of the buddhas shake.

The buddhas are all overjoyed and call the new bodhisattva "child of the buddhas" because they are just like a prince destined to become a great ruler. Even before being able to communicate or walk, a prince is still more important and more revered than the highest noble because of his potential; although still a baby, he has the power to control a whole kingdom. In the same way, the new bodhisattva has the potential to realize enlightenment and serve all sentient beings. Nothing could make the buddhas happier.

3. We Outshine the Arhats

The third benefit of bodhichitta is that with it we outshine the arhats, who have incredible qualities but lack the great will of the bodhisattvas, the supreme determination to lead each and every sentient being to full enlightenment.

It is not that arhats have no compassion for other sentient beings. Compared to the tiny compassion we might have, theirs is enormous. They have the strong wish that all sentient beings be free from suffering and have happiness, but what they lack is this extra wish, this responsibility that they take the whole burden upon themselves. This is the quality that makes the difference and that makes even a new bodhisattva outshine the arhats.

Pabongka Dechen Nyingpo explained that arhats enter a completely blissful state of peace in equipoise meditation, and because they are habituated to the taste of absorption in that blissful state, they don't attempt to generate bodhichitta. For an arhat to even try to generate bodhichitta would be difficult; because they have totally transcended suffering, they can no longer use their own suffering as an example to understand the suffering of others. It's good to understand this point. Without experiencing suffering an arhat has difficultly generating compassion for others.

When arhats are absorbed in the blissful state of peace, they experience such inconceivable happiness that they remain in equipoise meditation for many eons before awakening to attain enlightenment. During the length of time an arhat stays in that blissful state, a sentient being in the hells could have experienced the suffering of the hell realm, fully exhausted that karma, been reborn as a human with a perfect human rebirth, entered the Mahayana path, and achieved enlightenment. It says in *Liberation in the Palm of Your Hand* that somebody who hears

Mahayana teachings but is born in hell due to developing heresy for the Mahayana will still achieve enlightenment more quickly than somebody who has received the Mahayana lineage but then enters the Hinayana path and achieves arhatship.[54]

For instance, the *shravaka* Kashyapa taught the Hinayana path to sixty monks who achieved arhatship. But Manjushri had also given them Mahayana teachings that didn't suit their minds, and so they developed heresy and were subsequently born in the hells. When Kashyapa asked the Buddha why this was so, the Buddha said that Manjushri had done well; that his teaching had been skillful.

Many students of the one-month Kopan courses drop out after a few days, but I still feel it's far better they do that than not ever come to Kopan. Because of those few days their lives are much richer than that of somebody who has never been. Everything they did for the course was very positive—preparing for the trip, paying for the flight, coming to the *gönpa*—even if they just lasted *one* day. Attending a course for just a couple of days and hearing about bodhichitta is incredibly fortunate. The merit created in those days is something that could never happen in hundreds of years otherwise.

Although the arhats have incredible qualities like the sky, they can still make mistakes in guiding sentient beings because they have not abandoned the four unknowing minds and so are still unable to see the very subtle karma of sentient beings, something only buddhas can do. Therefore, if we want to do perfect work for sentient beings, we must attain enlightenment.

Because arhats are continuously absorbed in a state of great bliss, a state they never want to arise from, attaining this level of commitment is almost impossible. They are like somebody drunk on wine never wanting to be sober. Or maybe like we are on a cold morning, reluctant to get out of our warm, comfortable bed! Somehow the warmth of the bed seems more desirable than the prostrations and meditation that are waiting for us. If we can't see the urgency of our practice for our own sake, of course we can't see it for the sake of others. This is why it is so difficult for an arhat to achieve bodhichitta.

4. We Become a Supreme Object of Offering

The moment we attain bodhichitta we are revered by all and become a supreme object of offering, which is the fourth benefit of bodhichitta. The ground where a bodhisattva walks, the footprint in the dust, becomes an object of prostration for gods and humans due to the power of this precious thought, bodhichitta. Even universal kings of the gods, Indra and Brahma, touch their crowns to the footprint of a bodhisattva in respect.

Spending our whole life in retreat, reciting mantras, living in silence in a cave, never talking to other people, never coming out, not eating— such practices might be very beneficial but they have none of the benefits that training in bodhichitta has. Therefore no matter how difficult it is or how long it takes, trying to develop bodhichitta is much more worthwhile than undertaking the greatest austerity.

Even if it takes lifetimes, this is the great project we should determine to do. We should concentrate only on this, putting all our energies there. We should be like a great architect who works for many years on a huge project, such as a skyscraper, until it is finished, ignoring concerns about what others might think or whether such an enormous project could ever be completed, just working, working, working, day and night, until the skyscraper is built. Like that, we should only work toward attaining bodhichitta, even if it takes lifetimes. This life is gone very quickly so we might fail to attain bodhichitta before we die, but then, if we keep working, we can certainly attain it in the next life.

A bodhisattva has yet to eliminate all gross and subtle delusions or develop all positive qualities and so attain full enlightenment, but even so, he or she is still an object of respect for all the buddhas. It is said in the sutras,

> You should pay homage to the new moon and not the full moon. Likewise, anybody who draws inspiration from me should pay homage to the bodhisattvas and not the tathaga-tas. . . . When a bodhisattva mounts a chariot, they [the

buddhas] will provide delight for their five senses and enter-
tain them. Should there be no one else to pull the chariot, the
buddhas themselves will even draw the chariot by a rope tied
around their own heads.[55]

An arhat might have attained the blissful state that lasts eons, but they
do not earn the same respect as a new bodhisattva because the bodhisattva is only concerned with the welfare of others.

Because of the incomprehensible merit we generate by showing
respect to a bodhisattva, that bodhisattva becomes the supreme object
of offering for us. Through offering to the bodhisattva, we swiftly complete the two types of merit: the merit of wisdom and the merit of
method. Shantideva said,

> The world honors as virtuous
> one who sometimes gives a little, plain food
> disrespectfully to a few beings,
> which satisfies them for only half a day.

> What need be said then of one
> who eternally bestows the peerless bliss of the *sugatas*[56]
> upon limitless numbers of beings,
> thereby fulfilling all their hopes?[57]

When somebody helps us, we feel gratitude and wish to repay that
kindness in some way. If even temporary help for worldly problems is
considered a thing of admiration, then so much more so is the work of
the bodhisattva, who profoundly helps countless sentient beings without being asked and without wish for reward.

When we ask a normal person for help, we either fail to get it or
we get it with strings attached, but the help we get from bodhisattvas
comes without depending on us asking for it, because of the incredible
compassion that bodhisattvas feel for us and all sentient beings. Having
dedicated their whole lives to helping us sentient beings, they care more

about us than themselves. Without us asking, bodhisattvas cause us to create positive karma so we can be saved from suffering. Therefore, why wouldn't we admire these bodhisattvas far more than the most helpful worldly being?

Seeing this, we should determine to repay their great kindness. But how? Physically offering to holy objects or making beautiful things without transforming the mind cannot please them that much. To do the same actions, however, with a virtuous motivation—in other words, for our actions to become Dharma—*that* pleases them very much. Trying to transform our mind from self-cherishing to cherishing others and trying to realize emptiness are the best offerings we can make to them.

The whole body of a bodhisattva, from the tip of every hair on the head down to the toes, becomes an object of veneration, a holy object, a relic. Even whatever comes from the body—blood, pee-pee, or kaka—becomes blessed. When other beings use it, it purifies them, they are healed.

For example, in the Mount Everest region below Lawudo, where people claim I was a meditator in my past life (although I suspect I was a rat in the Lawudo Lama's cave, sleeping and stealing his *torma* cake), there is a monastery, a branch of Sera Mey. The founder of the monastery was a great bodhisattva who, when he joined the monastery, was given the job to collect and sell grain from the surrounding villages. He completely failed in this business, but his failure made him generate renunciation for samsara. After taking lamrim teachings and an initiation, he lived in a mud hut in the mountains for seven years where he achieved calm abiding and realized emptiness. He built a monastery for both monks and nuns. From time to time he would take the aspect of sickness, vomiting blood that filled a pot. His disciples then made pills out of the blood and people with colds and so forth would take these pills and completely recover.

I have also heard of a *sadhu*, a Hindi yogi, in India whose kaka was extremely beneficial for curing leprosy. It was so sought after that it became very rare.

The story of Saint Francis of Assisi, the Italian saint who lived around the same time as Milarepa, is very similar. Some of the monasteries kept the relics of saints, usually their clothes. Sick people would be given a small piece to eat, causing them to vomit and eventually recover. This is the power of the mind, the power of loving-kindness and compassion. Such stories are common.

Such things happen because of the power of bodhichitta within the mindstream of those beings, no matter what their external appearance. Therefore, a bodhisattva is considered a supreme object offering.

5. WE ACCUMULATE ENORMOUS MERIT

With the fifth and sixth benefits of bodhichitta, we create incredible merit and purify all our delusions, destroying the negative karmic imprints that have been left on our mindstream since beginningless time. That means we can quickly accomplish whatever actions we wish and complete the path to enlightenment, unbothered by any hindrances.

The fifth benefit of bodhichitta is that we accumulate enormous merit, quickly completing both the merit of method and the merit of transcendental wisdom. The path to enlightenment is divided into two aspects: the practices that develop the method side of the path, such as love, equanimity, and so forth; and the practices that develop the wisdom side, the realization of ultimate reality. We need both collections of merit to attain enlightenment.

How quickly we attain enlightenment depends on how strongly we purify obscurations and collect extensive merit, and the very best method to do this is to train the mind in bodhichitta. Just doing a breathing meditation with bodhichitta, effortlessly breathing in and out, creates merit as infinite as space. Chatting with other people, when done with bodhichitta, becomes so beneficial for us and for others; giving medicine with bodhichitta becomes powerfully effective. That is because with bodhichitta everything we do is dedicated to the ultimate welfare of all the beings in all the innumerable universes, all the hell beings, hungry ghosts, animals, humans, demigods, gods, and intermediate-state beings. Because the number is infinite and because the action is completely free from self-cherishing, the merit we create is infinite.

Generally, our actions are always clouded by partisanship. We benefit one person because they like us, and we hold our help back from another because they don't. Even giving a rupee to a beggar in India involves our partisan mind, choosing one beggar because they look pitiful and kind of gentle over another who looks rough and angry. There are always limitations in what we do.

With a bodhichitta motivation, on the other hand, we never show any discrimination. No matter what the situation is or what the other being does—even hating us and trying to hack us to pieces—we are always only concerned with freeing that being from suffering and the causes of suffering. Accordingly, no action we do can bring any harm or confusion.

Talking about how beneficial bodhichitta is, Shantideva said,

> If merely a benevolent intention
> excels veneration of the buddhas,
> then what need to mention striving to make
> all beings, without exception, happy?[58]

In *Adornment of the Mahayana Sutras*, his commentary to Maitreya Buddha's teachings, Arya Asanga[59] said that benefiting one sentient being is more meaningful than making offerings to buddhas and bodhisattvas equaling in number the atoms of the world. This is because helping sentient beings is the very best offering we can ever make to the buddhas. The buddhas cherish all beings, and the only motivation for anything they do is to best benefit others, therefore if we are helping others, we are doing the buddhas' work. It is like a mother seeing her child helping the neighbors and feeling such joy that the child is being so caring. Because she cherishes her child, she selflessly rejoices when she sees her child working with a good heart.

If helping sentient beings without having bodhichitta has this effect, then doing the same with bodhichitta multiplies the merit innumerably.

Even if we make offerings to all the enlightened beings, filling as many buddha fields as there are grains of sand in the river Ganges with seven kinds of jewels and offering it to that many buddhas, it cannot compare to the mind of bodhichitta. Making such extensive offerings to such powerful beings creates unbelievable merit, but how can that action done without bodhichitta compare to even the smallest action done with bodhichitta?

Offering charity, no matter how vast, will always have limits without bodhichitta; offering with bodhichitta, no matter how small, is limitless. I remember once when His Holiness the Dalai Lama was teaching on perfect human rebirth at Drepung Monastery in South India, and there were many dogs in the monastery that people fed. One tiny scrap of food to a dog brings us infinite merit and infinitely benefits the dog. But additionally, His Holiness said that because some of the monks in the monastery had the realization of bodhichitta, the connection the dogs made meant they received incredible purification and they would become liberated. This was through the power of the monks' bodhichitta.

Lama Atisha, in his *Lamp for the Path to Enlightenment*, said,

> If it possessed physical form,
> the merit of the altruistic intention
> would completely fill the whole of space
> and exceed even that.

> If someone were to fill with jewels
> as many buddha fields as there are grains
> of sand in the Ganges
> to offer to the Protector of the World,

> this would be surpassed by
> the gift of folding one's hands
> and inclining one's mind to enlightenment,
> for such is limitless.[60]

Can you imagine? If we purify so many eons of negative karma and create such incredible merit every second we meditate on bodhichitta, then what can we accomplish if we actually have bodhichitta? Just putting our palms together and saying the refuge and bodhichitta prayer creates infinite merit, far surpassing the most amazing offerings we could ever imagine.

A bodhisattva wants to cure all sentient beings of all physical and mental sufferings entirely, not just headaches. Because the number is infinite, the merit is infinite. All bodhisattvas are working tirelessly to help all sentient beings realize their full potential and gain boundless happiness and full enlightenment. Is it any wonder that at every moment a bodhisattva creates infinite merit?

We have to do daily actions such as eating and buying food, but even so, by maintaining a bodhichitta motivation as we do them, we can use such actions on the path to enlightenment. With a bodhichitta motivation, if we recite the *Praises to the Twenty-One Taras* once, it becomes a hundred thousand praises. If we offer one butter lamp, it's like offering a hundred thousand butter lamps. If we recite a Vajrasattva mantra once, it's like reciting a hundred thousand Vajrasattvas—instead of the three months that would usually take, all we would have to do would be to set up the altar, sit down on the cushion, and say the mantra once. The retreat would be over, and we would have plenty of time for other things!

In *The Jewel Lamp*, Khunu Lama Rinpoche said,

> Just like the lotus among flowers
> is bodhichitta supreme among all virtuous thoughts.
> Since having it brings immediate and final happiness,
> one should make every effort to produce it.[61]

Because we think of a lotus as the most beautiful flower, we revere it over all other flowers in the same way that we consider the diamond to be the most valuable of all gems. Likewise, bodhichitta is the most wonderful mind; it's the most important thing in our life. An action that grows from bodhichitta is the most beneficial action there can be, so nothing is more worthwhile than developing bodhichitta.

It is natural for us to always want the best, so we should determine to have the best possible mind: the mind that is called bodhichitta. All other practices, such as concentration, renunciation, and so forth, are ways of bringing about this most amazing mind.

Every action we do with a bodhichitta motivation is inestimable. Rising from our bed, every step we make toward our meditation place is worth infinitely more than a bag full of a million golden coins. Switching on a light, sitting down, whatever we do, becomes highly meaningful. With every word of the refuge prayer we say, our perfect human rebirth becomes highly meaningful; the unimaginable negative karma we have accumulated since beginningless rebirths is purified, and we collect infinite merit. The same thing happens when we recite mantras: each recitation becomes the cause of all sentient beings' peerless happiness. This is far greater than attaining nirvana for ourselves alone.

Like having vaults full of money in the bank that accrue great interest every year, having bodhichitta is a great treasury of merit that grows all the time. The merit we collect with bodhichitta doesn't stop until we reach enlightenment and continues even after that. We continuously experience the result: our mind in the state of peerless happiness. Not only that, as a result of the merit we collect with bodhichitta, we liberate numberless other sentient beings and bring them to full enlightenment.

Before the Buddha became enlightened he had a samsaric mind like we have. His attainment of enlightenment was not spontaneous; it didn't happen without him gradually developing his mind and achieving the realizations on the path to enlightenment. Through bodhichitta, he steadily overcame his delusions and increased his positive qualities, his mind opening like a lotus until his obscurations were totally destroyed and his positive qualities were totally realized. The merit created by his bodhichitta did not stop when he reached enlightenment, however, as he continues to benefit sentient beings based on that realization.

6. WE RAPIDLY PURIFY NEGATIVE KARMA

Everything we do with bodhichitta becomes unstained by the eight worldly dharmas, which means we not only no longer create nonvirtue but we also rapidly purify the negative karma we have accumulated. In the *Precious Garland*, Nagarjuna explained,

> Desire, hatred, ignorance, and
> the actions they generate are nonvirtues.
> Non-attachment, non-hatred, non-ignorance,
> and the actions they generate are virtues.
>
> From nonvirtues come all sufferings
> and likewise all bad transmigrations.
> From virtues, all happy transmigrations
> and the pleasures of all lives.[62]

Whatever action we do becomes the cause of happiness or suffering depending on our motivation. If the action is tainted with one or more of the three poisons of attachment, anger, and ignorance, then it can only lead to suffering. Even if it outwardly seems to be a Dharma action, it is still nonvirtuous, still non-Dharma, because the motivation is nonvirtuous. Because of that it causes a disturbance in our mind, robbing us of peace. As long as we are ruled by the three poisons, and especially by the attachment of clinging to this life, nothing we do becomes Dharma.

We might be helping somebody else, such as cleaning the flat of an old person or shopping for our parents, but while our own happiness is paramount even these good actions become nonvirtuous. However many hours we work, if we work for our own interests alone, we only create the cause for more suffering. No matter how much money we spend, if we spend it in this way, we never receive any satisfaction, any inner peace, any inner happiness. And because of our attachment, all those other negative minds such as anger or jealousy can so easily arise, bringing more suffering.

If, however, our motivation *is* for the well-being of others, then the action is virtuous; it becomes pure Dharma. It is important to know this, and therefore we need to ask ourselves whether the good actions we do are done selflessly or with self-interest. With a good heart our everyday job becomes the Dharma, becomes a meditation. This is how important a good heart is.

With bodhichitta nothing can harm us; nothing can create negativity in our mind. In *The Jewel Lamp*, Khunu Lama Rinpoche said,

> Without arrogance when things go well,
> not depressed when times are hard,
> unharmable by anything—
> this bodhichitta gold.[63]

Without bodhichitta we can be puffed up with arrogance or proud of our accomplishments when things go well and, conversely, obsessed with our own misfortune when things go badly, jealous of those with more and angry at those who block our happiness. With the precious mind of bodhichitta, on the other hand, although there might still be times when things go well and times when they don't, there is no problem in the mind. Wealth doesn't lead to pride and poverty doesn't mean unhappiness.

We cannot trust samsaric things; they will cheat us every time. As long as we are in samsara, ruled by ignorance, we will definitely live with frustration and unhappiness. The one thing that will never cheat us is our own achievement of bodhichitta. Among all the minds, bodhichitta is the mind that is completely trustworthy.

Worldly friendships are never free from attachment, and the closest friend can become an enemy, a creator of problems. But with bodhichitta, we have our best friend in our mind; it cannot be stolen, destroyed, or killed, and we don't have to give it material things or flatter and pay compliments. With this inner best friend, the longer we live, the more subdued and happy our mind becomes. Our bodhichitta always helps us overcome negative minds, taking us closer to enlightenment.

Unlike samsaric friendships, a friendship begun with bodhichitta lasts because it doesn't depend on what we receive from other people. This is why we can be friends equally with all sentient beings, without discrimination. With this pure thought we see all sentient beings in beauty. We see them all as extremely kind. We don't see even one enemy, no matter what others do to us. There is no cruel mind that makes us want to cheat others or cause them problems in order to get our way. Deceitful people are never trusted, but because our intentions are always pure, people naturally trust us.

Like a Sword That Cuts All Delusions

The reason so few of us worldly beings have been able to overcome negativity is because the virtue we have created is so feeble in comparison to the nonvirtue and, specifically, because we haven't created the powerful virtue of bodhichitta. Unable to control the arising of negative minds, we are unable to avoid negative actions and the suffering that results from those actions. Only bodhichitta is strong enough to overcome these negative minds. In *The Jewel Lamp*, Khunu Lama Rinpoche said,

> The bodhichitta that serves as a sword
> to cut the shoots of the afflictions,
> is the weapon for the protection
> of all wandering beings.[64]

Like a machete that cuts easily through jungle undergrowth, bodhichitta is the sword that cuts all delusions.

None of the weapons ordinary people have—atomic bombs, rockets, rifles, and all other weapons—have the power to destroy our delusions and bring us happiness. Not even detonating every atomic bomb in the world could destroy or even diminish one single negative mind. The internal weapon, bodhichitta, is completely different. Destroying the real enemy, the self-cherishing mind, brings peace in our heart, meaning we are more able to help others and we become closer to our ultimate goal of enlightenment. Destroying the self-cherishing mind is the same as destroying all external enemies, because they all come from the self-cherishing mind.

Bodhichitta is so powerful. Without it our nonvirtues will always flourish; with it we can overcome them so quickly. All negative karma and obscurations are burned up completely in the intense fire of bodhichitta. In *A Guide to the Bodhisattva's Way of Life*, Shantideva said,

> Just like the fire at the end of an age,
> it instantly consumes all great wrongdoing.
> Its unfathomable advantages were taught
> to the disciple Sudhana by the wise Lord Maitreya.[65]

The "end of an age" Shantideva referred to is the end of this world system. At that time there is a great destruction where karmically created fire consumes everything, leaving not an atom of substance. To us, such heat is unimaginable. In the same way, the power of bodhichitta to destroy negativities is equally unimaginable. In one second bodhichitta has the power to purify all delusions.

Even if we have attained the completion stage of a highest yoga tantra practice, without effortless bodhichitta it is impossible to experience the union of clear light and illusory body, the final part of the completion stage, and so enlightenment is impossible. Just having effortful bodhichitta, just the motivation, is not enough. Becoming enlightened depends on many factors. We need the most subtle level of understanding of emptiness, that of the Prasangika Madhyamaka school, but to obtain that we need to have already greatly purified our mind—and the best way to do that is to develop bodhichitta.

Shantideva said,

> It is like the supreme gold-making elixir,
> for it transforms the unclean body we have taken
> into the priceless jewel of a buddha form.
> Therefore firmly seize this Awakening Mind.[66]

There is a story about how Nagarjuna, when he was the manager of Nalanda Monastery, produced a special elixir that turned metal into gold so he could help the people experiencing great famine. He could do this because there was such a huge difference between the value of base metal, which is practically worthless, and gold, which is incredibly valuable. In the same way, this normal, impure body we have is nothing compared to the body of a being with bodhichitta. Just as it seems impossible that cheap metal can be turned into priceless gold, when we think about the delusions we hold in our mind and the way we are controlled by karma and delusion, it seems impossible that in this very body we could attain bodhichitta and transform our body into the body of a buddha. It *is* possible, however. Through the power of bodhichitta, our body can become an enlightened being's body, completely without defects, completely pure, completely clean.

Our present body is impure. It is a bag filled with bones, marrow, flesh, blood, bile, excrement, and so forth. As a product of karma and delusion there is not an atom that is not impure, but that is not the way it appears to us. We see the body as clean, as desirable—the complete opposite of reality. All the things that fill up a septic tank come from this body. Food is clean before it enters our body, but as Khunu Lama Rinpoche said, nobody wants to eat it after it has left our body.

Bodhichitta can completely turn that around, turning this impure body into the holy body of a buddha. The vital ingredient—the elixir that turns metal into gold—is bodhichitta. Bodhichitta has that much power. The merit gained through attaining bodhichitta is so great that it has the potential to destroy all of the 84,000 delusions, eliminating all the gross and subtle delusions of our mind.

There Is No Better Medicine Than Bodhichitta

In *The Jewel Lamp*, Khunu Lama Rinpoche said,

> By relying on the medicine of bodhichitta
> all the diseases of delusions are cured.

So in all the world it is definite
that there is no other medicine like this.[67]

The diseases of delusions are not colds, cholera, or other physical ailments such as those but the diseases that arise from self-cherishing, such as anger, jealousy, greed, miserliness, and so forth. Delusions are called "all-arising" because whatever occurs in the mind is tainted by self-cherishing. It seems we have no control over our self-cherishing mind and yet, by relying on the medicine of bodhichitta, we can subdue it.

Bodhichitta is the medicine, the nectar, that cures not just the gross suffering we experience but also the subtle levels of suffering, the suffering of change and pervasive compounding suffering. Only when we can eliminate the very subtle delusions will we be free from pervasive compounding suffering. This comes about by destroying self-cherishing, which is what bodhichitta does. Therefore, the only medicine that will completely cure the unbearable disease of samsara is bodhichitta. Being the one complete antidote to all of samsara, there is no greater cure to suffering than this.

Scientists in America tested groups of people and found that those who are generally goodhearted have less health problems than those who are selfish. A generous person is less uptight and less likely to get worried about their own comfort or possessions, and of course, this means their life will be happier and easier. I sometimes suggest to students to try to live two days with the thought of bodhichitta, only thinking of others, and then two days only thinking of themselves, and then check which of the two days were happier and more fruitful.

Generally, our health depends on our attitude to life. One way of thinking makes the body and mind sick; the other way of thinking, having a positive attitude, makes the body and mind healthy. I think that because anything happening in the body is an expression of the mind, the best way to take care of our health is to take care of our mind. Even though external factors such as pollution can affect the body and mind, there is a reason that they do so; it doesn't happen without cause and conditions.

7. We Accomplish Whatever We Wish

The seventh benefit of bodhichitta is that we accomplish whatever we wish. That means any work we undertake will be completely successful. Not only that: because we are working solely for others, whatever we do will be completed without much effort. In *The Jewel Lamp*, Khunu Lama Rinpoche said,

> If you want to help yourself, produce excellent bodhichitta.
> If you want to help others, produce excellent bodhichitta.
> If you want to serve the doctrine, produce excellent bodhichitta.
> If you want the path to bliss, generate bodhichitta.[68]

When we develop bodhichitta, we not only help ourselves and others but we also serve the Dharma and generate the path to happiness. Serving the Dharma does not necessarily mean working for a Dharma center; it can be whatever we do in our daily life. No matter what we do, we can transform our attitude and do it with the mind of cherishing others rather than for our own well-being alone.

With a selfish mind, we wake up with the thought, "I am going to work for my own happiness. I must have breakfast to get off to work to earn lots of money to have a comfortable life. This is what life is all about." However, instead of keeping busy day and night trying to fulfill the wishes of this self-centered attitude, concerned only with our own mundane happiness, we can work for others.

With bodhichitta there will be fewer problems at work because we no longer create any negative karma in our relationships with others. Instead of being in competition with others, we will see ourselves as their servant, happy to do whatever will help them. If we are an employee, we think we are working to help our boss and his customers; if we are an employer, we think we have developed our company in order to help our employees and our customers. It's all a matter of transforming our attitude.

Many worldly problems that we find difficult to overcome—harm from humans, nonhumans such as spirits, and the elements—can be easily overcome when we have bodhichitta. We would find it incredibly difficult to control an epidemic or a flood, no matter how skilled we might be, but for somebody with bodhichitta it would be easy; such a person wouldn't even have to recite mantras. A bodhisattva can cure others' diseases very easily by simple actions such as giving leftover food or drink or blowing on a sick person. Even drinking the pee-pee of a bodhisattva can cure diseases.

There is the story of the bodhisattva Monlam Pelwa who stopped a flood near Lhasa that nobody else could stop. He wrote on a stone, "If Monlam Pelwa is a bodhisattva, then by that truth the water will be turned back." He then left the stone in the path of the oncoming water, and before the flood reached the stone it receded. Just through the power of bodhichitta, without having to recite prayers or do special practices—simply writing on a stone—he was able to turn the flood back.

In the refugee camp Buxa Duar, where I spent eight years, the local Indian people suffered greatly from either too much rain or not enough, depending on whether the monsoons came or failed. The people began to rely on the monks to help them. When there was a drought the monks would go down to the river and do a short *puja*,[69] and very often before they had returned to the monastery there would be rain. Whether it rained or not depended on spirits such as *nagas* interfering with the lives of the farmers because they were disturbed in some way, and by the monks doing pujas, through the power of the bodhichitta generated, the spirits would be pleased and so the rains could come.

The main reason for generating bodhichitta, of course, is not to benefit worldly beings in mundane matters but to lead all beings to enlightenment. This is the greatest goal we can accomplish with bodhichitta. Shantideva said,

> Those who wish to destroy the many sorrows of [their] conditioned existence,

those who wish [all beings] to experience the multitude
of joys,
and those who wish to experience much happiness
should never forsake the Awakening Mind.[70]

Here are both levels of attainment that are possible when we generate bodhichitta: the final, complete elimination of our own suffering and the ability to relieve all beings of theirs. Whatever happiness we wish is ours, from mundane happiness to the happiness of the god realms, from the great happiness of nirvana all the way to the ultimate state of full enlightenment.

If we want ultimate happiness for ourselves, we must cultivate and keep bodhichitta. If we want ultimate happiness for all others, we must cultivate and keep bodhichitta. Bodhichitta should be the motivation for everything we do.

Mundane solutions will not rid us of the countless sufferings of samsara that have been with us all since beginningless time. The best solution, the only solution, is to generate bodhichitta. In this verse Shantideva reminds us how with bodhichitta, by focusing solely on the welfare of others, we are able not only to benefit them hugely but also to ultimately benefit ourselves.

In *The Jewel Lamp*, Khunu Lama Rinpoche said,

If you want to be a scholar learn bodhichitta.
If you want to be a noble person learn bodhichitta.
If you want to be a decent person learn bodhichitta.
If you want to be of benefit to others learn bodhichitta.[71]

Having bodhichitta, we know exactly what qualities need to be cultivated, and we easily achieve them. As Maitreya explained in *Ornament for Clear Realizations*, those who wish to benefit others must understand the entire Buddhadharma, both the paths of the individual-liberation practitioner and of the Bodhisattvayana[72] practitioner. With that motivation we study whatever subject we need in order to be beneficial to others: astrology, hygiene, languages, handicraft, art, and the like. Although we might have no inclination to follow other religions, if studying them benefits others, it's very important that we do. A classic example of this is His Holiness the Dalai Lama, who not only champions interfaith dialogue but also has yearly science seminars, where he has deep discussions with eminent scientists to make links between the ancient mind science of Buddhism and the new mind science of the modern world.

Bodhichitta inspires us to do whatever is beneficial, and of course, besides subjects such as these, we need to study the really vital subjects such as emptiness and the other realizations on the path. When we have bodhichitta, all these realizations pour down on us like cooling rain, without much effort at all, until we become an arya being. From that we develop further, destroying even the subtle delusions and completing all the realizations until we become a buddha.

The simplest thing has utmost meaning with bodhichitta; the highest education is meaningless without it. We could be learned in all the sciences such as biology, chemistry, or psychology, speak all the different languages and so forth, yet still our mind would be empty of the ultimate good heart, bodhichitta, and we would have no peace or real happiness. With or without an education there are the same dissatisfied thoughts, the same relationship problems.

"Noble" here in Khunu Lama Rinpoche's quote means a moral person, somebody with love and compassion for all sentient beings, somebody who is self-disciplined. It is very difficult to maintain self-discipline without bodhichitta because there is always a conflict between our external moral actions and what our self-cherishing mind wants. Conversely, when we do everything with a bodhichitta motivation, everything becomes highly meaningful.

Although we still have to work for money in order to survive, we no longer do it out of self-interest but in order to best help others. So however many hours we work are that many hours practicing the Dharma and creating the cause of happiness for ourselves and for others. The bodhichitta attitude gives meaning to life.

8. We Are Not Bothered by Hindrances

The eighth benefit of bodhichitta is that we cannot be harmed either by internal disturbances, such as distractions, or by external harms, such as other humans and nonhumans. A bodhisattva is always protected, not by a bodyguard as is a powerful king, but by the power of bodhichitta. It's said in the teachings that the universal kings, the extremely rich and powerful kings of the gods, must have many protectors to guard them while they are sleeping, but a bodhisattva naturally has twice as many protectors protecting them day and night, keeping them safe from spirits and other distractions. This is not something they aim for but is just a byproduct of attaining bodhichitta.

To protect practitioners living in a pure Dharma practice, there are different aspects of Dharma protectors appearing in different manifestations. Usually the meditator has to invoke the protector, to make offerings and say specific prayers in order to receive the help. The bodhisattva, however, receives help from the protectors even without asking.

Outer disturbances are controlled by bodhichitta in that it destroys the main distraction that lives within our own mind, the delusions. Both the external hindrances, the spirits and so forth, and the inner hindrances, the delusions themselves, are unable to disturb the bodhisattva.

There was a Kadampa geshe called Geshe Kamlungpa from Pembo, in Tibet, where there are all sorts of spirits, especially a very powerful type of spirit called *tsen*. These spirits can be in human form; they are sometimes even monks. They had great power in a previous life, but because they failed to subdue their mind, they became very spiteful, despite possibly being very learned in the teachings. It's said that many of these tsen can recite prayers they learned in previous lives. There were even geshes who became tsen because, despite their great learning, they had not taken care of their mind by training in the lamrim.

While Geshe Kamlungpa was in Pembo, spirits came, intent on doing him great harm. When they entered his cave where he was meditating, however, one of them who had certain powers saw the concern he felt for them and told the others they must not harm him because of his loving, compassionate mind. This was all because Geshe Kamlungpa was practicing bodhichitta.

When a bodhisattva comes to a place, even one made terrible with spirits' malevolence, that place can be transformed, made very quiet and tranquil, losing its violent atmosphere. The droughts, famines, and catastrophes that occur because of the spirits are stopped by the bodhisattva's influence. The weather improves, and the crops become bountiful. Walking through a forest full of dangers such as tigers or poisonous snakes, a bodhisattva is protected by the precious thought of bodhichitta; the wild creatures become subdued.

The great saint Francis of Assisi showed this. There was a wolf living in the forest giving a lot of harm to the people who had to travel through it. Saint Francis went to talk to the wolf, despite the warnings of the people that he would be killed. When he approached the wolf, however, it became very meek, like a dog who wants food from his master, lying in front of him and licking his feet.

There is also the famous story of how the Buddha calmed a crazy elephant King Magyeda had released in his path while the Buddha was on his alms round. People were terrified as the elephant charged. The other arhats there with the Buddha used their psychic powers to fly away in all directions to protect themselves, but the Buddha stayed calmly in the path of the elephant. By his great power he was able to subdue the elephant, who stopped in front of him and bowed down to him respectfully.

This is the power of bodhichitta.

9. We Quickly Complete the Path

The ninth benefit of bodhichitta is that we quickly complete the path and become enlightened. As I have said, there are more than ten benefits—if we were to explain all of them, we would never finish—but this ninth benefit encompasses the entire path to enlightenment.

I once asked Geshe Jampa Wangdu, a great meditator in Dharamsala who had actualized not just the three principal aspects of the path but also the generation and completion stages of highest yoga tantra, what the quickest way to actualize lamrim realizations was. He replied that because we are blocked from realizations by ignorance, practicing the antidote is the quickest way—and that means destroying the self-cherishing mind. These few words are like an atomic bomb. Removing every obstacle to achieving every happiness—both temporary and ultimate—relies on destroying our self-cherishing mind, which means attaining bodhichitta. That means that every action we do that is an antidote to self-cherishing leads us straight to all the realizations on the path to enlightenment.

Whichever Mahayana path we take, the Paramitayana path or the Vajrayana path, bodhichitta is the vital ingredient. We can spend our whole life progressing through the two stages of Vajrayana, the generation stage and the completion stage; we can control the psychic winds and open the chakras and all these things; but none of this is even a Mahayana action let alone the cause for enlightenment without bodhichitta.

In his *Guide to the Middle Way*, Chandrakirti[73] neatly explained how a buddha arises from a bodhisattva, who arises from bodhichitta. Even the arhats—the shravakas and *pratyekabuddhas*—attain nirvana based on the wisdom of the Buddha, and so we can say that they too are born, or arise, from the Buddha. In this way, bodhichitta becomes the holy field from which all sentient beings' happiness arises. All this depends on bodhichitta, which in turn depends on developing great compassion: seeing the suffering of all sentient beings and taking responsibility to free them from that suffering.

With bodhichitta every action creates infinite merit, so we naturally attain the entire path to enlightenment quickly. Becoming a bodhisattva, we engage in the six perfections and the four means of drawing disciples to the Dharma, and we quickly progress through the five paths. Then we are quickly able to complete the two merits of wisdom and method and achieve the two kayas, the dharmakaya and the rupa-kaya, the holy mind and holy body of a buddha. Without bodhichitta we might be able to complete the merit of wisdom but never the merit of method.

Enlightenment Is Impossible without Bodhichitta

As we have seen, we can't enter the Mahayana without bodhichitta, and without bodhichitta enlightenment is impossible. Khunu Lama Rinpoche said,

> If one is without the vital juice of bodhichitta
> one cannot even enter the Mahayana.
> If such is the case, how will one get
> to the supreme stage of buddhahood?[74]

Bodhichitta is like the vital life force that allows us to achieve all realizations and attain enlightenment. Without it the other realizations are impossible, just as how without our life energy none of our sense organs could function. Therefore we must always take care of our bodhichitta in the same way we now take care of our body and health.

We might think that bodhichitta is such a vast mind that we cannot possibly achieve it; we might become frightened even thinking about it. We need to listen to somebody wiser who can tell us it is possible. As Lama Yeshe, who is kinder than the buddhas of the three times, once said,

> Our problem is that inside us there's a mind going, "Impossible, impossible, impossible. I can't, I can't, I can't." We have to banish that mind from this solar system. Anything is possible; everything is possible. Sometimes you feel that your dreams are impossible, but they're not. Human beings have great potential; they can do anything. The power of the mind is incredible, limitless.[75]

Just like how a father who has a university degree explains to his child who wants to drop out of school how persevering will bring so many benefits, our teachers explain to us how even though bodhichitta seems impossible to us at the moment, by being shown the great benefits and the method to achieve it, we see it is possible and we develop the courage to try.

Lama Tsongkhapa described the two Mahayana paths to enlightenment, the Paramitayana and the Vajrayana, as like the sun and moon. Both paths, based on bodhichitta, lead us to enlightenment, but the length of time each takes is very different.

The Paramitayana is called the causal vehicle because we practice the method and wisdom sides sequentially, whereas the Vajrayana is called the resultant vehicle because with it we skillfully combine method and wisdom in one practice by imagining ourselves as an already enlightened deity, making the time taken to realize the path incredibly short if we do it correctly.

It is said in the texts that it takes three countless great eons to attain enlightenment within the Paramitayana. That means that sentient beings have to suffer for that long until they receive our help. To leave them suffering one minute more than we have to is unbearable. This is where the lightning-quick route of Vajrayana becomes vital. If we can do it skillfully and if all the conditions are there, it is possible to attain enlightenment not in three great eons but in one lifetime of this degenerate age.

The final practice of highest yoga tantra just before we attain enlightenment is the unification of clear light and illusory body, and for that we need not just a direct realization of emptiness but the realization of bodhichitta as well. Without bodhichitta we can have realizations of the generation stage but not of the completion stage because we are unable to destroy the subtle defilements. Trying to gain the unification of clear light and illusory body without bodhichitta is like trying to make pizza without flour or ice cream without milk.

10. WE BECOME A SOURCE OF HAPPINESS FOR OTHERS

The last of the ten benefits of bodhichitta is that we become a source of happiness for others. The *Flower Garland Sutra*, which contains teachings on bodhichitta, says,

> All kind of beings
> transmigrate through all the realms.
> Buddhas, not discriminating,
> liberate countless kinds.[76]

The Tibetan term used here for "transmigrators" is *jigtsok latawa* (often shortened to *jig ta*), which refers to the view of the changeable aggregates that all sentient beings hold: that the aggregates, which are transitory by nature, are solid and unchanging. From this fundamental wrong view all other wrong views and negative emotions arise, keeping them forever transmigrating from one realm to another. One definition of a sentient being is a being who depends on this wrong view of the changeable aggregates and hence is trapped in suffering. By destroying that self-view, bodhichitta has the power to destroy samsara.

This verse says that all the happiness of all worldly beings—beings trapped by this wrong view—comes from bodhichitta, as does the destruction of all the defilements. Arya beings, those beings free from samsara such as the higher bodhisattvas and buddhas, are not included here. Although they still depend on their aggregates, they do not suffer.

This is how incredibly beneficial our bodhichitta is. All transmigratory beings rely on our bodhichitta for all their happiness, just as the numberless past, present, and future buddhas rely on Guru Shakyamuni Buddha's bodhichitta to become enlightened.

The reason I so often start my talks with an explanation of bodhichitta is not only because of its importance but also because even hearing about bodhichitta fills us with joy. It is so important to see that the source of all suffering is the self-cherishing mind and the source of all happiness is the mind of cherishing others. Therefore, even hearing about bodhichitta is so important.

In every city and town in the world there are so many temples, churches, stupas, monks, priests, and so forth, but hearing the teachings on bodhichitta is so rare. It's like being in a top-class jewelry shop with all the diamonds and gold displayed—but in order to find the most valuable jewel of all hidden in the back, we first must know it exists.

PART II
DEVELOPING BODHICHITTA

....

If you desire to benefit others
you should cultivate bodhichitta.
If you desire to benefit yourself, to take the joyous path,
you should cultivate bodhichitta.

—KHUNU LAMA RINPOCHE,
THE JEWEL LAMP, VERSE 286

4 : AN OVERVIEW OF THE WAYS TO DEVELOP BODHICHITTA

....

THE TWO MAIN METHODS FOR DEVELOPING BODHICHITTA

HAVING SEEN that bodhichitta is the sole gateway to the Mahayana and hence the sole route to attaining enlightenment and profoundly benefiting others, we then practice either one of the two principal methods of developing it—the seven points of cause and effect, or equalizing and exchanging self and others—or we practice a combination of these two methods. The first of the two methods for developing bodhichitta, the seven points of cause and effect, was transmitted from Guru Shakyamuni Buddha through Maitreya Buddha, Asanga, Chandrakirti, and the other pandits. Lama Serlingpa[77] passed it on to Atisha, and from him the lineage passed to the Kadampa geshes and then to Lama Tsongkhapa. I will use Lama Tsongkhapa's explanation of the seven points.

The other technique, equalizing and exchanging self and others, also comes from Guru Shakyamuni Buddha, passing to Manjushri and to those other pandits such as Shantideva and Atisha, who handed the lineage of these teachings to his disciple Dromtönpa. Then it passed to Potowa and from him to his disciples, Langri Tangpa and Sharawa.

During those times, the equalizing and exchanging technique was kept secret because it is very profound and it was thought that ordinary people of limited intelligence would be unable to understand it and so fall into heresy. However, when he received the technique from Sharawa, the Kadampa geshe Chekawa[78] was worried that the technique would be lost if it remained a secret. Because of that he propagated the technique. That doesn't mean he publicized it with big ads in newspapers and magazines, but rather than just giving the teachings on it to one or two people, he gave public teachings to big groups in the monasteries.

It's generally considered that the seven points of cause and effect is best suited to a person of lower intelligence, whereas equalizing and exchanging self and others is for a person of higher intelligence, whose mind can handle the concepts of exchanging oneself with others.

The details of these two practices will be covered in subsequent chapters.

These two techniques are usually seen as quite separate, but Lama Tsongkhapa put them together. This combined method starts with the equanimity that is the prerequisite for either method: seeing all sentient beings as equal. From there we see all beings as having been our mother; we see their great kindness and then resolve to repay that kindness. These steps all come from the technique of the seven points of cause and effect.

We then equalize ourselves with all others. How are we equal? We usually think of ourselves as special, and we take care of ourselves better than we take care of others, thinking our life is somehow more important than theirs. In this method we see that there is no reason for this and that all others are just as important as we are. In that way we equalize them in our mind.

Then we generate compassion and love for them and develop the special intention, which leads to the effect of bodhichitta.

Types of Bodhichitta

As we discussed in chapter 1, bodhichitta can be divided into conventional bodhichitta (*kundzop jangchup sem*) and ultimate bodhichitta (*dondam jangchup sem*), the spontaneous wish to attain enlightenment for all sentient beings and the direct realization of emptiness within the mindstream of a bodhisattva, respectively. We also saw that bodhichitta can be divided into effortful bodhichitta and effortless bodhichitta—

bodhichitta that requires analysis and meditation and is part of the conceptual mind, and bodhichitta that is completely spontaneous and felt constantly in the heart, respectively.

Furthermore, the bodhichitta that is effortless and spontaneous can either be *aspirational bodhichitta* (*mönpa semkye*) or *engaging bodhichitta* (*jukpa semkye*). Aspirational bodhichitta is genuine bodhichitta but before the practitioner has taken the bodhisattva vows and engages in the six perfections, at which time it becomes engaging bodhichitta.

Aspirational and Engaging Bodhichitta

Aspirational bodhichitta is also called *aspiring* or *wishing bodhichitta*. In *A Guide to the Bodhisattva's Way of Life*, Shantideva described the difference between these two levels of bodhichitta:

> In brief, the Awakening Mind
> should be understood to be of two types;
> the mind that aspires to awaken
> and the mind that ventures to do so.[79]

Shantideva further said,

> Although great fruits occur in cyclic existence
> from the mind that aspires to awaken,
> an uninterrupted flow of merit does not ensue
> as it does with the engaging mind.[80]

The aspiration to achieve enlightenment for the sake of all sentient beings has incredible benefits, but it lacks the uninterrupted flow of merit of engaging bodhichitta. For this reason the bodhisattva engages in the practice of the six perfections of generosity, morality, patience, enthusiastic perseverance, concentration, and wisdom.

This decision to follow the activities of a bodhisattva continuously creates unbelievably powerful merits that are constantly increasing— every moment, day and night, awake or asleep—no matter what they do. Even in a coma they would still gain infinite merit. This is the power of the bodhisattva vows.

Accomplishing enlightenment is impossible by maintaining aspirational bodhichitta alone, without keeping the bodhisattva vows and performing the bodhisattva's deeds as a heart practice. The highly realized pandit Kamalashila explained in *Stages of Meditation*,

> The bodhisattva who has generated bodhichitta realizes that without subduing his own mind he cannot subdue the minds of others.

Conventional and Ultimate Bodhichitta

A verse in Panchen Lama Chökyi Gyaltsen's *Guru Puja* says,

> In short, no matter what appearances happen, be they
>   good or bad,
> I seek your blessings to transform them into the path
>   ever enhancing the two bodhichittas,
> through the practice of the five powers—the quintessence
>   of the entire Dharma—
> and thus to meditate only on mental happiness.[81]

This clearly shows us that by generating the ultimate good heart that cherishes all others, we will always keep the mind in true happiness, peace, and satisfaction. Here is the answer to the question of how to practice in everyday life. We can quickly progress to ultimate happiness if we can transform whatever experience we have into the path by developing ultimate, or absolute, bodhichitta and conventional bodhichitta, or bodhichitta for the all-obscuring mind.

Conventional bodhichitta is the altruistic mind that wishes to attain enlightenment for all sentient beings. Ultimate bodhichitta is wisdom, the wisdom that directly perceives emptiness. So with the two bodhichittas, one is wisdom and one is method. Therefore, the verse shows that we can use whatever situation we encounter, of good or bad appearance, to realize emptiness and develop our compassion by cherishing others and taking on the responsibility to work for them. Just as we need two legs in order to walk, to take us where we want to go, we need these two for enlightenment—not just conventional bodhichitta and not just a realization of emptiness, but both.

In *Eight Verses on Mind Training*, the first six verses are instructions on transforming the mind from self-cherishing to cherishing others, and the last two refer to the two bodhichittas, the seventh verse to conventional bodhichitta and the last verse to ultimate bodhichitta:

> In brief, I will train myself to offer benefit and joy
> to all my mothers, both directly and indirectly,
> and respectfully take upon myself
> all the hurts and pains of my mothers.
>
> By ensuring that all this remains undefiled
> from the stains of the eight mundane concerns,
> and by understanding all things as illusions,
> I will train myself to be free of the bondage of clinging.[82]

For both conventional and ultimate bodhichitta we need intense purification and great merit. The thought-transformation practices explained in the preceding verses are supports to eliminate the obstacles to achieving these two bodhichittas. For instance, one verse on patience explains how to see the enemy as our best friend and so overcome anger.[83]

EQUANIMITY

The prerequisite for both the techniques for developing bodhichitta is equanimity. In the seven points of cause and effect we must see all sentient beings as our mother and most dear, and that cannot happen when we place one sentient being above another. In equalizing and exchanging self and others we see ourselves as completely equal to all sentient beings, which, again, is impossible while we retain feelings of partiality.

We train our mind in equanimity by seeing how we must overcome the deluded categorization of beings into friend, enemy, and stranger, and how all beings are completely equal in wanting to have happiness and avoid suffering. We start the training by taking the example of three people: somebody we like, somebody we don't like, and somebody we have no feeling for. We then explore the inappropriateness of these categories. When we have done that, we see it in a wider circle of people, and then expand that to more and more beings, until we can take in all sentient beings.

The equanimity that is the foundation of the seven points of cause and effect is cutting off our attachment—the mind that discriminates some sentient beings as being close to us—and our anger—the mind that discriminates some sentient beings as being far from us. This equanimity is the general or common equanimity and is also within the teaching of the Hinayana. There is also the special Mahayana equanimity used in the equalizing and exchanging technique where we see ourselves as being completely equal to all other sentient beings. Through investigation we see that we are no different from a dear friend, such as our partner or parent, and then by extension, we are no different from any other sentient being in that all any of us ever does is try to be happy and avoid suffering. We will look at this in detail later.

Practicing equanimity is very important not just in a meditation session but also in our daily life. This is a remedy to stop the confusion and problems we have dealing with people. Any time we are with others is the actual time to practice; it is not something we should put off. Just as a soldier trains hard in order to effectively defeat the enemy in battle, we need to train in equanimity in order to defeat the enemy of self-cherishing, which sees some beings as friends and some as enemies. Every day we meet people who help us and people who harm us, and so we are always ready to discriminate between friend and enemy, but by doing the equanimity meditation we can overcome our deluded partiality.

We need to equalize all sentient beings. In our innumerable past lives they have all given us help and harm, but even when they harmed us, it was due to ignorance, caused by past karmic relationships we have had with them. This is the reason we discriminate against them as an enemy. The main point is to see all sentient beings in the aspect of being most dear, like a loving mother feels for her only beloved child. As the first verse of *Eight Verses on Mind Training* says,

> Determined to obtain the greatest possible benefit
> from all sentient beings,
> who are more precious than a wish-granting jewel,
> I shall hold them most dear at all times.[84]

The aim of this practice is to see the inappropriateness of the mind that generates attachment and anger based on the help one person has given and the harm another has given. How can we differentiate friend and enemy based on this? If somebody were to give us a present of a thousand dollars in the morning and beat us up in the afternoon, do we designate them "friend" or "enemy?" Do we base our label on the most recent action or the biggest action? Do we count the money as being more important than the attack and designate them "friend," or do we feel their harm is more important and designate them "enemy"? If we feel they are our friend, have they always been our friend? If we feel they are our enemy, have they always been our enemy? Which designation is the correct one? Investigating in this way, we can see how we create the label based on the transient help or harm a person gives and how we then see that person as an inherently existing friend or enemy, despite the transiency of their actions. Can the same person be a permanent friend and enemy?

As we are unable to remember past lives, of course we cannot remember all the relationships we have had in those past lives. We fail to understand that a person who has become our enemy recently has almost definitely been a good friend in a previous life. It feels as if that enemy has always been an enemy, but that is not at all so.

The permanent friend, designated on somebody who has recently benefited us, and the permanent enemy, designated on somebody who has recently caused us suffering, are just concepts, but we believe them to be real—a real friend and a real enemy—whereas there are no such beings existing anywhere without depending on our mind labeling them as such. The friend is not a friend from their own side; the enemy is not an enemy from their own side.

If we accept that it is inappropriate to label somebody "friend" or "enemy" based on their recent treatment of us, then that would apply to all sentient beings, because in previous lives they have been both kind and unkind to us. This person we consider a dear friend in this life has killed us, beaten us, criticized us, done every terrible thing to us, but they have also been our mother, our father, and our friend. Seeing today's enemy, we fail to see the friend of yesterday, and seeing today's friend, we fail to see the enemy of yesterday. There is simply no reason to feel anger or attachment. If we get angry at somebody, we are no different from a tiger, who retaliates unthinkingly when somebody threatens it.

Attachment is often described in the texts as a cannibal because it cheats us so badly, posing as a dear friend when all it ever wants to do is make us suffer. The cannibal makes friends with us, giving us gifts and making us trust them, and then when we are completely off our guard, they eat us.

We should always try to see all sentient beings in equanimity. That does not mean we see all beings as identical or as being both friend and enemy; it means seeing them as equal from their side, equal in only wanting happiness and never wanting suffering. As long as we discriminate based on how they treat us, we can never see this, and so we need to train to eliminate our discrimination.

Developing equanimity in this way overcomes the deluded notion that whatever disturbs our world is inherently bad. Many people live in this fantasy. Whatever brings problems is bad; whatever brings comfort and lack of problems is good. For such a person, the world is never right. Regardless of what they have, there is still something missing. They make their life a misery by demanding perfection and never getting it. With either attachment and aversion it is very difficult to develop our mind. When we have the object of our attachment, our mind is agitated, lifted up, and we are unable to practice the Dharma; when we are frustrated and overwhelmed with problems, our mind is miserable and angry and we are unable to practice the Dharma. We can change this whole attitude around by seeing how what we now label as a "problem" can be a situation that is invaluable for helping us grow and so should be appreciated and even liked. By changing our attitude, the whole problem is solved.

The meditation on equanimity is fundamental to all Mahayana practices, both in Sutrayana and Vajrayana.

When we no longer have attachment to some beings, aversion for others, or indifference to the rest, when that lack of discrimination arises spontaneously, then we can say we have realized equanimity. Then we can progress quickly in all the other points of the techniques for developing bodhichitta. Therefore the equanimity meditation we do as part of our mind training is extremely important.

We need to start in a realistic way, equalizing our feelings for those immediately around us: our parents, friends, colleagues at work, and so forth. When we get to the stage where in meditation we see those people as being equal in our feelings, with no discrimination between friend and enemy, we can expand that to others, bringing in strangers as well, and slowly increase that to include all sentient beings.

Then, in our daily life, whenever a pleasant or unpleasant situation arises and there is the potential to view somebody as a friend or an enemy, the stability we have gained from the equanimity meditation will help us overcome any feelings of discrimination and there will be no problems of attachment or anger. In that way, we won't create negative karma and our life will be happy and peaceful.

While there is still discrimination there can never be real peace. We don't go to our friends or enemies and demand that they all become equal. That is ridiculous; it just doesn't work. We can't place ads in the paper pleading with people to become equally our friend and enemy; we can't go on television and demand this happen; we can't protest in the street or try to equalize them by force. Neither, of course, can harming our enemies stop them from being our enemies. Even killing them all does not mean an end. The more enemies we destroy, the more enemies we create, because all this comes from the mind.

The peace that comes from equalizing friend, enemy, and stranger is the result of changing our perception of the people we encounter, not trying to forcibly change external circumstances—such as one nation trying to impose its will on another by force, which never succeeds. We can only change things by changing our mind. This mind of equanimity is the foundation of world peace, the exact opposite of the discriminating, partial, greedy mind that is the cause of so many of the world's problems.

When we look at how troubled and violent these times are, we can see how vital the practice of equanimity is. There is so much discrimination, so many extreme views, where one side hates the other side because they have opposing ideas. Forcing other people to not be our enemy by suppressing them or destroying them is not a solution; it only creates more enemies and perpetuates the suffering.

A Bodhisattva Sees Everybody in Equanimity

What sets bodhichitta above all other minds is that it covers all sentient beings equally. In *The Jewel Lamp*, Khunu Lama Rinpoche said,

> Bodhichitta pacifies one's own mindstream.
> Bodhichitta pacifies the mindstreams of others.
> With bodhichitta one respects everyone.
> With bodhichitta one sees everyone as equal.[85]

Bodhichitta doesn't just subdue our own mind; because we respect all others equally and treat all others with complete impartiality, we create no causes for them to be disturbed by us, and so our own bodhichitta helps pacify them too. By teaching or by example, we can lead them toward this precious mind, and of course, when they in turn attain it then their own minds will be thoroughly pacified.

His Holiness the Dalai Lama tells the story of Lama Serkangpa, which means "Lama Golden Leg." Once, when he was going around villages for donations, he and his servants were attacked by robbers who beat him severely and strung him up by the neck and legs in order to see if he really did have a golden leg. The shock of the attack was so severe that soon afterward Lama Serkangpa gave up his servants and went to a solitary place to do retreat. The unbelievable thought of renunciation came, and he realized the shortcomings of samsara, all due to the beating the robbers had given him.

This is how bodhichitta changes our life. Whatever the circumstance, whatever happens to us, we place the other being above us, and instead of receiving harm, we only ever receive the cause to further subdue the mind. If we have bodhichitta we respect all sentient beings, whether they are rich or poor, religious or irreligious, and whether they treat us well or badly. Seeing all beings as equal in desiring only happiness and freedom from suffering, all other differences fall away: race, color, sex, religion, class, social standing, and wealth. This thought of complete equanimity arises spontaneously and effortlessly.

Learning to respect all other beings, in turn, we gain respect from all others. Seeing all beings in equanimity, there can never be any thought of partisanship, where we wish to benefit one in favor of another. Of this, Khunu Lama Rinpoche said,

> The precious gem of bodhichitta
> does not discriminate between rich and poor,
> does not differentiate between wise and foolish;
> it benefits equally the high and the low.[86]

Bodhichitta does not discriminate between the rich and poor or the wise and foolish. No matter how wise some beings seem or how stupid others seem, all are the same in wishing to be free from all suffering and the same in being unable to avoid it because of fundamental ignorance.

Buddhas and bodhisattvas, who have perfect equanimity, see all beings equally and work tirelessly for all beings without discrimination.

Whether the beings beat them, criticize them, or even kill them, or whether they make extensive offerings and show incredible devotion to them, the buddhas and bodhisattvas show equal love and compassion.

Even if a sentient being, overcome by great hatred, wanted to kill the Buddha, the Buddha would only see that being as his beloved child, like a loving mother sees her only child, his compassion millions of times greater than the compassion the murderer would feel for themselves.

Devadatta was the Buddha's cousin, and although he ordained into the Buddha's Sangha he always felt intensely jealous of the Buddha. On different occasions he actually tried to kill the Buddha, and once he almost killed himself because of his jealousy.[87]

On this occasion, the Buddha's physician had given the Buddha some medicine that was incredibly powerful. Even though the Buddha was free from the cause of sickness, he sometimes manifested illness for the sake of other sentient beings. Devadatta heard that if anybody less advanced than the Buddha took this medicine, it would be too powerful for them and they would die. This incensed him, and he determined that he would prove he was as powerful as the Buddha by also taking the medicine. He swallowed the medicine and, as the doctor had predicted, became gravely ill. It was obvious that his life was in terrible danger. When the Buddha heard this, he went to Devadatta and put his hand on his forehead and said that if he, the Buddha, had equal love and compassion for Devadatta as for his own beloved son, Rahula, then he should get better. Just by the power of the truth of these words alone Devadatta became better immediately.

Explaining the Equanimity Meditation

Just as a farmer cannot plant seeds in a barren, rocky, uneven field, we need the field of our mind to be level in order to plant the crop of bodhichitta. Unless we can destroy all feelings of aversion and attachment, we will be forever stuck in partiality. While there is any sense of discrimination we cannot control our mind completely.

There are different ways of doing the equanimity meditation, depending on the lineage of the lama giving the teachings. One way is to try to equalize your feelings for a stranger first, then an enemy, and then a friend. Another way is to place all three in front of you and go through the points of meditation. Yet another way starts with the friend.

No strong feeling tends to come up when we think of a stranger; it's usually a feeling of indifference. Think about how when you happen to see somebody on the street who is neither a friend nor an enemy, just a completely neutral person, the mind simply doesn't react one way or the other. A stranger is somebody who treats you neither well nor badly. Thus equanimity for that stranger is very easy. This is the feeling you should develop toward those you think of as friends and enemies. Without equalizing the objects of attachment and anger, you cannot overcome attachment and anger, which is the whole point of the equanimity meditation.

Even if you could honestly say that at present you have no enemies at all, in the future there will be new people, people who could disturb your mind. You should see what the mind has aversion to, especially what is the most harmful thing happening to you, and use that as the object of your meditation. Does somebody criticize you, blaming you for being selfish or calling you stupid? Does somebody deliberately try to hurt you? When you have a specific object for your meditation, then use that to develop equanimity. But if you are unable to find one, use whoever comes to mind and imagine that person criticizing you or doing whatever you find the most harmful. Then check how your mind reacts.

In the same way, take a friend and examine how you think about them. Why do you think of them as a friend? Besides just calling them "friend," what is the feeling there? See the degree of clinging in the relationship. Why do you cling? Is it because they make you feel good by complimenting you and saying how much they like you?

When you have done that, remember that in the past the same person also harmed you, and so explore how your relationship is constantly changing—friend, enemy, friend, enemy, on and on. Even if this hasn't happened so far in this life, if you look at how you have had countless previous lives, then in past lives this switching from friend to enemy must have happened countless times with this one person. Numberless times they have been your friend, helping you, making you feel happy; and numberless times they have been your enemy, mistreating you, disturbing you, making you unhappy. In the same way, your current enemy has been your friend numberless times in the past, and somebody who is currently a stranger has been both friend and enemy numberless times.

From that, the natural conclusion is how pointless clinging and aversion are. Then try to equalize the feelings you have for that person. When you are able to get some feeling of equanimity for them, with neither clinging nor aversion, your mind becomes very loose, very light.

With a sense of equanimity there are far fewer problems. Even if people harm or help you, the mind doesn't discriminate as before. Then anger and attachment don't arise, or if they do, you can control them. Before, you became angry so easily whenever the object of your anger appeared. Now, using this technique for an hour, a few minutes, or even less, your whole way of seeing things completely changes, and that person you thought of as an enemy becomes a good friend again, and you can help each other without either anger or attachment. This is extremely useful.

5 : THE SEVEN POINTS OF CAUSE AND EFFECT

THE FIRST OF the two techniques for developing bodhichitta described in the texts is the seven points of cause and effect. As a reminder, the seven points are the following:

1. recognizing that all beings have been our mother
2. recalling the kindness of those beings
3. resolving to repay that kindness
4. developing loving-kindness
5. developing compassion
6. attaining the special attitude
7. bodhichitta

From the state of equanimity described in the previous chapter, we see that all sentient beings have been our own mother and we remember their kindness and then we develop the wish to repay that kindness. From that arises the feeling of great love or loving-kindness; we start to see all sentient beings in beauty. This has nothing to do with the outer beauty of the body but the inner beauty of the being, how precious they are to us. Then great compassion arises, the wish that all sentient beings be free from all suffering, and from that we develop the special attitude: the determination to free them from suffering. We completely take the responsibility of freeing all sentient beings by ourselves alone. These are the six causes that lead to the one result: bodhichitta.

This technique leads us first to develop effortful bodhichitta. Training in this way, in meditation we have strong feelings of bodhichitta, but outside of meditation they don't arise. We are licking the skin of the sugarcane rather than the sugarcane itself. But by unceasingly training the mind, this feeling arises continuously and spontaneously—while walking, eating, working, talking; all the time—and that is the actual realization of bodhichitta. That is the sweet inside fruit, the actual sugarcane.

After attaining bodhichitta, we become a bodhisattva. Then we will cherish all other sentient beings more than we cherish ourselves now. Every single sentient being becomes so precious, so important; each becomes the most precious and important person in our life. Every single thing we do is purely for their sake. Our life is pervaded with this attitude of bodhichitta. This is the goal of this technique.

1. Recognizing That All Sentient Beings Have Been Our Mother

To be able to see how all sentient beings have been incredibly kind to us and therefore to wish to repay that kindness, we first have to logically understand that they have all helped us throughout our infinite lives. We do this by seeing that all sentient beings have been our mother, not just once but countless times.

The mother is usually used for this point because it's easiest. Although some people may have had a difficult relationship with their mother, for most of us the mother of this life is the object of our great love and the person who has shown us the most love and kindness, more so than even our father. When we look at animal and bird mothers, we see the great instinctive love that the mother has for the child and the child has for the mother.

I remember once, when I was quite a young child, my mother became sick. She was an old woman but what she cried out was "Ama! Ama!"— "Mother! Mother!" At that time, my grandmother was still around, although she was probably about eighty, with completely white hair, but my mother still cried out for her when she was sick.

This is why the mother has been purposely chosen in the seven points of cause and effect technique to represent all that is best in beings. It helps us develop strong love and compassion for all sentient beings based on the feelings we have for the mother. That it doesn't use the father doesn't mean that the father isn't kind or that the father hasn't been our mother in countless previous lives. When we remember the kindness of the mother, we are also remembering the kindness of the father; it's just that we are using a different label.

The main point, though, is to remember somebody who has been incredibly kind to us. Even if it was an aunt or a foster parent rather than our birth mother, the point is that somebody brought us up, and seeing that, we can generate incredible gratitude for that person and wish to repay that kindness.

When we think about how a being passes from one life to another in a continuous stream of life after life after life, we can see how although in this present life we have this present mother, in previous lives other sentient beings have been our mother, and how because our lives have been numberless, our mothers have been numberless. All the people in our family have been our mother in previous lives; all the people and all the animals, flies, mosquitoes, birds, and so forth in the neighborhood and in the world have been our mother; all the beings in the ground, in the air, under the ground, in the seas have been our mother. Our dog has, and the fleas on our dog have; the worms under the ground have, and the fish in our pond have. All the sentient beings in the six realms have been our mother—and they have been our mother numberless times.

We can't remember this because we can't remember previous lives. Separated as a tiny baby, a child will be unable to remember their mother when grown up, but that does not mean they never had a mother. In the same way, we can neither remember how our present life's mother has been our mother countless times in countless past lives, nor can we remember how all other beings have.

As Nagarjuna said in *Friendly Letter*,

A heap of all the bones each being has left
would reach to Meru's top or even higher.
To count one's mother's lineage with pills
the size of berries, the earth would not suffice.[88]

Not only have we been reborn in every realm countless times and hence had countless mothers, but due to different karmic imprints, our present life's mother has not always been our mother. Perhaps when she was an elephant, we were an ant, born from a mother ant; or when she was a flea, we were a yak, born from a mother yak, and so forth. She has, however, been our mother countless times: a mother turkey to our turkey chick, a mother cow to our calf, and so forth.

There is no realm in samsara, from the lowest to the highest, in which we have not been born countless times. We have known innumerable forms of existence born to innumerable mothers. Sentient beings have been our mother since beginningless time. There has never been a time when they weren't our mother. This is something that not even a buddha's omniscient mind can see, and so, of course, our limited mind cannot see it.

Why is this realization the crucial first step to developing bodhichitta in this technique? Because attaining bodhichitta depends on having the special attitude that takes the sole responsibility to free all sentient beings from suffering and place them in peerless happiness. That comes from having great compassion, the compassion that wishes to free all beings from suffering, which in turn is a result of the mind of loving-kindness that sees all beings in beauty, with heartfelt love for each and every one.

Like a mother loves her child, we love all sentient beings, not just the ones who help us. Where does that feeling arise from? From seeing the incredible kindness all beings have shown us and wishing to repay that kindness, and that can only come when we understand that all sentient beings have been our mother.

At present, whenever we see our present life's mother, the intuitive feeling of "Oh, this is my mother" arises. We have attained the first of the steps of the seven points of cause and effect when the same feeling arises—that this is our kind mother—for each and every sentient being we encounter—each insect, bird, person.

2. Recalling the Kindness of Those Beings

Having established that all sentient beings have been our mother, the next step is to remember the kindness of those mothers, and by extension of all sentient beings.

A child usually feels so much respect for their parents. They feel that their mother and father are so kind, so precious, that automatically the thought of loving-kindness arises toward them. If we feel that a person has given us a lot of help when we have been in great difficulty, we naturally see that person in the light of loving-kindness. Knowing their great kindness, we wish them to be free from problems, like a mother does for a son or daughter. The more we feel their kindness, the more compassion we have; particularly when they are ill or have mental problems, and we wish them to be separated from those problems.

The Four Ways Our Mother Has Been Kind
As Thokmé Sangpo said in the *Thirty-Seven Practices of the Bodhisattva,*

> When your mothers, who've loved you since time without
> beginning
> are suffering, what's the use of your own happiness?
> Therefore to free limitless living beings
> develop the altruistic intention—
> this is the practice of Bodhisattvas.[89]

Traditionally, the kindness of the mother has been discussed using these four points:

1. the kindness of giving us this body
2. the kindness of protecting us from life's dangers
3. the kindness of leading us in the path of the world
4. the kindness of bearing many hardships and accumulating negative karma for us

When we are poor and somebody gives us a meal or a cup of coffee, we feel so grateful; we feel that person is incredibly kind. If they give us some money to spend a night in a hotel rather than on the street, we are filled with gratitude for their great kindness. We automatically feel we would like to repay that kindness by helping them in the future. Our mother of this life has been much, much kinder than the kindest friend or stranger. We need to understand this deeply and apply it to all sentient beings.

Looking at all the examples in our own life where our mother has been kind to us, our meditations on the kindness of the mother will become very effective. We have this amazing opportunity because we have this precious body, which our mother has given us by undergoing so many hardships. If we don't use it in the most meaningful way, we are wasting all the effort our mother has made and causing her great trouble.

We are not making up some fantasy to trick ourselves into compassion; this is according to reality. Every sentient being has been our mother and has been kind to us in these four ways, and when we can see this we will naturally see every sentient being in beauty.

When we have meditated on our present life's mother in this way, we can meditate on our father, seeing that he has also been our mother numberless times, and he has also been incredibly kind to us in these four ways in previous lives. Then we can do the same with our friends and then with our enemies and finally with all other sentient beings. All the sentient beings have been our mother numberless times and have been extremely kind to us in these four ways.

Then, no matter what situation we find ourselves in, our mind will remain strong, and attachment and anger will not easily arise.

When a mosquito lands on our arm and drinks our blood, we think, "Oh, here is my mother." Even if it's a flea on our clothes, a snake under the bed, a mouse eating our food, we still think this; we still have the same feeling we have for our present life's mother. Should a terrifying animal such as a tiger confront us, the thought of it being our real mother still arises without any effort. We will be like the great bodhisattva Atisha who, whenever he saw an animal suffering, said things such as, "Oh, my mother is exhausted. My mother is sick. My mother is suffering." This came from his own experience, not from imitation.

The four ways the mother has been kind to us are each further divided into four parts:

1. looking at the kindness
2. seeing that she has been kind countless times in previous lives
3. thinking that we can never repay that kindness
4. seeing that all sentient beings have been kind in this way

Thinking like this, a meditation on the four ways our mother has been kind becomes incredibly powerful.

1. The Kindness of Giving Us This Body

The first way our present life's mother—and by extension all mother sentient beings—has been kind to us is by bearing us for nine months and giving birth to us. If our mother had not created the karma to give birth to us, or if she had but then had an abortion, we wouldn't now have this precious human body, which has incredible freedom to experience not just worldly pleasures rather than the great suffering of the lower realms but also the freedom to practice the holy Dharma. This is all due to the great kindness of the mother.

If our mother had not cared for us when we were in her womb, if she had not loved us even then, none of these incredible advantages would have happened. We wouldn't have had the opportunity to meet the infallible teachings, the complete lamrim teachings that show us clearly the entire path to enlightenment and cause the Dharma wisdom to grow in us. We wouldn't have known about karma and the causes of happiness and suffering and thereby known how to avoid suffering and cultivate happiness. All the great advantages we now have are only there because of her incredible kindness.

With this body we can gain success in whatever we want; we can obtain happiness for ourselves and develop our mind fully so we can work to eliminate the suffering of all sentient beings. We can help one sentient being, then ten sentient beings, then a hundred, a thousand, a million, then countless, until our full potential is realized and we become a buddha, able to spontaneously work to free all beings. This is all due to the kindness of our mother, who gave us this precious human body.

Unlike the beings of the lower realms or the gods, we are able, through practice, to develop generosity, morality, and the other states of mind needed to attain another perfect human rebirth and so continue to develop on the path to enlightenment. This is all due to the kindness of our mother.

All beings have buddha nature. The mosquito has it, the turtle has it, the tiger has it, but they do not have the body that is needed to realize that potential. We do. If they heard the Dharma, they wouldn't understand one word. They cannot distinguish between virtue and nonvirtue; they are powerless to not create nonvirtue and ensure future suffering. We are able to choose between the two and always create virtue. When somebody explains the cause of happiness to us, we understand it immediately, even if we are not able to stop all our nonvirtuous activities right away. With that understanding, we have the power to transform our life into virtue. We have that freedom; it's completely in our hands. Within each day, each hour, each minute, each second, we have the freedom to abandon suffering and attain happiness. That is the great advantage of having this perfect human rebirth.

Attaining another perfect human rebirth, renouncing the whole of samsara and destroying forever the slightest suffering, developing the precious mind of bodhichitta and undertaking the bodhisattva's deeds, and then attaining full enlightenment—these all come from having this potential and this precious human body that we only have because of the kindness of our mother.

In all our countless lifetimes this has almost never happened before, so this is most amazing. The more we know of the value of this life, the more we can appreciate just how kind our mother has been, bearing us, raising us, suffering such hardships for us.

Even after our consciousness had joined with the sperm and egg to become a fertilized egg in her womb, she could have thought more of herself and aborted us. But she didn't do that. Not only that, she cared for her unborn baby as best she could. For our sake she only ate the right foods, and she gave up cigarettes and alcohol. She moved carefully so we wouldn't be jarred. She sat down so we would be comfortable. She made sure the room wasn't too hot or too cold for us. She tried not to lift or carry heavy things in order not to hurt us, and she never wore tight clothes or tight belts. She always moved carefully, watching out for dangers that could be fatal for us. She did everything she could to make our time in the womb as easy and comfortable as possible.

Nobody who is not a mother can imagine what carrying a baby around in the womb for nine months is like. It's unbelievable. There were the pains and the worries of pregnancy she had to bear, the discomfort and the worry that she might become sick and lose her baby. She always wanted to rest but could never find a comfortable position; she was always exhausted and getting fatter and fatter. Because of her concern for us, she accepted that her pregnancy would cause her to lose her outer beauty—but this wasn't important to her, only our well-being was.

When it was time to give birth to us, when the fetus turned around for the birth, she endured incredible pain, as if her body was cracking in two. During the whole birth process she suffered terribly, but afterward, when somebody asked her about the birth, she didn't complain at all.

Perhaps after we were born our mother abandoned us and we were raised by somebody else. If that were so, we might feel we are justified in thinking that the person who raised us was wonderful but our birth mother was so cruel, so heartless, totally bad. But even if all she did was keep us in her womb for nine months and give birth to us, that is an incredible kindness. Just having this human body is the most precious thing; it's up to us to fulfill its potential. We have all these opportunities due to our mother's kindness.

If she hadn't endured the suffering of carrying us and giving birth to us, where would we be now? We could be a bird sitting in a tree, desperately looking for a worm to eat; or we could be that worm, sliding along the ground, trying to escape the bird—or maybe even already torn in two and carried away in its beak. We could be a lizard completely covered by ants, being eaten alive; we could be a frog, half in and half out of the mouth of a snake, about to be swallowed whole. We could be a cow who, because her milk has dried up, is going to the slaughterhouse. We could be a fish caught in a fisher's net or in the beak of a pelican. We could be a mosquito, buzzing around people, desperate for their blood, or a crocodile, a rhinoceros, a hippopotamus—any being at all. We could be a hungry ghost or a hell being, where besides not ever hearing the name of the Buddha, we wouldn't even hear a human voice. We are none of these, however; we are a human being with this incredible potential.

If our mother hadn't carried us the full nine months and given birth to us, we wouldn't have had any opportunity at all to meet the Dharma and study with the highly qualified virtuous teachers such as His Holiness the Dalai Lama, or hear the complete path of the sutra and tantra, or take initiations into a tantric deity, the lightning-quick method to attain enlightenment. None of this could have happened.

Once we have considered the kindness of our present life's mother in having given us this body, we contemplate the rest of the four ways our mother is kind.

We consider that this is not the first time she has been kind by giving us a human body. Because we have lived innumerable lives, she has been our human mother innumerable times and given us innumerable human bodies. So we should feel from our heart that even the buddhas, whose holy minds are omniscient, cannot see the depth and the beginning of this kindness.

Then, feeling the depthless kindness she has shown in giving us this precious human body numberless times, we naturally feel we must repay that kindness, but we realize that even if we sacrificed all the lives we have had since beginningless time, as many lives as there are atoms, that doesn't even start to repay the kindness of our mother.

The fourth point of each aspect of kindness expands the thought even further. Our mother of this life has been kind to us in this way, but because we have had countless lives, we have had countless relationships with every sentient being, and so every sentient being has been our mother and has been so incredibly kind to us in this same way, by giving us this body numberless times.

Like us, all sentient beings have been higher and lower in samsara, and when they were human beings they were our mothers, bearing us and giving birth to us and caring for us, just as our present life's mother has. We should think of every being in every realm and see that each has been that kind to us. We should feel this for every hell being, every hungry ghost, every animal, every human being, every demigod, every god, and every intermediate-state being. We should remember even the tiniest creatures, those tiny biting flies that swarm around our sweating body. They too have been our unimaginably kind mother.

2. The Kindness of Protecting Us from Life's Dangers

The second kindness of the mother is that after we were born she protected us from all of life's dangers.

As a baby we were completely helpless. Unless our mother had been there constantly, guarding us, protecting us, we wouldn't have lasted five minutes. There are so many dangers, so many obstacles, that if she had just looked away for a second, we could have easily been killed. Even in one day our mother must have saved us from life's dangers hundreds of times.

When our birth went well she was so happy, like she had been given a wish-granting jewel. She took such incredible care of this big piece of flesh that was squirming like a worm. For me, a new baby is kind of scary, making me think, "I also came out like this." If we think about it, this is really true; we were just a big piece of flesh with some hairs on top, not knowing anything: how to walk, how to speak. Just like a big fish. Our mother was the one who made us a human being. She even trained us how to make pee-pee and kaka.

As a baby we were completely ignorant. We knew nothing of what was harmful and what was helpful. She always carefully placed us on a soft, comfortable bed, wrapped in the softest blankets she could find. When she lifted us up she did so with both hands, incredibly carefully, holding us to her so we would be warmed by her body.

She constantly watched to see that we were okay, checking whether we were hot or cold or in a draft, whether we had a fever or we had made a mess. If she didn't watch us every minute, we were in constant danger. We could fall off the bed or fall down the stairs. Any object we could get hold of was a danger. We could put a dangerous knife in our mouth or swallow a spoon; we could drink a dangerous liquid or put our hand into a fire. Fatal things seemed like a magnet to our hands, so she had to keep a constant vigil. Outside there were even more dangers—cars, animals, poisonous thorns, sharp objects. There were dangers to our life everywhere. She had to watch us with the concentration of a meditator watching the mind.

I saw in a newspaper once how the parents of a small girl returned home one day to find she had caught a snake and was eating it. She was literally chewing on the live snake's head as they walked through the door. I think when the television crew interviewed the father and asked him why she did it, he said something like he thought she saw it as a challenge.

We were so helpless, without teeth to eat any substantial food, without any means to survive. Just as she had nourished us when we were in her womb, giving us so much of her own energy and nutriment, after the umbilical cord was cut all she ever thought about was how to feed and nurture us. When we are thirsty and somebody gives us a cup of tea, we are very grateful, thinking of them as some kind of jewel, as some wonderful benefactor. And this is just from one cup of tea, which is not even from their body! This is absolutely nothing compared to our mother, who has nurtured us over countless lifetimes with oceans of her own breast milk. Even all the oceans of this earth are nothing compared to the milk she has given us; it would fill all of space.

Later, our mother made sure we had just the right food, prepared in just the right way—food that made us strong and healthy. Like this, she watched our diet month after month for many years. In many countries where people don't have blenders, the mother first chews all the food in her mouth and, like a mother bird, passes it from her mouth to the baby's mouth. I remember in Solu Khumbu, Nepal, where I was born, mothers would even clean the babies' snotty noses with their mouths. I don't personally remember being fed from my mother's mouth but I know I enjoyed the baby food very much. It was still tsampa, the staple food of the region, but mixed with milk and a lot of butter; it was delicious.

We are grateful when we are traveling and hungry and a stranger gives us a sandwich or something; we remember their kindness for a long time. And yet our mother fed us the most nutritious and delicious food year after year. This food didn't magically fall from the sky. She had to work unbelievably hard to buy it. She bought our food, clothes, toys, schoolbooks, and all the things we have taken for granted all our life. She underwent such incredible physical and mental difficulties in order to make life as perfect as possible for us.

Our mother took care of us as if her heart were on the outside. We were like an object of meditation for her, always at the center of her heart. She thought of us constantly day and night, even if she was far away from home, wishing only for our own happiness, all the time cherishing us like a priceless jewel. Sometimes she herself didn't have the time to look after us because she had to go to work to get food, so she hired another person to look after us. Even though she had many other things to do and so many other problems, she protected our life from hundreds of harms and mortal dangers.

When I see a mother taking care of her children, it really makes me think about her kindness. In the same way that she is taking care of them now, she has also taken care of me in the past. Since the continuity of lives is beginningless, she has definitely been my mother and definitely taken care of me like this. Like this, we should all feel the kindness from the very depths of our heart. It's very effective for our mind when we apply this to ourselves.

We conclude by thinking about this aspect of the kindness of our present life's mother by thinking that she has been this kind not just in this life but from beginningless rebirths. She has been our human mother countless times, giving us this precious human body and nourishing us and protecting us in these ways. Even the omniscient mind of the Buddha can't see the beginning of this kindness. We should feel this from the depths of our heart.

We would feel so grateful to a doctor who had cured us from a dangerous disease or a brave person who had rescued us from a mugger with a gun, but that is nothing compared to the kindness our mother has shown us in this life and in all the countless lives when she has been our mother. Even if we sacrificed our lives as many times as there are atoms in all the oceans of the world, we would not even start to repay her incredible kindness.

But she has not just been our human mother countless times, showing us incredible kindness, but also when we have had other types of bodies. In our infinite lives there is not one type of rebirth we haven't taken numberless times. Our present life's human mother has been our mother in these types of rebirths countless times. There is no samsaric rebirth we haven't had when she has not been our mother countless times.

For example, just as we have had a dog rebirth countless times, our present mother has had a dog rebirth countless times and been a dog mother countless times, so she has been our dog mother countless times. She has raised us as her pup countless times, according to her limited intelligence, keeping us warm under her body, trying to take care of the puppy us, licking our head and body to clean us, despite how filthy we might be, protecting us all the time from attacks by other dogs, people, or other predators.

We can take any animal we like and follow the same reasoning. A mother bird is an excellent example. She has been our bird mother countless times, showing our chick self incredible kindness. While we sat in the nest squawking impatiently, she tirelessly flew back and forth all day, collecting insects and worms for us to eat, feeding them patiently into our beak one by one. We were helpless in the nest, just waiting for her return, but she always did. When we think about how difficult it is for a tiny bird to make a safe and comfortable nest for her chicks, we can see how dedicated she is to the welfare of her young, picking up tiny bits of twigs, grass, and dirt in her beak and bringing them to the nest flight after flight to make it as perfect as she can. I saw a news program on television in Australia once where a mother bird stayed on her nest right through a bushfire to try to keep her eggs safe. Such incredible bravery. There are hundreds of thousands of different species of birds, and we have been born to bird mothers of each of these species numberless times. Can you imagine that?

Like this we can go from our present life's mother's kindness as a human mother to all the lives she has been our mother in all the other samsaric rebirths she has had. We can look at this in whatever way is most effective and most powerful for us.

When we have recognized this, we can then expand that to understand that, just like our present life's mother, each and every sentient being has been our mother countless times. Every sentient being has been our mother and been unbelievably kind to us countless times. The kindness of our present life's mother in this life alone is inexpressible, but inexpressible too is the kindness of all sentient beings who have also been our mother countless times. Every single ant, every single mosquito, every single cockroach, every single rabbit, bird, cow, tiger, fish, every being so tiny we need a microscope to see it, every whale—every being—has been so kind to us countless times.

For somebody who has attained this realization, the feeling is stronger even than what we feel for our present life's mother, because the understanding of the kindness is much stronger. Then whatever being that person encounters is seen as their precious and kind mother, no matter what type of being it is. Whenever they encounter a sentient being, that instinctive feeling arises—"This is my mother"—and that incredible feeling of the kindness of the mother is there. No matter how fearful or repulsive that being is, because of this feeling they only see them in beauty.

3. The Kindness of Leading Us in the Path of the World

The third aspect of the great kindness of our present life's mother is the kindness of leading us in the path of the world, which means teaching us what we need to know to be a real human being. If she hadn't led us in the path of the world, teaching us life skills and giving us an education, we wouldn't have been able to even survive, let alone call ourselves an independent, mature adult. We wouldn't have been "in the line of human beings," as the texts say.

She taught us all the skills we needed to be a human being. While she was feeding, clothing, and protecting us, she was also teaching us how to walk, talk, distinguish right from wrong, and all the social skills we need in everyday life. She showed us how to read and sent us to school, encouraging us to study and understand. Without an education, we wouldn't have the life we now have, with qualifications allowing us to have a good job and a good standard of living. While we took school for granted, without the education our parents worked so hard to give us, how could we study the Buddhadharma? This is an unbelievable kindness.

When we were children and our parents made us do things we didn't want to do, back then we might have seen them as persecutors, as blocks to our happiness, not realizing they were doing it for our own good. Instead of repaying their incredible kindness with love and compassion, we repaid it with fights and anger. Now we are independent adults, and it is completely wrong to think that this all came by our own doing, that we were solely responsible for our education, our degree, finding a good job, getting a home, and so forth. We must remember that if it were not for our parents, we would still be like worms crawling on the ground.

As with the previous kindness, we then think that this is not the first time our present life's mother has led us in the path of the world like this. She has been kind like this numberless times, so many times that even the omniscient mind of the Buddha is incapable of seeing the beginning. If we sacrificed our lives so many times that it equaled the number of atoms of all the oceans, we could not repay that kindness.

And not only our present life's mother but all sentient beings have been kind to us in this way, including our present life's enemies.

4. The Kindness of Bearing Many Hardships and Accumulating Negative Karma for Us

The fourth kindness of the mother is the kindness of bearing many hardships for us. Furthermore, in order to give us all the things she wanted us to have, she often had to create negative karma.

Always calling us by a sweet name, always looking at us with a smiling, loving face and with eyes of compassion, this was how our mother brought us up. She always chose our happiness over her own, remaining hungry and thirsty while we ate and drank, feeling cold or hot while we were comfortable, allowing herself to get sick in order to ensure we were always healthy. If she had had to die to save us, she would have done so; if she had had to choose between her enlightenment and ours, she would have chosen ours. In fact, if she could, she would give us enlightenment and still be looking for more to give us.

It's impossible to comprehend the hardships she endured for us. As we have seen, she endured great hardships during pregnancy and our birth, and after our birth she tirelessly looked after us, sacrificing her life for us, giving us a good education and all the things we needed. Looking after us was a full-time job, but on top of that, she had to go to work to pay for everything, making herself sick and exhausted. She spent her life constantly trying to make us happy. Whatever she did, even the most boring office work, she did with our happiness uppermost in her mind.

Not only that, she willingly created negative karma if it meant she could get us what we wanted. She stole to give us food to eat or lied to ensure we had a good reputation, telling others we were good, clever, beautiful, and so forth. (I remember my own mother telling other people how wonderful I was so they would think well of me, despite me being very naughty and not at all wonderful.)

Our mother would even kill if that were necessary for our welfare, assuring herself a rebirth in the lower realms and an unimaginable length of time of suffering. There was nothing she wouldn't do to make us happy. From our own side, we caused her to become angry, creating even more negative karma and again having to experience the suffering results.

Seeing how much our mother suffered to bring us up and seeing the negativities she created doing this reminds us of her incredible kindness and helps us develop love and compassion. Just thinking back to the deprivations both our mother and our father had to face is a strong reminder of their kindness. Tracing back all the struggles and sacrifices they both made from the time we were conceived to when we gained our independence, we can see their unbelievable kindness, even though at the time we probably took them for granted, seeing them almost as servants. These are the two people we have the closest possible connection with, especially our mother, who carried us in her womb for nine months.

It's heartbreaking when we think of this. Not only did she have to bear all those hardships for us, but because she had no idea of the Dharma, despite the great love she had for us, she also created so much negative karma out of ignorance. She has had to suffer like this for us. Therefore, from our side, we *must* do whatever we can to save her from this.

As with the other three kindnesses, we conclude by seeing that not only has our present life's human mother been incredibly kind to us in this life, but she was also incredibly kind to us when she was our human mother in countless previous lives. Even the omniscient mind of the Buddha cannot see the beginning of the times she has been our mother and been unbelievably kind to us. There is no way we can ever hope to repay that kindness, even if we sacrificed our lives as many times as there are the atoms in this earth.

This is just thinking of our present life's human mother. When we think of all the other rebirths we have had and all the other times she has been our nonhuman mother, then it's even more tragic. Think of when she was our bird mother, killing worm after worm in order to feed us, creating incredible, inconceivable negative karma for us.

When we think of any type of animal, bird, insect, or fish, we can easily see that in order to protect and nurture their young, they commit all sorts of negative actions, suffering all sorts of hardships and ensuring that their future will be even more suffering. The wildebeests in Africa brave attacks by lions and tigers while defending their young ferociously. Rather than let the young calf die, a wildebeest runs around and around and lets herself become the target of the attack, getting pounced on first by one big cat and then another. From the lions' side, they kill to let their children eat, the whole family becoming so full they can hardly walk, just leaving a pile of bloody bones for the vultures and hyenas. We have been born as a wildebeest calf, protected from the lions by our mother sacrificing her life; we have been born as a lion cub fed on wildebeest meat by our mother. We have been born as a vulture chick, waiting for our mother to steal the precious meat from the lions for us.

Dependent on a womb to take samsaric rebirths in these realms, we have been born to our present life's human mother when she was in countless different forms, and likewise we have been born to every single sentient being in every type of rebirth, and in each rebirth our mother has endured incredible hardships and created terrible negative karma in order to protect and nurture us. This has been going on from time without beginning.

Therefore we must make the best possible use of this precious human body, given to us through much hardship by our mother, and the best way we can do that is by practicing the Dharma. In particular, we must do whatever we can to attain bodhichitta and then full enlightenment in order to repay the kindness of all sentient beings and lead them from suffering to the peerless happiness of enlightenment.

In thinking about all the four ways our mothers have been so kind, we use our current life's mother as the template and then expand it out to all sentient beings. This mind is vital to take us to the next step—determining to repay that kindness—and from there to love, compassion, and the special attitude that determines to take sole responsibility to free them all from suffering.

3. Resolving to Repay That Kindness

All the mother sentient beings who have been so incredibly kind to us countless times in our infinite past lives are suffering because they lack Dharma wisdom. What must we do? It is as Chandragomin said in *Letter to a Disciple*:

> If we were to see our dear ones
> fallen into the ocean of samsara
> as if into a whirlpool,
> swiftly whirling around,
> emerging, and then again disappearing
> in the cycles of birth and death,
> and if we were to ignore them and go away alone—
> how could there be anyone more shameless?[90]

Sentient beings are also often compared to our old, crippled mother, her mind completely crazy, her body full of disease. Blind, she is unable to see the road, and so each step she takes brings her closer to a precipice and the bottomless abyss beyond. She thinks she is getting closer to safety and happiness, unable to see she is going in completely the wrong direction, closer to the edge rather than farther from it.

If our own mother were like this, and we were the only one who could help her, it would be totally shameful to not help her, to instead relax in a beautiful park, singing, lying in the sun, enjoying ourselves while she fell to her death.

This is the state of all sentient beings, blinded without the Dharma, stumbling with each step toward the abyss of the lower realms and unendurable suffering. They have no Dharma wisdom, they have no guide; they are completely crazy with delusions, believing attachment to sense objects to be happiness. Each second, each minute, each hour, they stumble toward the precipice that divides this life's suffering from the far greater suffering of the next life. These sentient beings have been our mother countless times and have been incredibly kind, so if we don't do whatever we can to try to save them from that abyss, we are completely shameless. Having met the Dharma, we have the means to free ourselves; other sentient beings do not. If we don't do whatever we can to repay their great kindness, there is nothing more selfish and ungenerous.

We must work hard to ensure all sentient beings are free from suffering. Giving them food, clothing, and material things is not the best way to repay them, because they have had all these things numberless times in their past lives. Numberless times they have been like Indra, the king of the god realm, having unimaginable enjoyment and incredible material power, but still they are not liberated from the suffering of samsara. Seeing this, we must make the heartfelt determination to repay all the mother sentient beings by liberating them from the suffering of samsara and leading them to full enlightenment.

Just as the buddhas cannot liberate us by pulling us from samsara—they can only guide us—we cannot physically free our kind mothers. Instead, we must show them how to free themselves by revealing the truth to them. The best service we can therefore offer others is to study the Dharma, to practice it, and to actualize it, attaining the realizations of the path to enlightenment. There are numberless beings who have a karmic connection with us and depend upon us to guide them from suffering toward liberation and enlightenment.

Every second in the hell realm a hell being must endure heat that is utterly unbearable, and yet it must be endured for eons. If we had already attained bodhichitta, we would have been able to help not just that one hell being but every hell being with a karmic connection with us. Therefore, even when we think of that one hell being who is experiencing unimaginable suffering, it becomes urgent that we attain bodhichitta without the delay of even a second.

We can think exactly the same way about the beings in the other realms. One hungry ghost has to endure unendurable sufferings of hunger and thirst, of heat, cold, and exhaustion. If we had already attained bodhichitta, not just that one hungry ghost but all the numberless hungry ghosts with karma with us would already have been freed from suffering. Similarly, every animal we have a connection with, if we had already obtained bodhichitta, would have been freed from suffering by now instead of having to bear the terrible sufferings of the animal realm. Every human being, now suffering the three types of suffering, would have been free from suffering. Therefore, it's urgent that we *must* generate bodhichitta without the delay of even a second, not just for one animal or one human but for the numberless animals and humans, as well as the numberless gods and demigods. Our mother and every sentient being have endured such incredible hardships for us life after life after life, since beginningless time, so giving up our body infinite times still won't come near to repaying their kindness. The only thing we can do is lead each of them from suffering and to peerless happiness. We really have no choice. We have no time to lose, no time to only be concerned with ourselves. All we can do is work tirelessly for our kind mother sentient beings.

Seeing how every second of our survival is dependent on the kindness of countless sentient beings, we must only work for this. What else is the purpose of living? What else is the purpose of our education? Why else would we go to work and earn that big salary? Why else would we own a big house and spend so much money keeping ourselves healthy and fit?

The job, house, car, clothes, medicine—all the things that are part of our life—only make sense when we use them to make our life most meaningful and beneficial for others. With this attitude, we can lead the same life, working in the same job, doing the same things, but instead of doing them from our own selfish interests, we do them for all other sentient beings. With this attitude, everything we do becomes a service for all sentient beings. Before, even meditating and studying the Dharma was just for our own peace and happiness. It was nothing special. But now, the same meditation is only in order to benefit others.

Everything we do becomes the preparation for achieving full enlightenment. With this perfect human rebirth we have the choice to make every second infinitely meaningful. Freeing all sentient beings, which are as infinite as the sky, is the meaning of life. That is repaying their kindness. They are incapable of freeing themselves; it's entirely up to us.

4. Developing Loving-Kindness

The followers of the Hinayana, the shravakas and pratyekabuddhas, have such strong loving-kindness and compassion we couldn't even conceive of it. In the Mahayana tradition, loving-kindness and compassion go even further; we're supposed to take the responsibility for releasing all sentient beings from suffering and bringing them to enlightenment. As the incomparably kind Lama Yeshe often used to say, "Act! Don't just say the words, all that talk, talk, talk about others' suffering. Act! Do something. Take the responsibility yourself." Taking this responsibility is difficult; talking is easier. I can talk. I can talk a lot! There are many who talk of love and compassion, but the number of those who take the responsibility and act is like stars in the daytime.

Having a strong feeling that all beings have been our mother and so kind, we generate the mind of loving-kindness, which in Sanskrit is *maitri* and in Tibetan is *yiong jampa*.[91] *Yiong* means "beautiful" or "affection," and *jampa* means "loving-kindness," so we can translate it as the "loving-kindness of seeing others in beauty."

It can also just be called "love" or "affectionate loving-kindness," but the latter is not an exact translation because that links the affection to the sense of loving-kindness, the subjective state, whereas in the Tibetan it refers to the object itself, the sentient beings, and so it means a good, kind, beautiful being. A mother naturally sees her child as having these qualities, and so loving-kindness includes both these aspects, seeing the beauty in sentient beings and wishing that they have only happiness.

When we say "beautiful" here it's not that the nose is beautiful or the shape of the body is beautiful; we are referring to the inner beauty. When asked once what this love is like, Geshe Potowa explained to a mother, "That love, mother, should be like the love that you feel for your only beloved son." The child could be horribly deformed, but their mother would still see them as beautiful because she can see beyond the external deformity. Like a mother loves her child, we love all sentient beings, seeing them all in beauty, in an aspect most dear. They are the most precious things in our life, and we want to do everything possible to bring them happiness.

As you can see, this is not an easy term to translate into English.

Thinking of the pitiful state of all sentient beings, we think how wonderful it would be if all our kind mother sentient beings could have happiness and the cause of happiness. This is the realization—the wish for their happiness as intense as a loving mother for her only child— with the basis that they are all most precious, most dear to us. We want all sentient beings to attain enlightenment, and we determine we will do everything we can to ensure that this happens.

This love has nothing to do with the love we worldly people normally talk about, which involves how much happiness the other sentient being can give us. For us, feeling good ourselves is more important than others feeling good. We see a beggar deformed with leprosy, without a nose, with filthy rags, and we are repulsed. Somebody with loving-kindness, on the other hand, would be filled with compassion, love, and the deep wish that that beggar only has happiness and never has suffering. When we can appreciate how the beings of the lower realms and those of this realm who are suffering have all been our mother and have shown us such incredible kindness, we can generate this great loving-kindness for them.

If we can remember the benefits of practicing loving-kindness, our mind becomes very happy, and that in turn inspires us to practice it. In *Precious Garland*, Nagarjuna explained the eight benefits of practicing loving-kindness:

> Even three times a day to offer
> three hundred cooking pots of food
> does not match to a portion of the merit
> in one instant of love.

Though [through love] you are not liberated
you will attain the eight good qualities of love—
gods and humans will be friendly,
even [non-humans] will protect you,

you will have mental and many [physical] pleasures,
poison or weapons will not harm you,
without striving you will attain your aims,
and be reborn in the world of Brahma.[92]

Besides other people being our friend, we are befriended and protected
by the samsaric gods and by spirits. We are always happy, always protected from any harm by things such as dangerous diseases, poison,
or weapons. We will achieve whatever we want effortlessly. So even if
we fail to become liberated in this life, we receive these eight benefits
and then, after death, we attain another fortunate rebirth as a human
or god.

On the night the Buddha attained enlightenment under the bodhi
tree, at dusk millions of maras attacked him, taking on many terrible
forms in order to harm and distract him. However, the Buddha's body
remained utterly unmoving and his mind remained in loving-kindness.
Loving-kindness is our best weapon, our best protector, keeping us from
harm. When there is no internal enemy, there can be no external enemy.

Pacifying the suffering of others and bringing them happiness is our
universal responsibility, the meaning of being a human. Whatever we do
should be solely to fulfill this universal responsibility. We can remember the kindness of the people who employ us, allowing us to earn the
means to stay alive, and so we can work for their happiness rather than
our own. If we work in a factory we can think that the product we are
making will bring happiness and comfort to thousands of others; if we
teach we can feel we are giving our students the education they need
to fulfill their own potential and become happy themselves and bring
happiness to others; if we are a builder we can think that the house we
are building will be a place of security, comfort, and happiness for the

people and animals who will live in it. We should remember that we are serving others rather than using them for our own pleasure. We are not the master but the servant; others are our master. Our life is dedicated to pacifying their suffering and to obtaining their happiness.

Simply smiling at somebody brings that person happiness. In turn that person feels close to us, which then makes us feel happier. When I was living in California I had to exercise every day for my diabetes. I remember one day there was a young guy on a skateboard coming the other way along the street, so I just smiled at him and said hello. It was dusk, so I couldn't see his reaction, but I heard later that he asked our cook who I was and when she explained he said "good, good." He had obviously been affected by that smile.

Whatever we do, if we do it from the heart, with loving-kindness, it will have a very positive effect. We can smile, but if there is a political, self-serving motivation behind the smile, people will be aware of it and it won't make them happy. It all depends on our attitude. Regardless of what we do, if we do it from the heart with a sincere, loving motivation, it will bring great benefit to others. Whether we study Buddhadharma or not, whether we believe in any religion or not, having a sincere motivation, doing things with loving-kindness, is so important.

The next Buddha after Shakyamuni Buddha is Maitreya, from the Sanskrit for *loving-kindness*, and so Maitreya is the embodiment of all the buddhas' loving-kindness. That loving-kindness is the source of all the peace and happiness of all of us, of all sentient beings. It's the source of peace and happiness of every hell being, every hungry ghost, every animal, every human being, every demigod, every god, and every intermediate-state being. Loving-kindness is the essential element that brings all beings happiness, and this is the vital importance of Maitreya. Even if there were millions of religions in the world, without loving-kindness they would be incapable of giving peace and happiness to sentient beings. So Maitreya Buddha is connected with all religions, not just Buddhism, because the essence of any religion is loving-kindness.

This is why we are building a big Maitreya statue in Bodhgaya, the holiest place in the world. Bodhgaya is where Shakyamuni Buddha, the fourth of the thousand buddhas of this fortunate eon, attained enlightenment and where Maitreya Buddha and all the other thousand buddhas will attain enlightenment. Even though this is the holiest place for Buddhists, the statue is being built to benefit everybody, Buddhist or not. To see the statue will help generate the precious mind of loving-kindness in people and plant the seed of all the realizations of the path to enlightenment. Then slowly, through purifying the mind and collecting extensive merit, loving-kindness will be realized in everybody.

Whether other beings receive happiness or harm is completely in our hands. Each one of us is responsible for the happiness and suffering of all beings. Each one of us has this universal responsibility.

Even if our partner is very selfish and impatient, by practicing loving-kindness rather than causing harm, we will bring them peace and happiness. We develop a strong mind and a stable life and become an example, gradually helping our partner also develop loving-kindness. With loving-kindness we don't return anger with anger and we don't return criticism with criticism, so even if the other person doesn't practice loving-kindness, there is still peace and happiness in the relationship. With our family, with our friends, at work, in any situation where we interact with people, we have the responsibility to ensure that the situation is peaceful and happy—and that comes through our loving-kindness.

Starting with those close to us, we can gradually extend that loving-kindness to include all beings in our area, in our city, in our society, in the whole world. Because of his realization of loving-kindness, His Holiness the Dalai Lama is able to bring so much peace and happiness to millions and millions of people in this world, the majority of them not Buddhists. Similarly, Mahatma Gandhi-ji brought so much happiness—first to the people of India and then to the whole world—by setting an example for all of us.

5. Developing Compassion

Compassion, which is *karuna* in Sanskrit and *nyingjé* in Tibetan, is the wish that others will be free from suffering. It is the source of happiness in life, the essential means of ensuring our own happiness and the happiness of others. Without compassion there is no peace or happiness in the family, in society, in the country, or in the world. Generating compassion is also the source of a healthy mind and a healthy body, the most powerful way to heal ourselves and other living beings. And from a Mahayana perspective, compassion leads to great compassion, the mind that wishes to free *all* sentient beings from suffering, which is the prerequisite to the peerless mind called bodhichitta and to attaining the state of buddhahood.

Chandrakirti started his great treatise *A Guide to the Middle Way* with a praise to compassion. He said,

> The Shravakas and those half way to buddhahood are born
>   from the Mighty Sage,
> and the buddhas take birth born from the mighty heroes.
> Compassion, nonduality, and the wish for buddhahood
>   for other sake
> are the causes of the children of the Conqueror.
>
> Of buddhahood's abundant crop, compassion is the seed.
> It is like moisture bringing increase and is said
> to ripen in the state of lasting happiness.
> Therefore, to begin I celebrate compassion![93]

Here, Chandrakirti showed how compassion is vital wherever we are on the Mahayana path: whether we're at the beginning, middle, or end.

Without the seed we cannot enjoy the fruit, and so compassion, the seed that leads to the fruit of enlightenment, is vital at the beginning of the path. Without compassion we cannot attain bodhichitta, enter the Mahayana, engage in the bodhisattva's deeds, progress through the five paths, or attain the ten bhumis. Without compassion we cannot eliminate both the gross and the subtle defilements or complete the two merits. Our mind will always be distracted by self-interest, and so calm abiding and the realization of emptiness will be impossible.

Like water for a plant, in the middle of the path compassion sustains us, taking us all the way. It is vital as we progress through the paths of merit and preparation to the path of seeing, and even while we're on the path of meditation, the path of the higher bodhisattvas.

Finally, compassion is needed even after enlightenment. An arhat abides in perfect peace for eons but a buddha is not like that; a buddha does not abide in that state for even a second but ceaselessly works for all other living beings until they are all brought to enlightenment.

An Education in Compassion Is Our Contribution to World Peace

In Western culture, and especially in science, the important topics of karma and compassion seem to be rarely mentioned. Without an understanding of karma, how can we see that happiness and suffering are products of our own mind? Science uses rational analysis, and so the concept of cause and effect is there, but even in modern psychology karma, which is cause and effect related to the mind, is not mentioned.

Similarly, the mention of the need for compassion in modern psychology is extremely rare. It's as if psychologists are trying to find ways to help us to be happy but ignore the one infallible element, the thing most urgently needed: compassion.

When there is compassion, even if there are guns and bombs, there is no harm. Without compassion, even words without weapons can hurt others. His Holiness the Dalai Lama often says that human beings have so much more intelligence than animals, but we use it in the wrong way, to harm others. Even one person lacking compassion can cause terrible harm.

Everything that has been developed to protect us and make life happier can bring more complications and more suffering if compassion is missing. Even institutions created to make us safe and happy can become dangerous and cause great suffering. The army and the police, for instance, which are there to protect us, can become our oppressors when there is no compassion.

If the people in power lack compassion, they can use their power to threaten the world; if they have compassion, on the other hand, then the benefit they can be to the millions of people and the billions of animals of this world is infinite. Because of their compassion, all the beings of this world will be protected from being harmed and killed, and there will be peace. So such a person has great responsibility for world peace.

For instance, if Osama bin Laden had practiced a good heart, there is no way the attack on the World Trade Center would have happened. Those thousands of people wouldn't have died, and the airlines and companies wouldn't have lost all that money. The problems in Afghanistan and with terrorists and everything that followed—all that stemmed from one man's anger. Bin Laden himself was just a thin man with a beard; he wasn't gigantic like a mountain, but his anger brought unbelievable harm.

Compassion should be a vital subject in schools to teach children how to generate a good heart and benefit others. Just as many countries support each other in practicing war, everybody should come together so that this special education emphasizing the good heart can be brought into the schools in their own country. And at home, parents should also teach this to their children and practice it themselves, becoming examples to their children.

Each child will then grow up with a good heart, patience, and universal responsibility, feeling they are responsible for freeing others from suffering and bringing them happiness. When they grow up in this way, that child will bring so much peace to their parents and to the rest of their family. When that child then becomes a parent, they will be able to educate their own children by being an inspiring example.

I heard from some teachers in London that, while meditation worked for them, when they tried to teach it, some of their students became confused because of the clash between the basic philosophies of Buddhism and the modern world. It seems many people feel compassion and self-interest are contradictory. We need to analyze what brings us long-term happiness, in this life and in all the coming future lives. The causes of happiness and suffering come from within our own mind; the external circumstances are just conditions, not the actual causes as we now think of them. That is the reality.

There is a real need for education in compassion in this world. The more people are educated in compassion, the more peace there will be in the world. World peace is impossible without compassion. Refusing to fight out of fear of weapons and violence is not real peace. Having stockpiles of atomic bombs but not using them doesn't mean we have peace. His Holiness says that real peace can only come from within, not by force, not by us trying to control the enemy, but by compassion, by the good heart.

The world's problems involve two factors. The first is the result: people are experiencing the result of the negative actions they created in the past. The second is the cause: they are still creating negative actions and so still creating the cause of future problems. All problems, from wars and killings to economic and environmental disasters, come from negative karma. Because studying compassion shows how to prevent the cause and not experience problems, it is important to teach people about compassion, to plant the imprints so they will slowly move away from the selfish, grasping mind that harms themselves and others.

Our contribution to world peace is to develop compassion within our own heart and to teach compassion to others, by showing them how happiness and peace come from within. We need to see our own suffering fully and through that see the suffering of others, not just compassion for the poor and homeless or the cute, exploited animals, but also the predators and the human exploiters. We need compassion for all beings.

It won't stop war immediately, but when we educate one person in compassion and that person practices a good heart, they can pass that vital education on to another person, and that person to others and so it spreads, to twenty, to a hundred, and to thousands, and then the message of compassion will spread to millions and millions. *This* is the way we can stop the world's problems.

But just reading about compassion isn't the real education; people must want to develop compassion. We all need to know *how* to develop compassion. Compassion doesn't just fall from the sky like rain, unfortunately. We must actively develop it. Even rain has causes and conditions, so we need to develop the right conditions for our compassion to grow. This is where the whole graduated path to enlightenment is vital to show the way we must go if we are to overcome our self-cherishing and be of real benefit to others.

This is why practicing the Dharma is vital. Doing retreats, doing practices, taking the eight Mahayana precepts[94] are all vital to help us develop compassion. This is the *real* solution, the *real* way to bring about world peace. When we live in the Dharma, especially keeping the various levels of vows we can take, we give no harm at all to other beings, and we are doing all we can to help them. By actualizing the various lamrim realizations, we are working toward the ultimate way to end the suffering of all beings. And that includes all the terrorists. Actually, our self-cherishing mind is the only real terrorist, the only one we need to ruthlessly destroy. We have the ultimate terrorist in our mind, and by following that terrorist we blow up our liberation, we blow up our enlightenment.

Whether we consider it a religious action or not, we need to turn every action into the Dharma by doing it selflessly, doing it only for others. This is what I call a "healthy mind." Otherwise, the mind thinking only of its own benefit and so harming ourselves and others is not at all healthy; when it's ruled by attachment, anger, jealousy, and the other negative emotions, it's really a sick mind.

When we're only concerned for others, the immediate effect is that we feel very happy and satisfied, that our life is very worthwhile; the long-term effect, the consequence of our altruistic actions, is great happiness in the future. Even if it is not our intention, the result is a long life, a healthy body, wealth, contentment, receiving help whenever we need it, being respected by others—all the things that a worldly mind craves. Even if we don't want such things at all, they just happen, as a consequence of our compassion.

Because compassion is the key to bodhichitta, an education in compassion is the root to the end of all suffering and to full enlightenment. This is not an intellectual education but an education that transforms the mind, taking us from selfish concerns to being concerned only for others, and this is the most important thing in the world. This is the antidote to every problem, every suffering experience; to disease, poverty, oppression, war.

Practicing compassion means more than not harming others; it means only ever helping them, which, in turn, becomes the cause of our own success. When we see everybody as our friend, we feel close to everybody, even if they are physically distant from us. Without compassion there is no closeness; people feel distant even if they are in the same room. Seeing others as competitors and enemies, we lose what friends we have; even members of our own family can become enemies. There is no real peace or satisfaction in our life. Our heart is like a barren desert. Lack of compassion brings loneliness, depression, and many other problems. When asked about depression in an interview, His Holiness the Dalai Lama replied that depression basically comes from not having affection for others.

Our compassion is the source of peace and happiness for all other living beings, starting with the people and animals closest to us. Conversely, all other beings are the source of our happiness. On a simple level we can see how we are affected by those around us: happy when somebody smiles at us, even a stranger, and upset when somebody frowns at us or treats us unkindly. Even seeing somebody walking along a street immersed in misery and problems depresses us. In the same way, our behavior affects those around us. When we are relaxed and caring, others are relaxed and happy, even animals. Even mice! At first wary and scared, they soon come to trust us when they sense our kindness.

I have a lot of karma with mice. Even if there were previously no mice in a place, they usually appear soon after I arrive. Once when I was doing a retreat in Adelaide, Australia, several mice would appear every night, climbing up next to me on the bed and ducking behind one of the pillows, where I think they had made a nest in the warmth. One night one of the mice climbed up onto the table in front of me. Of course, this didn't happen because I am kind or goodhearted but because at that time I had no intention of disturbing the mouse. Seeing

I was no threat, its face remained very soft and happy-looking. After some time it went away.

Our education, no matter how vast, will only cause us problems if we are motivated solely by self-concern. Instead of bringing us happiness and satisfaction, it will cause pride, anger, and other unhealthy minds to arise. We will not enjoy life or see any meaning in it. In the same way that atomic power can be used for good or harm, what we get from our education depends on how we use it. The real reason for an education is to serve others.

The first step in practicing compassion is to stop harming other living beings, starting with the people and animals around us, which means that others receive peace from us. With a compassionate mind, we radiate loving-kindness, and our external appearance is very peaceful. When we look on others with love, they find so much peace just being near us.

That does not necessarily mean we only ever do what others want. As I have said many times, whether an action is virtuous or not depends on the motivation. We need to check our motivation and ensure we do only what is the greatest benefit. There are times when we might see that doing what the other person wants will harm them, and we need to do the opposite. Other times, being gentle with somebody might fail to stop them from hurting themselves, and so we need to show a wrathful attitude. Even though it may appear on the surface as anger, our motivation is pure compassion, the wish to benefit.

The more compassion we have, the more we will dedicate our life to helping others. All other living beings will then receive peace and happiness from us, either directly or indirectly. This is how each of us is responsible for the peace and happiness of each and every living being. Therefore, everything we do should be to develop compassion. We chant *om mani padme hum* to develop compassion; we build temples to develop compassion. We collect merit and purify obscurations to develop compassion. We take initiations and practice a sadhana, we make offerings to holy objects, we listen to teachings—all to develop compassion. We develop compassion so the numberless sentient beings we harmed in the past will no longer receive any harm from us at all.

The Healing Power of Compassion

Compassion has the power to heal. Merely seeing the face of a compassionate person helps heal us because it brings us peace and happiness, relieving us of whatever worry or problem we have. We are delighted when they come into a room and happy to even hear their name.

My mother was a very compassionate person. Everybody liked and respected her, not because she was my mother but because she was always concerned about others. Whenever I saw her she talked about the problems of other people. I can hardly remember her ever bringing up her own problems. When she was blinded by cataracts she did once ask me to recite mantras and blow on her eyes, but normally she would never discuss her own needs.

My mother would never let anyone leave her house empty-handed. She gave to people all day long. When we were driving she was upset by the people she saw walking along the road barefoot, concerned they were too poor for shoes. She was once invited to Tushita Meditation Centre in Dharamsala where the cooks always made pancakes for breakfast. Every day, after eating a little of her pancake, she would fold up the rest and put it in her pocket and then walk down from Tushita, which is high up on a mountain, to circumambulate His Holiness's residence, where she would share her pancake among the many lepers who begged on the circumambulation path.

Because my mother was so compassionate, everyone was happy to meet her and talk to her. Whenever we see someone who seems generous and warm-hearted, even if we don't know them, we feel like sitting down and talking to them. This is our natural response to compassionate people, to those who always put others before themselves.

If our doctor is gentle and compassionate, we naturally relax in their presence and have confidence that they will do their best to help us. Simply by talking to us and examining us, they make us happy and that lessens our pain. Even if the medicine they prescribe is not the best quality, it will still benefit us. Everybody in the healing profession needs compassion above all things. And the best healer is somebody with the realization of bodhichitta. A sick person can recover just from the breath of a bodhisattva.

External medicine is needed to cure a physical sickness, but we need the inner medicine of compassion to heal the actual cause of the disease—our negative mind—and ensure we never have to experience that illness again. Developing our mind in compassion is the way to cure ourselves of all diseases.

At present we are limited in everything we do; our power, knowledge, and compassion are all limited. When we develop these to their utmost, when we become an enlightened being, we achieve ultimate freedom and have the ultimate means to benefit all beings. When the sun rises, its light is naturally reflected in everything, in every body of water, every lake, every stream, every ocean, every dewdrop. Likewise, since all the gross and subtle obscurations are eliminated, the omniscient mind naturally pervades everywhere. Whenever somebody's positive imprint ripens, the omniscient mind of a buddha can immediately manifest in whatever form suits the level of mind of that person. If they have a pure mind it manifests in a pure form to guide them; if they have an impure mind it manifests in an impure form. In that way the omniscient mind, seeing all existence at all times, can manifest at once to help guide beings from happiness to happiness, to the peerless happiness of full enlightenment. This is the meaning of perfect power.

With perfect power we need to generate perfect compassion for all living beings so we can develop all other positive qualities. This transformation of the mind is ultimate healing. The healing comes through our positive thinking, through our own wisdom and compassion.

Compassion Brings Real Success

If we are looking for meaning in our life, we have no choice but to practice compassion. Not only does it bring peace, but it also brings whatever success we want as a byproduct.

Having a compassionate mind is the cause of wealth. With compassion, because we naturally want to help others and are therefore natu-rally generous, that generous mind is the cause of wealth in the future. With self-concern we only ever do something for our own welfare. We either never give, and our stinginess is the cause of future poverty, or we give but with a selfish motivation—to improve our business or get on the right side of somebody—and so there can only be a negative result.

The protector of morality and wealth in Tibetan Buddhism is Namtösé,[95] and with this protector our practice is generosity. Unless we create the merit by giving to others, there is no way the protector can do anything for us—and therefore it is impossible to benefit from obtaining wealth.

In the same way, having a compassionate mind is the cause of a long life. By giving up harming others we are causing them to have a long life, and that, in turn, becomes the cause for our own long life. And, as we have seen, compassion is the cause of peace, because we relinquish harming others and so stop being harmed by them in turn.

Having a compassionate mind is also the cause of success. The selfish mind can only ever lead to failure; it cannot become the source of any kind of happiness. Any success a selfish person is experiencing now is only the result of positive karma collected in the past. The person is living off of that, but it is constantly dwindling, just as money saved in a bank constantly diminishes if it is squandered without any being put back. That type of life is very sad.

On the other hand, even though a goodhearted person might fail in a business venture, that is just one failure; they haven't lost the merit they created benefiting others. Even if their business completely col-lapses, they still have all that merit in their merit bank, in their mental continuum, which is the cause of success in this life and in future lives, of having a good rebirth for thousands and billions of lifetimes.

I remember that many years back Lama Yeshe advised a student to take care of his family, to look after their financial interests and do whatever was necessary to help them. He followed Lama's advice with devotion, working for his family's happiness by investing in their busi-ness. However, sometime later the business collapsed and the family lost millions of dollars. He became an object of criticism for the whole family. Externally it was a disaster, but what happened in his heart was very different. Working through the whole situation, his devotion to Lama Yeshe increased and his renunciation of samsara increased. His inner life, his lamrim realizations, developed in his heart because of this.

This is how we should judge success, not in material gain but in spiritual gain, in the change that happens in our heart. Progress toward liberation and enlightenment is the best success, the only real success in life. We might be a complete failure in the view of the worldly people who judge success by money or possessions—the view of ignorance—but from a Dharma point of view, the view of wisdom, we have real success.

Seeing the Suffering of Others

If we fell into the ocean with our mother, we would do whatever we could to free ourselves in order to get her out. Until we are free ourselves, we can do very little; we are drowning so we can't help her. She has to wait, tossed by the strong waves of delusion and karma, chased by the sharks of the three types of suffering, always in great danger. She won't be out of danger until we are free ourselves, until we are enlightened and can truly help her.

Thinking of the state of all our kind mother sentient beings, we are inspired to do everything we can to become enlightened in order to help them. Without even thinking of the more subtle sufferings that keep all beings trapped in samsara—the suffering of change or pervasive compounding suffering—when we consider just the suffering of suffering that the vast majority of beings must endure, we see how terrible samsara is. Even if we don't have a strong sense of past and future lives, just considering the suffering there is in this world today will show us how we must free ourselves from our own delusions so we can help others.

We can see pain all around us. Even when a baby is first born, we can easily see they must endure the great pain of being born and coming into the bright, noisy world. Just looking at the baby's face shows their suffering. The baby suffered their pain and the mother suffered hers, each experiencing the results of their own separate karma.

Similarly, when we think about the people trapped in the homes for the elderly, we can see how much suffering they must endure every day. We can see it in the eyes of the old men and women, sitting around lifelessly in chairs all day and all night, waiting to die but unable to. Their expressions are blank, like nothing is happening in their minds. They have no Dharma understanding, no way of making even this terrible time meaningful. They have no way of purifying negativities or accumulating merit. Unlike the poorest, most miserable beggar in Tibet, they can't even recite *om mani padme hum* or take refuge in the Buddha, Dharma, and Sangha. Not having met the Dharma, their mind is empty; they are just waiting for death.

In between birth and old age, we are still plagued by the suffering of suffering, getting what we don't want, not getting what we want, all the time having to be separated from desirable objects and having to meet undesirable objects, all the time overwhelmed by dissatisfaction. We can think of all the people suffering from sicknesses, especially all the people in hospitals. How pitiful they are. Each has a different disease, each has a different experience, but all are suffering. Even if they are not suffering from some terrible disease, just having to be in the hospital is suffering: unable to do what they want, having to eat tasteless food without choice, being surrounded by such suffering. For many, of course, the experience is truly awful; they get fed through tubes, have painful treatments, and know they won't get any better. We can generate compassion for all these people by just remembering how unbearable it feels when we have a stomachache or a headache. We'd do anything to get rid of it, even though it is nothing compared to what the people in hospitals have to suffer.

We don't have to go to hospitals to see suffering. Just observing the activities of the people in the city streets should be enough to convince us of the suffering of samsara and develop compassion. Everybody is running around, desperately looking for something, so busy, so confused, all chasing the eight worldly dharmas, all seeking happiness in objects that can only bring suffering. If just examining one person's suffering shows us how unbearable it is, how much more when we examine the suffering of all the people in the city, in the country, in the whole world, and then if we expand that to include the animals and the beings of the other realms. When we consider it deeply, we will certainly determine we *must* do whatever we can to release them all from this suffering.

When we see a mosquito we currently see a threat, something that is out to harm us, but we need to see beyond our own selfish concern. It is such a pitiful, tiny thing: so fragile, with a tiny body and long, thin legs, not great and strong like ours. And yet it has involuntarily taken a body that scares others, making others want to kill it just by seeing it. Just thinking like this, our mind has no choice; compassion must arise.

We can do the same thing with any being. There is no way we want to have the body of a slug for a second—simply looking at it is disgusting—and yet the slug has no choice. When we consider its pitiful life—so powerless, so fearful, reliant on the rain to stop from drying out and dying—then compassion must arise. We can take any animal and see how its life is suffering: a cow, a sheep, a snake, an elephant. Each is trapped in a suffering body, unable to do anything about it.

Compassion is like the fuel for a jet plane. A jet has the potential to take us wherever we want to go incredibly quickly, but it's useless without fuel. Without compassion there can never be great compassion, and so there can never bodhichitta, and so, of course, there can never be enlightenment. Compassion and bodhichitta are what propelled the Buddha's search for enlightenment, leading him through the stages of the path and especially the realization of emptiness that allowed him to attain buddhahood. Then, with his perfect compassion, he taught the Buddhadharma for over forty years. This is what all buddhas do; they come into our world system, engage in the twelve deeds from birth up to enlightenment, and reveal the teachings. What inspires all the buddhas is compassion.

The entire Buddhadharma comes from the compassion of the Buddha. All the hundreds of scriptures of the Buddha come from his compassion. All religions emphasize compassion but the compassion that

Buddhism teaches us is compassion utterly without discrimination, wanting to benefit not just some sentient beings but all sentient beings. This is why I talk so much about compassion.

Great Compassion

Great compassion, which is *mahakaruna* in Sanskrit and *nyingjé chenpo* in Tibetan, is even more than immeasurable compassion, which wishes all beings to be free from suffering. The label "great" is added when the thought also includes the wish that we ourselves should work to free all beings from suffering and its causes. If we exclude even one sentient being from our compassion, or if we lack the wish to free all beings ourselves, it means we have still not realized great compassion. Bodhichitta depends on having great compassion for all sentient beings.

In the lamrim texts great compassion comes after loving-kindness, but that is not necessarily the sequence. Whichever comes first, when we meditate on the kindness of all sentient beings, we generate the wish that they all have happiness and be free from suffering, and so loving-kindness and compassion both arise.

One of the most popular Jataka Tales is how, when he was a bodhisattva, the Buddha sacrificed his body for a starving tigress and her cubs. At that time Shakyamuni Buddha and Maitreya Buddha were brother bodhisattvas. One day, they came across the tigress and her four cubs in the jungle, starving to death. The tigress could only lie there, too weak to try to find any food for her cubs, and it was obvious that they would all soon die. Immense compassion arose in the minds of the two brothers. The one that would become Maitreya prayed hard that they would find a favorable rebirth and left, very upset with the plight of the animals. Shakyamuni, however, could not stand to think that there was nothing he could do, and so he went to the tigress and cut his flesh so she could drink his blood and regain her strength. Then he offered his whole body; she and her cubs were able to feed from him and so were saved from starvation. As the tigers were chewing his bones, eating his flesh, and drinking his blood, he prayed that not only would they manage to live from this sacrifice but also that in a future life they would become his disciples and he would be able to lead them to enlightenment. Because of his great compassion and the strong connection made with the tigers, this came true.

At this great act, the earth shook six times and the gods showered a rain of flowers from the sky. Although Maitreya actualized bodhichitta before Shakyamuni, Shakyamuni attained enlightenment first because of the strength of his great compassion.

Another famous story is of Asanga and the wounded dog. Asanga meditated for twelve years in order to see Maitreya but was unsuccessful until one day he saw a wounded dog, infested with maggots, and with great compassion tried to help it. He was going to remove the maggots when he realized by helping the dog he would hurt the maggots. He therefore cut a small piece of flesh from his leg and put it on the ground for the maggots, but then he realized that moving them with his fingers would hurt them and possibly kill them, so he did it with his tongue.

He did all this with such strong compassion that it became a huge act of purification, and the dog appeared to him in the form of Maitreya. It wasn't a dog at all, actually, but because his mind wasn't purified that was how he'd seen it.

A verse in the *Guru Puja* says,

> Having considered how all these miserable beings have
>   been my mothers,
> And have raised me in kindness again and again,
> I seek your blessings to develop effortless compassion,
> Like that of a loving mother for her precious child.[96]

A mother takes care of her one precious child like her own heart. Were they to fall into a pit of fire she would feel such incredibly strong compassion that she would do anything to save her child, including sacrifice her own life.

No matter how disrespectful, rude, or disobedient the child is, the mother's love will never diminish in the slightest. Even if from the child's side there is no loving-kindness, even if the child never helps at all but instead only goes out of their way to make life difficult, she will still feel great love and compassion. Her only concern is her child's happiness, and she will do whatever she can to ensure that. This is how we feel toward all living beings.

Whereas others will keep away from somebody with a terrible disease such as leprosy or who is deranged, deformed, or vicious, when we have great compassion, their suffering only generates more compassion in us. For worldly people, such a person can harm their self-cherishing, but with great compassion we see that person as so precious. These people who are shunned by society are objects of compassion for us.

In that way we equally cherish all sentient beings who are continuously migrating throughout the six realms, constantly under the control of karma and delusion, utterly without freedom. Seeing their plight, we feel great compassion for them all without any discrimination. Furthermore, we see them all as our friend helping us to enlightenment, as so kind, so precious.

6. Attaining the Special Attitude

After attaining the realizations of loving-kindness and great compassion, the sixth stage of the seven points of cause and effect is attaining the special attitude. This occurs when we actually take the responsibility for the happiness of all sentient beings by ourselves alone.

This is like in our daily life when we see a hard job needs to be done, and we go from thinking that somebody should do it to the decision that we ourselves must do it. Perhaps we see an old lady struggling with her bag in a railway station. The first thought might be that somebody should certainly help her by carrying the bag, but then we think that we ourselves should do it, and with that comes the determination to do it. We take the responsibility. Rather than letting the other person suffer, we take it on ourselves.

This is what we need to do. Otherwise it's like we are up in a tree watching while our old mother, who has been so kind to us from the time we were conceived, is on the ground being attacked by a tiger. Safe from attack, we look down on her plight, maybe laughing or singing a song. How cruel! How selfish! How thoughtless!

In the same way, because we're so fortunate in having met the Dharma and the perfect spiritual guide, we can see a way out of samsara. We have eyes—the eye of wisdom—whereas our kind mother sentient beings are blind and have no opportunity to help themselves. How can we refuse to turn back to help them out of the great suffering they are forced to endure? When we have this incredible chance to help not just ourselves but all sentient beings, to do anything less would be so shameful and ungenerous.

We must free all sentient beings from all the suffering they are experiencing and place them in the peerless happiness of enlightenment. With loving-kindness and great compassion, we determine we will do this; with the special attitude we take this one step further by determining we will do this *by ourselves alone*. That extra phrase "by myself alone" is so important. We should always remember that.

This is not just watching from the safety of the tree while our mother is attacked by a tiger and thinking *how terrible* but doing nothing. This is jumping down without thinking for an instant about our own safety and taking on that tiger in order to save her. With the special attitude, this is how we feel about all sentient beings every second. Like a mother is constantly aware of her child no matter what she is doing, constantly watching out for sharp objects, holes in the road, poisonous snakes—we constantly have the welfare of all sentient beings on our mind no matter what we are doing.

Pabongka Dechen Nyingpo explained that the difference between the wish to repay the kindness and the special attitude is like the difference between having the intention to buy something from a shop and developing the complete determination that whatever it costs we will buy it: "I'll pay for it and I'll take it!" This is the strength of the determination we have to free all beings ourselves.

We cannot physically take their suffering from them. As the Buddha explained in a sutra,

The Great Ones do not wash away sin with water;
  they do not rid beings of suffering with their hands;
  they do not transfer realizations of suchness onto others.
  They liberate by teaching the truth of suchness.[97]

To cleanse true suffering and the true cause of suffering by water is impossible. Even the Great Ones, the buddhas, cannot do that, nor can they physically remove our suffering, like pulling out a thorn stuck in our hand. Neither can they relieve our suffering by wiping all the negativities from our minds. If they could they would have done that eons ago, and samsara would be empty. We are the ones who must do that ourselves—but what they can do is perfectly show us the way to do this.

The buddhas have perfect power to direct all beings to enlightenment. Each beam emitted from their holy bodies can free infinite beings from suffering and lead them to happiness. Able to see the thoughts of every sentient being within all the three times, they work for them tirelessly, revealing whatever method is best suited to each sentient being.

But the perfect power that the buddhas have would be ineffectual without their great compassion. Perfect power and perfect compassion are what we are developing as we work toward a realization of bodhichitta.

With our special attitude we see that we must lead all beings from suffering and that the only way to do that is to perfectly show them the path. We cannot do this until we understand the infinitely various propensities of all the sentient beings—their different attitudes, thoughts, desires, levels of intelligence, personalities, and so forth—and know which methods will best suit them to allow them to develop the fastest. Because the only being who fully understands the minds of all sentient beings is a buddha, we ourselves must become enlightened.

We therefore determine to attain buddhahood in order to fulfill our wish for all beings. With that, we attain the effortless, spontaneous attitude that only ever works toward the happiness of all sentient beings and that is the mind called bodhichitta. At that moment we are a bodhisattva.

Whenever we listen to somebody explaining the Dharma, that goal should always be there. From the side of the teacher, they should explain the Dharma in order to lead the students to the peerless happiness of enlightenment; and from our side, the student's side, we should keep that great goal in our heart while we are listening. Then a Dharma talk becomes perfect; it becomes highly effective for the mind.

Our position is quite unique. We have a perfect human rebirth, we have met the perfect teacher, and we have all the qualities that will take us all the way to enlightenment if we put the effort into developing them. Therefore, we have this responsibility to others. It's up to us to develop our compassion and love until it becomes the special attitude that takes full and sole responsibility for the happiness of all sentient beings.

7. Bodhichitta

The final step of the seven points of cause and effect is bodhichitta itself, the effect. Having passed through the other stages, we attain this incredible state of mind. As we have seen, bodhichitta is a main mind, not a secondary mental factor, which means our whole being spontaneously and effortlessly wishes to attain enlightenment in order to free all beings.

Bodhichitta is the thought to benefit every single sentient being, without exception, without excluding one single hell being, one single hungry ghost, one single animal, one single human being, one single demigod, one single god, one single intermediate-state being. It's the thought to benefit every being on the ground, in the ground, in the seas, in the air—every ant on every mountain, every fish in every ocean, every bird and insect in every field, every single sentient being in all the six realms.

Whenever we say the refuge and bodhichitta prayer, we are vowing to generate bodhichitta, for instance, for all the countless shellfish on all the beaches of the world. Even on one beach the number of shellfish is uncountable and the wish to help even one shellfish is incredible, but we are vowing to help all shellfish on all beaches in all the oceans—and not just to give them some temporary help but to lead them to generate bodhichitta themselves and so attain enlightenment. Similarly, by saying the refuge and bodhichitta prayer we are vowing to free all ants from suffering and lead them to peerless happiness. Even in one garden alone there are an incredible number of ants, so multiply that by all the gardens in a community, in a city, in a country, and in all the countries of the world, all the ants on the ground, under the ground, in suburban gardens, in fields in the countryside, on mountains in the Himalayas, in the jungles and deserts—an uncountable number of ants—and we are vowing to free them all from all suffering and bring them every happiness up to enlightenment.

These are just two species among billions. Here, we think of all the beings in all the six realms and generate the thought to bring not just temporary benefit to a few of them, not just temporary benefit to all of them, but the ultimate benefit of enlightenment to each and every sentient being. This is such an unbelievable, incredible thought.

When we have attained bodhichitta, every action of body, speech, and mind is pervaded with this wish to benefit all sentient beings. This is why I say bodhichitta is the most incredible mind. That we have been able to meet the Mahayana teachings and hear about bodhichitta—and hopefully be working toward attaining this incredible mind—is amazing, astounding. It's hard to believe we have been this fortunate; it's like a dream.

Bodhichitta is not the final goal, but it is the vital step we must take if we want to attain enlightenment. When we consider who alone has the perfect power to lead all beings from suffering into happiness, we see it is only the buddhas, and therefore, with this heartfelt wish to benefit all beings, we determine we must attain enlightenment and become a buddha ourselves.

We Can Definitely Attain Bodhichitta

There is a story of Drupkhang Gelek Gyatso, one of the lamrim lineage lamas. Je Drupkhang had a guru called Atsara who was giving him teachings on bodhichitta. Although this was in Tibet—Je Drupkhang had a cave above Sera Monastery—it seems that this guru was not a monk but an Indian sadhu with long hair rolled up on top of his head. He lived in the forest and was quite ascetic, not fat, shiny-looking, or well dressed like we are.

One day, Je Drupkhang saw his guru next to his hermitage. He was crying, and without realizing his disciple was looking at him, he made a thumbs-up gesture. In Tibetan this means "very good," as it does in the West, but it is also a way of pleading for help, and as such it is a gesture that beggars make. Later Je Drupkhang asked his guru what he was doing, and he explained that he was reading Guru Shakyamuni Buddha's life story. In one of his lives the Buddha gave all of his eyes and limbs to sentient beings and how the people, seeing he was nothing more than a limbless trunk and therefore utterly useless, took the holy body outside the city and dumped it. But even there he was able to be of great benefit to the ants, flies, and other creatures that ate his body. Seeing this, the gods came down from the sky and made offerings to the bodhisattva's holy body.

Atsara said, "Guru Shakyamuni Buddha is his mother's son. I am also my mother's son, but look at the difference! We are the same in that respect but what incredible sacrifice and dedication he made for sentient beings, and look at me! Look at me! What do I do? What do I do for sentient beings? Look at the difference!" He cried to Guru Shakyamuni Buddha, "Sentient beings are born from mothers, and you are a worthy son serving them like that, but I haven't done anything for them." Saying that, he cried so much, knowing that he was unable to do as Guru Shakyamuni Buddha had done.

One of the last times they parted, as Je Drupkhang was leaving, Atsara again emphasized, "Don't forget the bodhichitta practice. Unless you practice bodhichitta, other paths won't come to anything." To that Je Drupkhang replied, "Bodhichitta is a causative phenomenon. I am also a causative phenomenon," meaning it is possible to change the mind. For example, with dough mixed from flour and water we can make noodles, chapatis, cakes, and so forth. Because it's a causative phenomenon, a dependent arising, we can change the dough into many different types of food. In a similar way, by creating the cause we are able to generate the result of bodhichitta within our heart, just as Guru Shakyamuni Buddha did as a bodhisattva. For three countless great eons he accumulated extensive merit, then achieved enlightenment and revealed the path in order to liberate sentient beings from all obscurations and lead them to enlightenment.

This is exactly what we should do. The purpose of our life is to benefit every sentient being. We should think, "Even if at present I cannot sacrifice myself for every sentient being as Guru Shakyamuni Buddha did, how wonderful it is that at least I am able to use my body, speech, and mind to benefit my family and make them happy. How fortunate I am! While I cannot actually offer my body as charity to other sentient beings, at least I am serving this small number of sentient beings and bringing them happiness." Like this, we should rejoice from our heart. Whether working in a family, at a Dharma center, in a hospital, or in the community, we should offer service to others with a sincere attitude and good heart, remembering their kindness. In this way our mind will be very happy all the time. Because all our activities will be done with loving-kindness and the thought of cherishing others, depression will never arise.

Just as Je Drupkhang saw how Guru Shakyamuni Buddha accumulated merit for three countless great eons by generating compassion in his past lives, practicing the first perfection of generosity, giving his holy body thousands of times, we too can understand that enlightenment is definitely possible if we first generate bodhichitta. And generating bodhichitta is definitely possible because it is a dependent arising; it arises in dependence on causes and conditions. Doing a negative action creates negative imprints that will ripen at some stage in the future in dependence on causes and conditions. On the other hand, doing a compassionate action creates the causes for future happiness, and so compassion is also a dependent arising. If things were not dependent arisings it would be impossible to develop bodhichitta we do not already have. However, things *are* dependent arisings, and so developing bodhichitta is definitely possible.

The more we familiarize ourselves with an attitude, the easier it is to develop; it's possible to completely train the mind in compassion and bodhichitta. Everything like this is a habit: when we follow the self-cherishing mind, we habituate ourselves to more and more negative attitudes and more and more problems; when we follow the altruistic attitude, we habituate ourselves to more and more positive attitudes and more and more peace, more and more happiness. It all depends on which direction we move our mind. The more we train ourselves in these amazing minds, the less effort we need to exert.

Because love, compassion, and bodhichitta are natural states of mind, there is no need to resort to reasoning to develop them. The only problem at all with bodhichitta is that we have not put the effort into trying to develop it. Once we start, it will become easier and easier, and then, at some stage, it will be completely effortless. We can see this is so when we understand the nature of the mind, that it arises in dependence on causes and conditions. It all depends on which causes we create.

6 : EQUALIZING AND EXCHANGING SELF AND OTHERS

··

BESIDES THE seven points of cause and effect technique, the other traditional way of developing bodhichitta is the technique of equalizing and exchanging self and others. The points of this technique are this:

- equalizing self and others
  - seeing the disadvantages of the self-cherishing mind
  - seeing the advantages of the mind cherishing others
- exchanging self and others
- taking and giving

Probably our life at present is predominantly one of self-interest, whether we live in a busy city or in the tranquil countryside, whether we live in a house or a Dharma center. When we examine it carefully it becomes incredibly clear that *all* problems arise from this self-cherishing. Because we have always cherished ourselves more than others, all our efforts at attaining happiness have been fruitless. Even chasing worldly pleasures has been of no avail, let alone practicing the Dharma.

Without consciously trying to transform our mind from self-cherishing to cherishing others, no amount of lamrim teachings can benefit us. Our mind remains like a stone that has sat at the bottom of the ocean for hundreds of years—the surface is a little bit wet, but the inside stays completely dry. We need to see how cruel our self-cherishing really is, how it denies us any chance at any happiness at all.

When we see a being like His Holiness the Dalai Lama, we can feel how his holy body is completely filled with compassion, completely of the nature of bodhichitta. Ours, on the other hand, is completely filled with selfish concern, where nothing matters but the interests of this I that rules us. The contrast between His Holiness's incredibly peaceful, happy presence and ours is stark. We have no space to think about the happiness of others, no way to think their happiness is as important as ours, let alone more important, which is the core of the thought-transformation practices.

In *A Guide to the Bodhisattva's Way of Life*, Shantideva said,

> If I do not actually exchange my happiness
> for the suffering of others,
> I shall not attain the state of buddhahood
> and even in cyclic existence have no joy.[98]

Unless we can replace the selfish attitude with one of genuine selfless-ness, even the happiness of this life will be beyond us, let alone the peerless happiness of enlightenment. This bodhichitta practice is not just for those who seek liberation or enlightenment; it's not just for those who accept reincarnation and understand karma. Even worldly people with no higher aim than seeking their own happiness in this life must practice a good heart, replacing self-interest with altruism, or they will be frustrated in their desire.

This is why we need to transform our attitude from self-cherishing to cherishing others, and the first step in that transformation is equal-izing ourselves with others: seeing that all beings, including ourselves, are completely equal in wanting happiness and not wanting suffering.

The Six Relative Reasons That Self and Others Are Equal

The first aspect of the technique of equalizing and exchanging self and others is the equalizing, which means seeing ourselves and others as completely equal in only wanting happiness and never wanting even the slightest suffering.

There are various reasons stated in the texts that clearly show us why this is so. These are often listed as the six relative reasons—three from our own side and three from the side of others—and the three reasons based on ultimate truth.[99]

The six relative reasons:

1. We depend on sentient beings for all happiness.
2. We depend on sentient beings to attain liberation and enlightenment.
3. Sentient beings are equal to the buddhas in the help they give us.
4. We are all equal in wanting to obtain happiness and avoid suffering.
5. We are all equal in needing help.
6. We are all equal in being tormented by delusions.

The three ultimate reasons:

1. "Friend," "enemy," and "stranger" are merely concepts conceived by our deluded mind.
2. "Friend," "enemy," and "stranger" appear permanent, but they are not.
3. I and others are interdependent, like "here" and "there."

1. We Depend on Sentient Beings for All Happiness

The first three of the six relative reasons, the ones that are relative to our own experience, show us how we depend on all other beings for all happiness, liberation, and enlightenment, and how in this way other beings are equal to the buddhas in the help they give us.

The first reason is that we depend on sentient beings for all happiness, for both our comfort and our worldly happiness. We can easily see this when we examine the relationships we have with people such as our friends, our family, and our colleagues at work. Just as we depend on them for our happiness, we similarly depend on all sentient beings.

In fact, this dependence is mutual because all sentient beings are reliant on us for their happiness. What we want from other sentient beings are things such as kindness, compassion, and practical help to solve our problems; what we don't want is the slightest harm from them. This is exactly what others want from us. If we treat others badly, they dislike us; if we treat them with loving-kindness, they like us. This is true of even strangers in the street. Every day we are responsible for the happiness of other sentient beings, and we are dependent on them for our happiness.

We depend on sentient beings for our comfort. There is no material thing we have ever received or pleasant situation we have ever experienced that has not depended on other sentient beings having to undergo some suffering.

Our home was built on the suffering of many sentient beings. Just laying the foundation meant many creatures were killed or were hurt or had their homes destroyed as the concrete was laid and the work was done. Without their suffering there is no way we could enjoy our home. And because the builders had to harm others in the process, they created negative karma. Unexamined, it looks as if this beautiful environment exists from its own side, without depending on any being's hardship, but one way or another it could only grow from the suffering of others.

We can follow the same line of reasoning with anything we own. Without the hard work, skill, and suffering of countless sentient beings, we would not be able to use and enjoy such things as our car, our television, our furniture, our computer, our phone, our clothes. We usually think that we acquired all these things through our own hard work and ingenuity—because of the education we received and the big salary we earn—but really they have all come to us through the hard work and suffering of so many unseen sentient beings. In all the factories all over the world, people are working long hours for very little money to ensure we have our comfortable standard of living.

This is also true of the clothes we wear that protect us from heat and cold. Of course, leather coats and shoes come from cows slaughtered for us, but even wool sweaters are made from the suffering of sheep. A sheep is grabbed harshly by all four legs and held down bleating while the wool is stripped from it, often causing it great pain and many cuts.

The most beautiful clothes are made of silk, but we rarely think of the silkworms that are boiled alive in the process.

Likewise, the food that keeps us alive each day comes from the suffering of other sentient beings. Meat is easy to understand—of course other sentient beings have suffered so we can enjoy eating meat—but even vegetarian food requires suffering. Even a simple thing such as a cup of tea involves the suffering of sentient beings. Within one mouthful of water there are many tiny creatures invisible to the eye, and so when we boil the water for our tea, all these creatures die or experience much suffering.

For one grain of rice, the field has to be plowed and fertilized, either with machines or animals. When we take a handful of earth from our garden bed, we can see how many tiny creatures are living there, and so when a whole field is plowed, countless creatures are harmed or killed.

So before we eat, we should always check and see whether we are eating solely for our own happiness, whether we are controlled by the self-cherishing mind. We should see how selfish that is and reflect on how many sentient beings have suffered so we could have that food. If we investigate thoroughly, this could take many hours and the food could be completely cold, but that's okay, we shouldn't hurry. (I'm joking!)

This is why I always emphasize the importance of making a food offering before we eat. When we eat with attachment, we create the causes to be born in the lower realms, but when we remember all those many, many sentient beings who have suffered in order for us to have that food, how can we eat with attachment, with self-cherishing? We should think that the food is due to the kindness of an incredible number of sentient beings who have suffered and maybe even died for us to have it. This is true of a huge meal or a glass of water.

Just as we depend on all others for our comfort, we also depend on sentient beings for our worldly happiness. At present, whatever success we attain in life is almost invariably at the expense of others. We might have a good education, a well-paid job, a nice house, a car, and plenty of money, and we might see ourselves as an independent, self-supporting person, but none of that has come without the kindness of others. Only when we have developed bodhichitta can we think of ourselves as self-supporting.

2. We Depend on Sentient Beings to Attain Liberation and Enlightenment

There is no single instance of happiness we have ever experienced that is not due to the kindness of other sentient beings. Whatever happiness we experience comes from only creating positive actions, which means following a moral life, not harming others, and trying to help them. Without this fundamental Dharma, all these things are impossible.

Where does this Dharma come from? It comes from the buddhas who come from bodhisattvas who are born from bodhichitta. Where does bodhichitta come from? From loving-kindness and great compassion, which in turn comes from understanding the suffering of all sentient beings. Therefore bodhichitta cannot be realized without depending on sentient beings.

We achieve bodhichitta and experience every single happiness due to the kindness of every single sentient being: the insect we step over in the street, the frogs we hear in the river, the humans working in the nearby factory—every sentient being. So every single sentient being is so unbelievably kind, so unbelievably precious.

3. Sentient Beings Are Equal to the Buddhas in the Help They Give Us

We feel great respect for the buddhas, but all sentient beings equally deserve respect because they are equal to the buddhas in the help they give us. At present we feel that kindness only extends to those friends who have helped us in some mundane way: by giving us presents, by praising us, and so forth. We don't see the incredible kindness of all the sentient beings who have worked so hard and suffered so much to make our life comfortable, and we don't see beyond this life. Furthermore, we don't see how sentient beings have helped us by allowing us to be virtuous. Our understanding of kindness is so limited, so narrow.

As Shantideva said in *A Guide to the Bodhisattva's Way of Life*,

> When beholding somebody with my eyes,
> thinking, "I shall fully awaken
> through depending upon this being,"
> I should look at that person with love and an open heart.[100]

We sincerely remember that being's kindness and a mind of loving-kindness naturally arises. We look at that sentient being and naturally think that because of them we will become enlightened.

Even if somebody is actively harming us in some way, we remember that we can attain enlightenment based on this sentient being, that all the happiness of the three times depends on them. As soon as we think in this way all our anger evaporates, like a water bubble popping in the hot sun. Then, rather than being a source of anger and future suffering, that person becomes a source of enlightenment. In that way, sentient beings are like the field where we plant the seeds of our virtuous actions in order to receive the crops of happiness.

People in this world understand the importance of land. Countries fight other countries so they can have more land. We can build our home on it, grow our food on it, take resources from it, build cities and factories, and create whatever we need to have a comfortable, enjoyable life. Because farmers' lives are greatly endangered when the harvest is damaged in some way, such as through floods, droughts, or plagues of insects, they do anything they can to protect their precious fields.

In the same way we should see all sentient beings as precious and protect and care for them. We should always ensure they are protected from any harm and that they receive the best care possible in order to ensure they never suffer in any way.

Why? Because without this field of all sentient beings it is impossible to grow the smallest crop of happiness. For farmers, the seeds, the fields, and the harvest are all important, but even for them sentient beings are far more important. Without sentient beings they wouldn't be able to buy the land or the seeds or sell the harvested crop, and there would be no way to have the material things they need: a house, food, clothes, and so forth. This all comes from the field of sentient beings, not from the crops they grow. In the same way, we can see that without the field of sentient beings, we wouldn't have this precious body to take us all the way to enlightenment; without them we wouldn't be able to sustain this body for even a day, let alone have an education to appreciate and study the Dharma, or experience any of the sense pleasures we currently enjoy.

Shantideva said,

> Therefore the Mighty One has said
> that the field of sentient beings is (similar to) a buddha field,
> for many who have pleased them
> have thereby reached perfection.

> A buddha's qualities are gained
> from the sentient beings and the Conquerors alike,
> so why do I not respect them
> in the same way as I respect the Conquerors?[101]

The beginning of our Dharma practice depends on the kindness of mother sentient beings; the middle of our Dharma practice depends on their kindness; even achieving enlightenment depends on their kindness.

Attaining the six perfections is impossible without other sentient beings. Without sentient beings how could we practice charity, which is the wish to give to others; or morality, which is refraining from harming others? And, of course, if there were no sentient beings, there would be nobody we could practice our patience on.

Enthusiastic perseverance depends on other sentient beings as well. If there were no sentient beings, how could we sustain the effort for three countless great eons, accumulating merit, purifying obscurations, and following the path to enlightenment? Only the unbearable compassion we feel toward all sentient beings gives us the incentive to undertake such a difficult journey. The perfections of concentration and wisdom are dependent on the previous four practices and so in that way are also impossible to attain without depending on sentient beings.

We cannot develop one quality on the path to enlightenment without sentient beings; therefore they are exactly equal to all the buddhas and bodhisattvas in deserving respect, although, of course, not equal in having the infinite qualities of the buddhas and bodhisattvas. This is the meaning of Shantideva's verses.

Whether we are able to realize emptiness in this life or not, as His Holiness says, if we live our life with compassion toward others, with the thought of benefiting others, even if we only have one day to live, that makes our life extremely meaningful, extremely beneficial.

The Kindness of the Enemy

Every happiness we have ever experienced or will ever experience is due to not only those we are close to but also those who harm us. Without depending on the kindness of the enemy, even the pleasure of a cup of tea or a drop of water when we are thirsty is impossible.

If we can understand this line of reasoning our whole attitude toward the person we perceive as an enemy relaxes and becomes more peaceful. We no longer see them in a negative light but instead see how incredibly helpful they have been to us, and we can even feel sorry that we have been upset in the past. Instead of anger and hatred toward them, we see them in beauty; we have a mind of loving-kindness for them. Seeing how their delusions make them harm us, how they are controlled by karma and delusion, we develop compassion for them. When we understand that they are the key to our enlightenment and so are more precious than skies filled with jewels, the wish to take care of them arises naturally, like a mother for her only beloved child.

We could argue that although all sentient beings have helped us in the past, they have also harmed us in the past. This is not a valid point. In the past they have helped us innumerable times and only rarely harmed us, so whatever benefit they have given us far outweighs any harm. We can see this even if we only consider this present life.

More importantly, the harm they have done us is actually indirectly a great benefit. As we have seen, without suffering sentient beings there could be no compassion and no bodhichitta, and therefore enlightenment would be impossible. All this has come from the suffering of all other sentient beings, from the harm they have done and the harm they have received.

Generating great compassion by having compassion for every single sentient being in all the six realms except this one terrible person, this enemy, is impossible, because great compassion encompasses all sentient beings. The *Guru Puja* says,

> The mind that cherishes all mother sentient beings and would
> secure them in bliss
> is the gateway leading to infinite virtue.
> Seeing this, I seek your blessings to cherish these beings
> more than my life, even should they rise up as my enemies.[102]

We should cherish those we consider enemies even more than ourselves because it is only through them that we can completely destroy the self-cherishing mind—the one true enemy—and attain enlightenment.

If we can learn to cherish the enemy—the mosquito that bites us, the person who criticizes us—if we can generate compassion for that being, it opens the door to all qualities and becomes the basis to achieve all the realizations of the whole path to enlightenment. If we don't cherish that enemy, there are no realizations.

The alternative to wishing our enemy to be free from suffering is either ignoring them or wishing to harm them, which is nonvirtue, and how can we expect happiness from nonvirtue? An ear of wheat comes from a wheat seed, not from a corn or an avocado seed. If we want avocados, we plant one thing; if we want wheat, we plant something else. Wishing for avocados and planting wheat won't give us the result we want, no matter how much we pray or prostrate or worry over why there are no avocados there. In the same way, expecting happiness from creating nonvirtue is crazy. Such a thing cannot happen.

Seeing how this one person is the cause of all our future happiness, our attitude is totally reversed. Before, because they somehow harmed our attachment, our self-cherishing mind, we saw them as bad, but now it is the opposite. Without a negative label, there is no sense of enemy; we don't see that person as bad. Now there are skies of reasons for seeing the enemy in a positive way. We see that the person we previously labeled "enemy" is, in fact, our best friend.

We see the good qualities of our friends quite easily. Because they make us feel good we label them "friends," but the benefit they give us is only for the happiness of this life, the happiness our self-cherishing desires. Our understanding is very limited, going no further than the immediate, short-term, transient pleasures.

In seeing somebody as an enemy, we have labeled the wrong object. We currently see our self-cherishing mind as "friend" and slavishly follow it, and we see this person as "enemy" and try to harm them, whereas it should be the other way around. By being a friend to our self-cherishing we are always opening the door to problems, inviting suffering into our life. Conversely, we see whoever blocks our desire as an enemy, and yet really that person, by obstructing our grasping desire and harming our self-cherishing, is our greatest friend.

When we overcome self-cherishing, every action we perform becomes a cause of happiness for all sentient beings. We are friends to all sentient beings without discrimination, whether they like us or hate us, whether they praise us or abuse us, whether they give us presents or cheat us.

For example, there are people who protest against His Holiness the Dalai Lama when he gives teachings, angrily criticizing him. He told a group of geshes in Australia once that every day he does a prayer that says, "I invite sentient beings as my guest to enlightenment." His Holiness said that when he did this prayer he particularly thought of those who were criticizing him, thinking of them inside his heart and making very strong prayers for them. This is due to having realized bodhichitta.

As Thokmé Sangpo said in *Thirty-Seven Practices of the Bodhisattva*,

> Though somebody may deride and speak bad words
> about you in a public meeting,
> look on him as a spiritual teacher,

bow to him with respect—
    this is the practice of Bodhisattvas.

Even if a person for whom you've cared
like your own child regards you as an enemy,
cherish him specially, like a mother
does her child who is stricken by sickness—
    this is the practice of Bodhisattvas.[103]

No matter how another being treats us, we should train ourselves to see that person as the dearest, most precious one, as unbearably kind, as the one who can help us purify all negativities and attain all positive qualities.

In a sutra the Buddha said,

I and sentient beings are equal in happiness and suffering.
I have attained the holy form body only for the sake of
    sentient beings,
and so harming sentient beings is the supreme harm to me,
whereas benefiting sentient beings is the best worship to me.[104]

Making a sentient being unhappy affects the Buddha, whereas making a sentient being happy is the best offering we can make to the Buddha.

Just as the Buddha strived for three countless great eons to attain all those unbelievable qualities and attain full enlightenment only for the sake of sentient beings, all the numberless buddhas have all done the same. This person we hate, they have cherished like a mother cherishes her own beloved child, like her jewel, her heart.

4. We Are All Equal in Wanting to Obtain Happiness and Avoid Suffering

Besides the three conventional reasons why we and all beings are equal that relate to ourselves, there are three reasons from the side of others. The first reason is that we and all sentient beings are exactly equal in only wanting happiness and not wanting even the slightest suffering. A wonderful verse in the *Guru Puja* says,

> There is no difference between myself and others:
> none of us wishes even the slightest of sufferings
> or is ever content with the happiness we have.
> Realizing this, I seek your blessings that I may enhance
>   the bliss and joy for others.[105]

Even in a dream, none of us wishes for the slightest suffering and only ever wants the very best happiness. We should always remember this whenever a negative emotion starts to arise, such as jealousy, anger, pride, and so forth. When we think how we are all equal in this way, that negativity just naturally disappears and we feel no difference between ourselves and others.

At present, if we have everything we want, we are happy, whereas if we don't but we see that others do, we feel jealous and unhappy; we dislike them intensely. Because we are all alike in wanting happiness, there is no reason to renounce some sentient beings and cherish others.

5. We Are All Equal in Needing Help

The next reason why we and all beings are equal is that we are all alike in needing help. Say we see ten beggars all equally needing something to eat. If we were to discriminate, thinking to give money to some but not to others, that is faulty thinking. They are all exactly the same in this most fundamental need to sustain themselves. In the same way, all sentient beings without exception are devoid of the most fundamental need: to have happiness and avoid suffering. Therefore there is no reason at all for us to renounce some sentient beings and only help others. We *must* work for the happiness of all sentient beings.

Using another analogy, we can think of a group of prisoners awaiting execution in the morning. As all need a reprieve badly, there is no point in giving help to some and not to others. All sentient beings including ourselves are trapped in the prison of samsara by karma and delusion.

Subject to impermanence and death, without exception we are all caught in the jaws of Yama, the fearful demon that holds the Wheel of Life, the jaws of death that can be snapped closed at any moment. Death is definite; the time of death is very indefinite—this is the death sentence that hangs over us all. Therefore there is no point at all in liking one person and disliking another, cherishing one person and renouncing another.

6. We Are All Equal in Being Tormented by Delusions

The last of the conventional reasons is that we are all equal in being tormented by delusions. For this example, rather than ten beggars, we can think of ten sick people. All are sick, all need medicine and treatment, so there is no point in giving medicine to some while denying it to the others.

In the same way, we and all sentient beings are exactly the same in being under the control of the three poisons of attachment, anger, and ignorance, and because of that we are constantly experiencing suffering. Even if there is less suffering of suffering, we still experience the suffering of change; we experience the samsaric sense pleasures that depend on external conditions and therefore have the nature of suffering.

Even with this optimum rebirth, we are still faced with old age, sickness, death, and so forth. Imagine if that could be stopped. There would be no need to stretch out the wrinkles, no need to dye the hair, no need to take endless pills, no need to pay health insurance. With no rebirth in samsara there would be no problem with meeting undesirable objects, no problem with attachment and dissatisfaction. While we are trapped in samsara, however, there are always undesirable situations happening: every day, every hour, every minute. We can easily see this when we examine our own life, and we can also see that all sentient beings are exactly the same as we are in this, all under the control of the three poisons that arise from the fundamental delusion, the root of samsara, ignorance. We are all equal in being sick with the sickness of samsara. Therefore there is no justification in feeling some sentient beings deserve our help and others don't.

THE THREE ULTIMATE REASONS THAT SELF AND OTHERS ARE EQUAL

Rather than using conventional logic as the previous reasons did, the next three reasons use ultimate reasoning, examining the three categories of "friend," "enemy," and "stranger" from the perspective of emptiness.

1. "Friend," "Enemy," and "Stranger" Are Merely Concepts Conceived by Our Deluded Mind

The first ultimate reason that self and others are equal is that these three categories are merely concepts conceived by our deluded mind and have no reality at all. Because somebody helps us we label that person "friend," and because somebody harms us we label that person "enemy." Having labeled in this way, whenever the first person appears we see an inherent friend, and whenever the second person appears we see an inherent enemy. There is no real friend or enemy from their own side; this is all a construction of the superstitious, hallucinating mind.

If these appearances were true, as they appear to our deluded mind, then a buddha would also have friends and enemies. But for a buddha, even if somebody offers perfume or a massage and somebody else cuts their flesh with an axe, there is no discriminating thought at all, there is no seeing one as friend and one as enemy.

If there were truly existent friends and enemies, then we could become happy by eliminating all our enemies. That would mean that the astronauts who landed on the moon were perfectly happy because there were no beings, and so no enemies, on the moon. We could kill every other person in the world, but we would still have no peace, because the unsubdued mind has not been controlled. Real peace is the cessation of greed, hatred, and ignorance.

When we are trying to live in the practice and do not follow the negative, unsubdued mind, even though we might not have achieved the elimination of our true enemy (ignorance), we no longer see people as inherent friends or enemies. When we have an equal feeling for all, there is no confusion. Rather than having a mind agitated and uptight, like water boiling, we are peaceful, happy, and relaxed and that influences others. We have fewer problems and we give others fewer problems.

2. "Friend," "Enemy," and "Stranger" Only Appear Permanent, But They Are Not

The second ultimate reason looks at the impermanence of things, how we feel that "friend," "enemy," and "stranger" have a permanence that they do not have at all. At present we have those we think of as our friends and those we think of as our enemies, and these two categories seem somehow fixed. We see our enemy and they seem our enemy forever, a permanent enemy; they have always been our enemy and they always will be. The same thing applies to our permanent, fixed friend; that person will be our friend forever.

If that were true, then there would be no opportunity to change. The enemy could never become our friend, and the friend could never become our enemy. But "enemy" and "friend" do change. An enemy becomes our friend when we see that they are benefiting us in some way. Even if they don't change their attitude to us, if we see them in a different light then we can start to see them as a friend. "Friend" and "enemy" are dependent arisings; they arise in dependence on causes and conditions and on label and base. When conditions change, the concept of friend or enemy changes, and our perception of them reverses. In fact, our relationship with others is constantly changing. Our relationship with each friend and enemy has changed from beginningless time until now and will change life to life. It changes within a lifetime, friend becoming enemy and enemy becoming friend within even a year, a month, a week, or a day—even within one hour.

In the *King of Samadhi Sutra*, it says,

> The father becomes son, the mother becomes wife,
> the person who was the enemy becomes the friend.
> All these have the nature of change;
> therefore nothing is definite in samsara.

This is illustrated by the story of the Buddha's disciple, Shariputra, who with his clairvoyance saw the situation of a family. The father of this family used to catch fish from a pond behind the family's house, and when he died he was reborn as one of those fish. The mother was so attached to their property that when she died she was reborn as a dog on that property. The enemy of the son was strongly attracted to the son's wife, and when he died he was reborn as her child.

One day while on his alms round, when Shariputra looked through the door of the house, he saw the father was now a fish that had been caught by the son and was being eaten by the family, while the mother, now a dog, was at the son's feet, chewing the bones of her former husband. Meanwhile, the son was cradling his former hated enemy—now their child—in his arms and beating the dog, his mother, with a stick. When Shariputra saw this he said, "Eating the father's flesh, beating the mother, cuddling the enemy—samsaric existence is laughable."

While we have strong relationships with our family, our pets, and our colleagues, those relationships are bound to change. One day we could be the pet. Because of this impermanence, it is pointless to discriminate and feel attachment to the friend of this moment and anger toward the enemy of this moment.

3. I and Others Are Interdependent Like "Here" and "There"

The last ultimate reason looks at the interdependence of all beings. Nagarjuna, in his *Fundamental Wisdom of the Middle Way*, explained that I and others are interdependent, like here and there.

Say we are chatting. I am sitting here, and you are sitting there. That is only from my perspective, of course. From yours, you think, "I am sitting here, and he is sitting there," and we both call these positions "here" and "there" as if they exist from their own side, as if they are independent, without relying on the position of the speaker.

If "here" and "there" were independent entities, then "here" would always be where I am sitting and "there" would always be where you are sitting. Then if I move to your side of the room, I would have to say, "I am sitting there." This mistake arises because of the sense of independence of things and events.

"Here" is only "here" depending on "there"; "there" is only "there" depending on "here." In that way, "here" and "there" are interdependent; they depend on each other. There can be no "here" without "there" and vice versa.

When we analyze it, it's easy to see that both "here" and "there" are only designated by the mind, merely imputed on the base by the thought. "Here" and "there" exist in mere name. When we see this, we can feel that the concrete "here" and "there"—the independent, real "here" and "there"—are empty.

Similarly, while both "I" and "others" appear as real, they are completely interdependent. If "I" and "others" actually existed as they appear to us, the "I" would be "I" and "others" would be "others" no matter what the perspective. Except for myself—this being I call "I"—every other being would be "others." From my side I am "I" and from others' side I am "I," and also from others' side they are "others" and from my side they are "others." So it becomes contradictory. The independent "I" and "others" as they appear to us now is a complete hallucination.

Nothing exists from its own side and therefore there is no reason to have a partial mind, to give up on some sentient beings and to care for others.

THE FAULTS OF SELF-CHERISHING

An important aspect of equalizing ourselves with others is an exploration of why self-cherishing is so harmful and cherishing others is so beneficial. By cherishing ourselves, as we have been doing since beginningless time, what have we achieved? What results of cherishing ourselves are we experiencing now and what will be the results in the future? If, on the other hand, we start cherishing others, what will be the effects?

It's actually very easy to predict what will happen either way, if we continue to cherish ourselves or if we start cherishing others. We don't need any special clairvoyance, any observations, any astrology. Guru Shakyamuni Buddha explained it very clearly and Shantideva dedicated many verses of his *Guide to the Bodhisattva's Way of Life* to illustrating it.

How has your life gone so far? Have you achieved the happiness you long for? From birth until now, have you been free from problems? This is a very important investigation, and I guess it's something you have thought about a lot. I'm sure, like most of us, if you investigate you will find that you have experienced a great deal of confusion and problems and a host of disturbing emotions such as jealousy, spitefulness, pride, and so forth, all triggered by the three poisons. Maybe you have been lucky; your body has been fairly healthy and you have never, until now, been seriously sick. But the mind has always been sick with the selfish attitude and disturbing thoughts.

Because we are controlled by delusions we have always suffered, and we are still suffering. In the future, too, we will continue to suffer. If yesterday there had been no delusions, no self-cherishing, we could not experience suffering today.

If suffering arose independent of causes, then there would be nothing we could do about it. It would be like planting a mango seed and watching a chili plant grow. Using that logic, we could follow the path to enlightenment and yet achieve no results, still tied to suffering despite our efforts. If that were the case, there would be little difference between somebody who practices the Dharma and somebody who doesn't; both the Dharma practitioner and the other person are subject to the same causeless suffering.

As great teachers such as Guru Shakyamuni Buddha and Shantideva have shown, happiness and suffering are not independent of causes; to have one and avoid the other is up to us. They have showed us that all suffering comes from having a selfish attitude, whereas to become happy and move to greater and even greater happiness depends on turning the mind toward cherishing others.

To understand the faults of self-cherishing we can study it under these headings:

- Self-cherishing keeps us trapped in samsara.
- Self-cherishing brings countless problems.
- Self-cherishing creates enemies.
- Self-cherishing prevents every happiness.
- Self-cherishing prevents us from practicing the Dharma and attaining enlightenment.

Self-Cherishing Keeps Us Trapped in Samsara

If we continue to take the side of self-cherishing, being a slave to its desires, what can we expect? The self-cherishing mind is like a butcher who slaughters our freedom, bringing us problems in this life and beyond, creating enemies, not allowing us to create virtue by following the Dharma, and causing anger and other negative emotions to rule us. Rather than leading us to happiness, it leads us instead to the lower realms. It's like a thief, stealing away any hard-earned merit we have accumulated, and yet we still want to follow it.

The selfish mind robs us of all peace. When we always want our own way, when somebody disagrees with us or says something we don't like, we immediately get angry with them. Instead of considering the other person's point of view, we fight and argue to have our way, scratching their face, bashing them over the head, throwing chairs at them—maybe even a plate of food or the whole table!

Here, I'm not talking about a movie fight, where everything is smashed up and fists are flying, and finally the police arrive with sirens sounding and guns blazing, and then everybody stops and they all start talking to each other. When somebody insults us in real life, real anger arises, and even though we might not smash a chair over that person's head, still we wish them harm for what they have done to us.

We can see that this all comes from our own mind, not the power of words alone. The words used in the insult in a movie might be exactly the same, but they don't cause anger to arise, whereas the words used by our enemy do. This selfish attitude is what has caused us to be endlessly reborn in the six realms of samsara, experiencing all of the various sufferings an infinite number of times. While we reside in the human realm, it is the cause of old age, sickness, death, and the other types of suffering we face every day. While in the other realms, it is the cause of all those sufferings.

Only Self-Cherishing Can Lead Us to the Lower Realms

An external enemy can also become a friend if, rather than fight them as is our habit now, we try to be of benefit by taking their side, giving them presents, and so forth. However, with our internal enemy, our self-cherishing, this is not so. No matter how much we take its side, no matter how much we follow its wishes, it never gives us one single benefit. The friendlier we become, the more harm it gives us.

Even if that external enemy harmed us terribly, maybe even killing us, still they would be powerless to send us to the lower realms. Only our own negative actions propelled by our self-cherishing can do that. Shantideva said,

> Should even all the gods and demigods
> rise up against me as my enemies,
> they could not lead nor place me in
> the roaring fires of deepest hell.

> Yet the mighty foe, these disturbing conceptions,
> in a moment can cast me amid (those flames)
> which, when met, will cause not even the ashes
> of the king of mountains to remain.[106]

Our self-cherishing mind is the only thing that can make us take an unfortunate rebirth and especially be reborn in the hell realm.

Shantideva said,

> Who created the burning iron ground?
> Where have the multitude of flames come from?

. . . .

The Mighty One has said that all this
comes from the evil mind.[107]

For the hell being, the terrible environment of burning iron ground and bleak ice mountains are products of its own mind, the ripening of the imprints from past negative actions. For us, positive and negative karmas are ripening all the time, and thus our world is a mixture of attractive and repulsive things, of lovely and harmful experiences. But the hell being's world only ever comprises terrible, negative things and events.

Nobody has created this world for the hell being. It's not as if there is this world, complete and uncaused, that the being is invited to step into. The fearful place it is born into is its own karmic vision, created by the deluded mind filled with hatred and anger.

Seeing how this is where the self-cherishing mind is leading us, we should reflect strongly on its shortcomings and determine never again to follow its wrong advice. All the problems we have experienced, are experiencing, or will experience are results of actions that grow from this self-centeredness.

Under the control of the self-cherishing mind we are like a fish caught by a fisherman. Think about how terrifying that would be, pulled from the water and gutted while still alive. That fisherman is the self-cherishing mind, harming us without thought, without care.

Similarly, we are like a sheep, having been sold to a butcher and lined up with other sheep, waiting our turn for the slaughter. Our four legs are securely tied and our cries fill the room as our neck is cut, but the butcher is unmoved, uncaring. The self-cherishing mind is so incredible, so harmful.

This great enemy, the self-cherishing mind, is the creator of the whole of samsara. For beginningless lifetimes it has forced us to wander in samsara and experience all the terrible sufferings of the six realms. It has blocked all forms of happiness and not allowed us to create any virtue, to attain any realizations, and, of course, to attain the precious mind of bodhichitta and the precious mind that realizes emptiness. Liberation and enlightenment are impossible when we are under the influence of the self-cherishing mind.

Self-Cherishing Brings Countless Problems

Panchen Lama Chökyi Gyaltsen in the *Guru Puja* said,

> This chronic disease of cherishing myself
> is the cause giving rise to my unsought suffering.
> Perceiving this, I seek your blessings to blame, begrudge,
> and destroy the monstrous demon of selfishness.[108]

If we are able to put the advice of this verse into practice, we can bring real happiness into our life. By recognizing the influence of the self-cherishing mind and by actively fighting it, we are doing this powerful puja all the time. Without this main puja of fighting self-cherishing, there is no end to the other pujas and practices we would have to do. By watching our mind constantly, we develop rapidly and our life becomes richer and richer.

Chökyi Gyaltsen called the self-cherishing mind a chronic disease because it is deep-rooted in our mind and causes us incredible suffering. We can do everything possible to rid ourselves of all the other problems that plague our life, but they are just the symptoms of this chronic disease. If we don't destroy the root, we will always be beset with problems. Rather than trying to vanquish some external enemy, we should blame, begrudge, and destroy the self-cherishing mind.

A dog barks while we are trying to meditate, and we think our inability to meditate is totally the dog's fault. The barking is a condition, but the real cause is a lack of concentration due to self-cherishing. This is the demon and it inhabits our mind and stops us from experiencing any happiness.

We should remember this whenever a problem arises and we instinctively look outside for the cause. We should look inside instead, laying the blame on the self-cherishing mind. We resentfully hold our enemies in our heart and spitefully wish them every harm, plotting how to destroy them. Of course, with external enemies this is totally the wrong thing to do, but with the self-cherishing mind it's wonderful to have such a spiteful mind. Instead of storing all the ills others have done against us in our heart and plotting revenge, we do that with self-cherishing. Thinking back on any problem we think, "The self-cherishing mind did this to me. He made me starve like this. He took my clothes. He criticized me in this way. He stopped me from meditating."

However, if we are really hungry because we are doing a *nyungné* retreat, we can't blame the self-cherishing mind for *that* hunger. But other than hardships faced due to practicing the Dharma, any other problem we have to experience, we can definitely blame the self-cherishing mind. Then instead of the mind being spiteful to other beings, we can be spiteful solely to the self-cherishing mind.

Perhaps we live in a dangerous environment where we are always afraid of being killed. It might be a war zone or a very rough neighborhood, where street fights and muggers are prevalent. Or perhaps we seem to have little control over whether we harm others or not; we kill other beings despite trying not to. These are the faults of the self-cherishing mind. How is that so?

In a previous lifetime the self-cherishing mind forced us to create the negative karma of killing others, and because of that, we are experiencing this result. Without the self-cherishing mind leading us into creating such negative actions, these results could never occur. We don't want these results. We don't want to live in a hostile environment. We don't want our life shortened, dying young because of accident or illness. We don't want to be killed. We want the opposite, but to do that we must create the causes. This is how the self-cherishing mind destroys even our chance to receive samsaric pleasures.

Self-Cherishing Brings Conflict and Lack of Harmony

Until we destroy self-cherishing, until we free ourselves from selfish concern, there will be no end to the problems we encounter. If we are in a relationship, there is lack of harmony and so there are always fights. We see this all the time. Couples fight constantly. Every few minutes something happens, they disagree, and another fight breaks out. The selfish attitude demands each has his or her way—when and where they travel, how the house is kept, how the food should be cooked, what they watch on television, and so on and so forth—meaning there can never be harmony.

Sexual misconduct is a direct result of self-cherishing, where one partner thinks that because their sexual needs are paramount, it is perfectly acceptable to carelessly commit nonvirtuous actions to satisfy them. If either partner were to develop a less selfish attitude, sacrificing more for the other, there would be more peace. It solves nothing for one to stubbornly decide not to change until the other person does. While both people become more stubborn and more selfish, there can be no peace, not even for a minute. It's like living in the hells, trapped in the red-hot burning house. No matter how beautiful the house, no matter how much luxury and comfort there is, how many bedrooms, showers, or swimming pools there are, the house is still on fire.

This hasn't been created by any external factor but by the selfish, wanting mind, which has no regard for the other person. This situation was not created by God or the gods, although perhaps we can blame the great god of self-cherishing, the one god we really worship. This is the god that we follow, that we offer service to day and night. Of course, this doesn't apply to everybody, but this is the way most of us live our life, dedicating ourselves to the self-cherishing mind.

Self-Cherishing Disturbs the Mind and Brings Illness
The nature of the selfish attitude is to disturb our mind. Through either attachment or aversion we have an uptight, agitated mind; there is no peace, no relaxation in our mind. These disturbing thoughts trigger nonvirtuous actions and the mind becomes even more polluted.

The mind is reliant on psychic winds that travel through our body, and with this pollution these winds get disturbed, causing the elements in our body to become unbalanced. The proper balance of the four elements of the body—wind, earth, fire, and water—is the foundation of Tibetan medicine.[109] When our deluded, agitated mind disturbs the balance of these four elements, we become ill.

The most terrible fatal disease is nothing compared to the self-cherishing mind. An illness can only kill us, which is only the separation of mind from body; it doesn't have the power to throw us into the lower realms. With the self-cherishing mind abiding in our heart, however, our next destination is almost definitely the lower realms.

Diseases such as cancer are very prevalent these days, but even so, we don't have cancer every lifetime. We do, however, have the cancer of self-cherishing every lifetime. Cancer will come and go—certainly it will go at death—but the self-cherishing mind remains to harm us life after life, staying to destroy all happiness while we continue to keep it in our heart.

When we are unable to control our mind, we not only become sick but our external environment also becomes unbalanced. The self-cherishing mind can also be blamed for the pollution and danger to this earth. The weather becomes agitated in the same way our mind does, and there are violent storms, floods, tsunamis, hail storms, droughts, famines, and so forth. So the self-cherishing mind can even be blamed for the environmental disasters that are becoming more prevalent.

During the twentieth century there was a huge danger of nuclear annihilation, where whole countries could have been destroyed within an hour. The real danger wasn't the nuclear arsenals but the delusions and the self-cherishing mind that created them. Without the self-cherishing mind there would be no delusions and hence no weapons, or even if there were weapons, there would be no danger without the deluded minds to use those weapons.

Without analyzing it, we can think that the self-cherishing mind is our friend. Western culture, in particular, advises us that self-cherishing helps and protects us. However, if we use our wisdom to check the truth of this, we see that it is a hallucination. In reality, self-cherishing constantly harms us; it destroys us and our happiness. It doesn't allow us to achieve temporary success, let alone ultimate success. Our self-cherishing never leaves us in peace, constantly torturing us. It also brings us the pain that comes from anger, attachment, jealousy, pride, and the other delusions.

Self-Cherishing Creates Enemies

With the self-cherishing mind we are unable to see the good in people, and so we create enemies wherever we are. Our parents, our Dharma friends, our gurus might all be showing us great compassion, advising us to not create any negative actions, but nothing goes in. Thinking our self-cherishing knows better, we are unable to accept any advice.

The self-cherishing mind causes us to judge others depending on our own egoistic standard. When we see somebody with more than us, we are jealous. Perhaps it's a friend with greater Dharma knowledge, a fellow student with higher grades at university, a businessperson who is richer and more successful. Seeing their success and judging it against our own lower status, we feel resentful and miserable.

When we encounter somebody on the same level, we feel competitive, and again there is suffering in our mind. We might be identical in education, race, class, looks, even body shape, but we must prove we are better, we must compete. If we can bring the other person down in some way, we will definitely do that.

When we encounter somebody lower than we are, we feel pride, despising them because they are lower. We feel we are rich, good-looking, well positioned in society, and the other person is far below us, poor, ugly, unable to succeed in the way we have. We have no compassion for them, but rather we gloat in their misery, heightening as it does our own specialness.

Looked at from the outside, it looks crazy, but when we have such an attitude it seems perfectly correct. We think what we want is right and justifiable and what the other person wants is wrong and they are outrageous even thinking they should have it. We feel we would miss out if we were to give anything away. It's either our happiness or their happiness, and of course, our happiness is much more important. In this world, with all these countless sentient beings, as long as this one single sentient being—me—is happy, then everything is okay.

The Self-Cherishing Mind Is Never Satisfied

The self-cherishing mind is never satisfied, always wanting more. Depending on how powerful we are, the number of sentient beings we can harm with this need, intentionally or unintentionally, is huge. One person, such as Hitler or Mao Zedong, can destroy millions and millions of people with his self-cherishing. After a dictator such as Hitler conquers one country, he wants another, and then another, and then the whole world, not caring who gets killed or who suffers for him to get what he wants. Not only does he create the most incredible negative karma, assuring himself eons in the worst possible suffering of the hell realm, but he also creates unbelievable suffering for countless beings.

Hitler is not the real enemy; Mao is not the real enemy; Osama bin Laden is not the real enemy. The self-cherishing mind is the real enemy. There is no external enemy; the only real enemy is the self-cherishing mind. This real enemy is the one that creates all the other enemies.

When the self-cherishing mind is strong, it is very easy to become angry. The stronger the self-cherishing mind, the more impatient and jealous we are. Many problems arise quickly and easily, one after another, giving us little time to relax.

It makes us intolerant. Sometimes people feel totally fed up living in a family with lots of people and want to be free from people. Some just want to go off into the forest by themselves and keep on walking to see what happens. I remember one of my students in Australia told me this. From an airplane you can see there are vast areas of Australia that are bush, without a single house or town. He just wanted to walk into the bush and keep going for days and days, and in this way he thought he would find peace. I had the feeling he wanted to find some new experience, not the Buddha.

With the self-cherishing mind there is no satisfaction at all. It's just like the leader of the Rolling Stones, Mick Jagger, said, "I can't get no satisfaction. Though I tried and I tried and I tried." I think that really illustrates our samsaric life.

Without practicing the Dharma we fail at whatever we try. We try to get pleasure, we try and try, we try and try, and we try and try, but we never get satisfaction. If there were no attachment, there would be no frustration and no reason to get angry. Many negative emotional thoughts arise like that. This creates hundreds of problems, millions of problems, problems that go on and on and on and on. Before one package of problems—relationship problems, work problems, and so forth—has finished, another has already started.

Self-Cherishing Prevents Every Happiness

When we are ruled by the self-cherishing mind, making any effort at all to help others becomes a heavy burden. Instead of feeling incredible joy at being able to benefit others, if we have to care for somebody else, we feel weighed down and miserable, as if we are being asked to carry a huge mountain on our head.

In *A Guide to the Bodhisattva's Way of Life*, Shantideva said,

> Whatever joy there is in this world
> all comes from desiring others to be happy,
> and whatever suffering there is in this world
> all comes from desiring myself to be happy.
>
> What need is there to say more?
> The childish work only for their own benefit
> while the buddhas work solely for the benefit of others.
> Just look at the difference between them![110]

If we check, we can see this so clearly. Because we have acted in this childish, selfish way since beginningless rebirths, we have always been caught in this endless cycle of suffering life after suffering life.

When we work for our own ends, we are children. Look at children playing in the sand. They make piles of sand and give them labels, calling one pile "my house" and another "my car." They believe in this and grasp on to it, and when challenged, they argue and fight, and anger, hatred, and attachment arise. Clinging to the eight worldly dharmas, we are just like those children. We selfishly grab at whatever we think will make "me" happy, disregarding the harm it does others.

When we use the term *childish* we generally mean somebody who unrealistically and selfishly grasps on to something meaningless, like a child does some toy, working hard solely for their own trivial goal. Doesn't that describe us? No matter how "big" we are—we might be a chief executive of a world-renowned bank or a famous scientist—and no matter how much education or influence we have, we are still childish in that we are only working for our own benefit.

The buddhas, on the other hand, by working solely for others, have renounced selfish concerns and overcome all suffering and attained full enlightenment. Guru Shakyamuni Buddha was similar to us, suffering, wandering in samsara, but then he renounced working for himself. By renouncing the self-cherishing mind, and instead cherishing others and working solely for them, he achieved enlightenment. Despite our similarities he is now enlightened due to cherishing others and we are still stuck in samsara due to cherishing ourselves.

I have already compared self-cherishing to a thief, but that is exactly what it is like. A thief sneaks into our house in the middle of the night while we are asleep and steals every single one of our possessions, leaving our house completely empty. When we wake up in the morning, we have no idea we have been burgled until we look about and see an empty house. Likewise, self-cherishing steals all our merit, not letting us experience the results of the positive karma we created in the past. We go to sleep with a whole house full of positive karma, and self-cherishing sneaks in and takes it all away in the sack of three poisons. Whatever positive potential we have is destroyed by our anger, attachment, and ignorance.

We can also think of self-cherishing as like an atomic bomb, something very dangerous, with the power to destroy an environment completely. The traditional analogy used here is somebody with black magic who might seem normal on the surface but who has the power to murder many people. Like an atomic bomb, when it lurks in our heart the self-cherishing can destroy our entire happiness and the potential to ever receive happiness in the future.

Self-Cherishing Prevents Us from Practicing the Dharma and Attaining Enlightenment

The self-cherishing mind destroys the happiness of this life, and worse than that, it prevents us from understanding and practicing the Dharma. It blocks any progress we might wish to make on the path to enlightenment, destroying any chance of realizations and making even another human rebirth impossible.

After Guru Shakyamuni Buddha attained enlightenment, an incredible number of followers also attained enlightenment or became arhats. Great Indian teachers such as Naropa, Atisha, and Nagarjuna attained enlightenment as well as many great Tibetan teachers such as Lama Tsongkhapa. But we have not attained one single realization, and this is all completely the fault of the self-cherishing mind.

Even though it demands that we constantly search for samsaric happiness, the self-cherishing mind fails to provide even that, and it ensures we have no Dharma happiness either. Because the self-cherishing mind relies on cherishing this life, the very opposite of the mind of the Dharma, we are totally unable to turn any action into a Dharma action and thus into the cause for happiness. If we define an enemy as somebody who harms our self-cherishing mind, then the Dharma is our great enemy. And bodhichitta, the mind that wishes to attain enlightenment for the sake of all sentient beings and so cherishes others more than ourselves, is the greatest threat of all to the self-cherishing mind, so bodhichitta is the greatest enemy of all.

THE NEED TO DESTROY SELF-CHERISHING

Shantideva asked why we cling to self-cherishing if it is the cause of all our problems.

> If all the injury,
> fear, and pain in this world
> arise from grasping at the self,
> then what use is that great ghost to me?[111]

We naturally reject anything that harms us and yet we embrace the thing that harms us the most. If we were given a bottle of deadly poison that could kill us with even a touch, we would utterly reject it, and yet this is what this ghost, this demon of self-cherishing, is asking us to do. So why don't we, likewise, reject it?

After checking where the source of all our problems lies, of course we want to destroy that source. We should think of the self-cherishing as like a red-hot burning poker thrust right into our heart. We shouldn't stand it for even a split second, let alone a minute, an hour, a year, or the countless eons we have lived with this demon. Actually, the feeling of needing to be free from the demon self-cherishing should be billions of times stronger than the wish to be free from a red-hot poker in our heart, which would surely only be a small discomfort compared with the suffering that self-cherishing has inflicted on us since beginningless time.

In the next verse, Shantideva said,

> If I do not completely forsake it
> I shall be unable to put an end to suffering,
> just as I cannot avoid being burned
> if I do not cast aside the fire (I hold).[112]

Just as we would drop a burning coal the instant we realized we were holding it, we must drop the self-cherishing attitude or we will surely suffer.

Overwhelmed by the worldly mind, we always seek worldly solutions to worldly problems, and so we are constantly running after satisfaction for the ego's desires, never realizing that this is an impossible task. *I am the most important person in the universe; my* needs are more important than anybody else's in the universe. If we were to examine the mind that holds these thoughts, we would see that it is a painful, tight mind, a mind without peace. Even leaving aside the suffering it will bring us in the future, that very mind is suffering.

The remedy is to renounce self-cherishing and instead to cherish others. Shantideva summed this up very precisely in the next verse,

> Therefore, in order to allay the harms inflicted on me
> and in order to pacify the sufferings of others,
> I shall give myself up to others
> and cherish them as I do my very self.[113]

These verses are very powerful, very effective for the mind. As soon as we change our attitude from self-cherishing to cherishing others, thinking of the kindness of others and determining to repay that kindness, there is great peace in our heart, great tranquility.

Blame the One Enemy

The core of mind training is the twin thoughts of placing the blame for all our suffering where it is due, on our self-cherishing, and contemplating the great kindness of all sentient beings. At the beginning of Chekawa Yeshe Dorje's *Seven-Point Mind Training* it says,

> When the world and its inhabitants boil with negativity,
> transform adverse conditions into the path of enlightenment.
> Banish all blames to the single source.
> Toward all beings contemplate great kindness.[114]

When we can recognize that whatever unpleasant experience happens to us is the result of our own karma, that it comes solely from our own mind, we can see that there is absolutely no external factor to blame for our own suffering. When somebody harms us in some way, this is an appearance of our karma, created by us and nobody else.

Because every negative thing, every problem and harm, is all the fault of self-cherishing, we should only ever blame this one enemy. This is the one who forces us to plant the seed of negativity in the field of the consciousness; this is the one who waters and fertilizes it to ensure a huge crop of suffering. This is the one who encourages our miserliness and ensures we are reborn as a hungry ghost, who keeps us stupid and ensures an animal rebirth, who forces us to become uncontrollably angry and takes us into the hell realm. The self-cherishing mind forces us to experience all these sufferings by obliging us to do all of the ten nonvirtuous actions again and again, to kill and steal and lie, all to satisfy its demands. Seeing this is the source of all our problems, we banish our blame of all other objects and only blame this single source.

The minute we do the thought-transformation practice, the problem we believe we have becomes nonexistent. Before, we thought the source of the problem was only external and never related it to our own mind. It existed purely from its own side, a real problem. Suddenly that problem is no longer there. Relating everything that happens to us back to our own mind, because we see it as the appearance of our karma and hence created by us, there is nobody we can point to who is to blame for our problems except our own mind, our own delusions, and specifically our own self-cherishing.

There is no need to look for this thing that is to blame for everything. We don't have to search the city and the country looking for it, putting ads in newspapers and asking the police for help. There is no need because it is right there inside us, the self-cherishing mind. Suddenly it becomes so easy to place the blame. *Everything* unwanted is the fault of this mind. That is the essence of these lines of *Seven-Point Mind Training*. It's unbelievably precious to train ourselves to think this way. By putting the blame on the one, we banish it completely.

The last line of the verse tells us to meditate on the great kindness of all beings. Rather than blaming others for our problems, we see how every happiness of the past, present, and future comes from the unbelievable kindness of others.

Shantideva said,

> Previously I must have caused similar harm
> to other sentient beings.
> Therefore it is right for this harm to be returned
> to me, who caused injury to others.[115]

We harmed that person in the past, which is why we are receiving harm now. But we are not really being harmed by them; it is our self-cherishing that harms us.

In Western psychology, the other person is usually seen as the cause of the problem rather than our own mind, whether it is a relationship problem, abuse, or whatever. Thought transformation, on the other hand, places the blame exactly where it should go, on self-cherishing, and shows us how to transform difficult situations into positive ones. As Langri Tangpa said in *Eight Verses on Mind Training*,

> When others out of jealousy
> treat me wrongly with abuse and slander,
> I will train to take the defeat upon myself
> and offer the victory to others.
>
> Even if one whom I have helped,
> or in whom I have placed great hope,
> gravely mistreats me in hurtful ways,
> I will train myself to view him as my sublime teacher.[116]

If somebody harms us and we harm them in return, trying to defeat that person, then we create the cause to receive harm for hundreds, for thousands of lifetimes. That is why this advice is so smart, even though ordinary worldly people, those who don't know the Dharma, would think we are totally wrong in doing this. By accepting the loss and offering the victory to others we make them happy, and so instead of harming us they help us and we also win.

Since beginningless time we have lived under the control of the self-cherishing mind, but now we have recognized it and we will never let it control us again. This false friend has been revealed for the demon it is. Now we can confront it and do whatever we need to do to destroy it. Shantideva said,

> For ages you have dealt with me like this
> and I have suffered long;
> but now, recalling all my grudges,
> I shall overcome your selfish thoughts.[117]

Now that we can see the self-cherishing mind for what it is, where can it hide from us? Kathmandu? The United States? (Actually, Shantideva didn't mention this.) Having been in the hands of the self-cherishing mind for countless eons, now the tables have turned and it is in our hands. It's as if we have finally captured the thief who has been stealing all our happiness and have locked him safely in a room. Now we can give him a really hard time; we can beat him up, squash him flat, or do whatever we want with him. From being completely arrogant, utterly sure he can get whatever he wants, he now cowers, certain we will take our revenge on him.

Overturning our habitual selfish traits and training our mind in working for others is the core of the thought-transformation practices. Without such a radical transformation we cannot hope to develop great compassion, bodhichitta, and all the minds that lead to full enlightenment. We need to see the truth, that every tiny happiness we have ever experienced, are experiencing now, and will ever experience, is solely due to the kindness of every living being, regardless of their relationship with us.

The Benefits of Cherishing Others

Real happiness in life starts when we cherish others. With compassion and loving-kindness toward others, we voluntarily and joyously work for others. That is the door to happiness and satisfaction in life.

With the mind of cherishing others, whatever problem occurs is immediately transformed into the path to enlightenment, making it no longer a problem. Bodhisattvas actually pray for problems to arise in order to more quickly develop on the path. Experiencing problems on behalf of other sentient beings creates limitless skies of merit in our heart and brings enlightenment in the quickest possible time. If we create countless enemies when we only cherish ourselves, it is completely the opposite when we cherish others. Filled with loving-kindness and compassion, with no ill will toward anybody, wherever we go there are only friends. No matter how hard we look we are unable to find one single enemy. As Khunu Lama Rinpoche said in *The Jewel Lamp*,

> How could someone in whom the bodhichitta
> of the supreme vehicle exists ever turn
> toward the poison of self-cherishing, even for a moment?
> How could they give up the nectar of cherishing others?[118]

When we wear the ornament of bodhichitta, there is no way we could ever harbor ill will toward any other being, no matter what that being might do to us. This is the power of bodhichitta. Our mind only ever thinks of benefiting other living beings, instinctively, spontaneously, without being told to do it. When we have a good heart—not even the realization of bodhichitta—we have no enemies because enemies are creations of our own mind.

With a good heart, we are treated kindly. People like us regardless of whether we are rich or poor, wishing us health and a long life. When we are with others, even if they have difficult, negative personalities, simply by staying with them we can have a positive influence on them.

Our loving, caring attitude will even influence extremely selfish people. A classic example of this is Lama Yeshe. People who were normally quite negative types became better when they were around Lama because of his tremendous loving-kindness and bodhichitta. Toward others they might still be quite selfish and impatient, with uncontrolled minds, but in Lama's presence they changed and were very loving to him, never thinking of harming him. In that way, Lama never found an enemy, a bad person, because Lama himself had that kind of personality, kind and concerned for everybody. Just seeing Lama's holy body, just hearing Lama's holy words, their negative thoughts were subdued and they naturally became kind.

Because a buddha has perfect compassion for each and every sentient being and, on top of that, perfect understanding and perfect power to reveal the perfect methods for sentient beings to be free from suffering, a buddha never misleads any sentient being. Even if the earth were to become the sky and the mountains were to become water, it would be impossible for this to happen.

I remember seeing an interview His Holiness the Dalai Lama did with Larry King, the guy on American television who always wears suspenders. When he asked His Holiness if he ever had emotions, His Holiness replied that any emotions were like waves on the surface of the ocean, they come and go, but below there was great stillness. He talked heart-to-heart like that, and Larry King was completely satisfied. His Holiness is so skillful like this, speaking at the level of whoever is talking to him. I think if he told people he was like God or something like that, he wouldn't inspire people at all, but when he presents himself as a simple monk with much the same problems and aspirations as we have, he has great power to inspire us to try to be like him.

Cherishing others is the foundation of all the positive qualities we develop on the path to enlightenment. Based on this, we become a buddha and have the infinite qualities of holy body, holy speech, and holy mind. Then we are able to offer perfect work for all sentient beings without the slightest mistake. This is the incredible benefit we are able to offer all beings due to having renounced self-cherishing and turned the mind to cherishing others instead.

When we consider it in this way we can see that our good heart that cherishes others—this one person's good heart—is most precious, like a wish-granting jewel, bringing happiness to every single hell being, hungry ghost, animal, human, demigod, god, and intermediate-state being. What we achieve is unimaginable, priceless. The *Guru Puja* says,

Since cherishing myself is the doorway to all torment,
while cherishing others is the foundation of all that is good,
I seek your blessings to make my core practice
the yoga of exchanging self and others.[119]

This is the essential practice. If somebody asks us what our main practice, our heart practice, in life is, we should say bodhichitta. Usually if somebody is asked what their main practice is, they will give the name of a deity or say it's *kundalini* yoga or concentrating on the winds and drops or something like that, but really, while everything else might be very worthwhile, the *main* practice must be bodhichitta.

No other education can compare to entering the Mahayana path. Even the eight common siddhis and the five forms of clairvoyance are nothing compared to this.[120] The higher bodhisattvas' qualities are beyond our imagination. They can travel to countless pure lands to receive teachings from countless buddhas and thereby attain enlightenment even more quickly. In order to benefit others, they manifest in billions and zillions of forms—teachers, crazy people, animals, bridges, or whatever—whichever are most suitable for sentient beings.

We too have this potential to achieve such amazing qualities because, like all sentient beings, we have buddha nature. The key that unlocks this potential is compassion, which leads us to develop one of the different techniques for attaining bodhichitta.

We should follow the examples of the bodhisattvas, seeing how they have trained to cherish others more than themselves. They should be our role models, showing us how they totally overcame all problems and attained sublime happiness for themselves and others. Like that, we too will become a role model for others. Through our positive, loving attitude, we influence others.

EXCHANGING OURSELVES AND OTHERS

The heart of the thought-transformation practice is exchanging our current desire for ourselves to be happy with the desire to give happiness to all other beings, as well as the willingness to take all their suffering. We do this in the profound meditation practice called *tonglen*, "taking and giving."

In *Thirty-Seven Practices of the Bodhisattva*, the great bodhisattva Thokmé Sangpo said,

> All suffering comes from the wish for your own happiness;
> perfect Buddhas are born from the thought to help others.
> Therefore exchange your own happiness
> for the suffering of others—
>   this is the practice of Bodhisattvas.[121]

This is the actual exchange of self and other. Enlightenment only comes from exchanging ourselves with others, from willingly accepting their suffering and giving them all our happiness. Thokmé Sangpo only mentions enlightenment here, but we can include all other forms of happiness, from the happiness of this life to liberation. There is no way we can totally purify all the gross and subtle obscurations and develop all the qualities to obtain enlightenment without this vital practice.

As practitioners of thought transformation, it is our job to always diligently watch our mind like a spy watches a potential traitor, day and night, to see if anything negative happens. Then when we see a negative emotion such as anger arising, we can train ourselves to avert it.

Years back we would have had no control over our anger. Even if we had studied the Dharma and knew the disadvantages of anger, still in our mind we would feel that we were 100 percent right and the other person was 100 percent wrong, and therefore our anger was justified. We might have heard the teachings on the kindness of the enemy but feel that they refer to some other enemy, not this one.

Slowly, however, through habituation, we have developed patience and compassion, and although anger might still sometimes arise, we can generally avert it. This is something we would have thought impossible a few years back. By continuing our training, at some time in the future we will find we no longer have anger. There will even come the time when we will feel great joy at the thought of taking on suffering for the sake of others.

In *A Guide to the Bodhisattva's Way of Life*, Shantideva said,

> There is nothing whatsoever
> that is not made easier through acquaintance.[122]

The thing is to change our mind. At present we have the wisdom not to stick a sharp knife into our body because we know it will harm us. We also know that if a foot is sore we do whatever we can to cure that pain rather than blame the foot or decide to cut it off to be rid of the pain. Shantideva asked us to extend that line of reasoning to all sentient beings:

> When both myself and others
> are similar in that we wish to be happy
> what is so special about me?
> Why do I strive for my happiness alone?
> . . . .
> —Surely whenever there is suffering
> the (sufferers) must protect themselves from it?—
> Yet the suffering of the foot is not that of the hand,
> why then does one protect the other?[123]

Say the foot has a thorn stuck in it. The hand naturally helps by pulling the thorn out without expectation of reward, seeing the foot as part of the same body and so part of what we think of as "me." In the same way, we should see all sentient beings as part of this universe that we all belong to and deserving of being helped without expectation of reward. The hand is not hurting but it naturally helps the hurting foot; we are not suffering but we naturally help the suffering sentient beings.

We can definitely habituate ourselves to this way of thinking. We have great attachment to our body, and yet this body is not the I. Because our consciousness entered the union of sperm and egg, causing the fetus to develop and become what we are now, we think of the body as ours. It is not ours at all; it is the product of the sperm and egg of our father and mother, and therefore, if anybody's, it belongs to them. Actually, it's just a label we give to this collection of parts. Of this, Shantideva said,

> Although the basis is quite impersonal,
> through (constant) familiarity
> I have come to regard
> the drops of sperm and blood of others as "I."

> So, in the same way, why should I be unable
> to regard the bodies of others as "I"?
> Hence, it is not difficult to see
> that my body is also that of others.[124]

In exactly the same way we can train our mind to see all other sentient beings' bodies and minds in a different light. Although at present we see "me" and "others" as two completely separate things, as we have seen, there is no such different intrinsic entity called "others" separate from "me." This entity we call "I" would not exist if it were not for the entity we call "others," something completely created by our mind.

Therefore, whereas now we see others' suffering as separate from ourselves and no concern to us, by using this logic we can see that this is nonsensical. We should help others simply because there is suffering, in the same way the hand helps the foot.

Taking and Giving

Tonglen is the quickest, most powerful way to heal ourselves. In this meditation we take the sufferings and causes of suffering of the numberless other living beings within ourselves and use them to destroy our self-cherishing mind, the source of all our problems; we then give other living beings everything that we have: our body, our relatives and friends, our possessions, our merit, and our happiness.

Although this is something we should practice all the time, it is particularly powerful to do tonglen when we are having a problem, because then we can use our own pain to develop compassion for other living beings. This way, we experience our problem on behalf of all living beings. Doing the meditation well often helps to stop our own pain, and it is not uncommon for it to even heal disease. The main point of taking and giving, however, is that it purifies the causes of disease, which are in our mind.

When we successfully do tonglen, if there were a choice, we would sincerely take on every suffering of every sentient being, including the suffering of suffering, the suffering of change, and pervasive compounding suffering. We would take on the sufferings of the lower realms and the sufferings of humans, such as old age, sickness, death, rebirth, and so forth, and all of the gods' sufferings. Tonglen involves having a will as powerful as that. Even before that, however, we can train to take on others' sufferings and give them our happiness in much smaller ways.

Saying the words of a prayer such as the refuge and bodhichitta prayer is not enough. We need to practice what the prayer says. Shantideva said,

> Therefore, I shall put this way of life into actual practice,
> for what can be achieved by merely talking about it?
> Will the sick receive benefit
> merely by reading the medical texts?[125]

With a strong selfish attitude, even to try to do a meditation on taking and giving can terrify us. For somebody like us, just reciting the prayer that says we are renouncing ourselves, such as "May I forever be the means of living for sentient beings," is scary. But we should use the words of the prayer as our guide to train ourselves as much as we can.

There is no doubt that if we take on the suffering of others, we create limitless skies of merit and purify lifetimes of negativity, depending on the strength of our compassion for the objects of our practice. Tonglen is such an unbelievable practice in this way.

The *taking* part of taking and giving must be done with compassion otherwise it simply wouldn't be taking. Nobody forces us to take the suffering of others. This is not something that can be imposed on us from outside, like a Communist dictate where we must share all our possessions with others whether we like it or not. The wish to take others' suffering can only come from a sincere compassion that wishes others to be free from suffering.

In the same way, the *giving* part of taking and giving must come from loving-kindness. First, we meditate on how sentient beings are devoid of happiness in all its different levels and then we generate the strong wish that we can bring them that happiness.

Even now, while we are still wrapped up in self-concern, we can train in this way. With the taking we can learn to see the suffering of others more and more, feeling how unbearable it is and determining to take that suffering rather than let them endure it. And with the giving we can see sentient beings more and more in beauty, recognizing their buddha nature and potential to become happy, and determining to give our happiness to them. So these two precious minds of compassion and loving-kindness are developed within the practice of taking and giving.

When we practice taking and giving, other important insights naturally come. Longdrol Lama Rinpoche from Sera Je Monastery was an extremely advanced practitioner who often saw Tara in his practice. One day Tara advised him to practice tonglen, to take others' suffering within himself in order to destroy his self-cherishing mind and offer all his happiness to them in order to attain infinite merit, saying if he did this the realization of emptiness would happen by the way.

After encouraging us to place the blame on the one enemy, the self-cherishing mind, *Seven-Point Mind Training* says,

> Train in the two—giving and taking—alternately.
> Place the two astride your breath.[126]

While thinking of the suffering of others and wishing to relieve them of that suffering by taking it on ourselves, it is extremely difficult at the same time to think of their happiness and give them all our happiness.

To effectively practice taking and giving, these two aspects should be done alternately. The way to do it is to "place the two astride your breath": taking the suffering of others in with our in-breath and giving them all our happiness and merit with our out-breath.

Because this is a secret practice, invisible to others, we can do it wherever we are: sitting on a chair, lying on the beach, and so forth. Wherever we are we can collect infinite skies of merit and purify infinite negative imprints just by breathing in and out with our normal breath.

To do the actual practice of exchanging ourselves and others, we start with the *taking*.[127] First we generate compassion by thinking how, because of their ignorance, living beings constantly experience suffering. We think, "How wonderful it would be if all living beings could be free from all suffering and the causes of suffering." Then we generate great compassion by thinking, "I myself will free them from all their suffering and its causes."

As we slowly breathe in, we imagine taking all the suffering and causes of suffering of other living beings in through our nostrils in the form of black smoke. Like plucking a thorn out of their flesh, we immediately free all the numberless living beings from all their suffering.

The black smoke comes in through our nostrils and absorbs into the self-cherishing mind in our heart, completely destroying it. At the same time, the false I that ignorance holds to be truly existent also becomes completely empty, as it is empty in reality. By meditating for as long as possible on this emptiness, the ultimate nature of the I, this becomes powerful purification.

Next, we do the *giving* part. We generate loving-kindness by thinking that, even though living beings want happiness, they lack it because they are ignorant of its causes or unable to create them. We think, "How wonderful it would be if all living beings had happiness and the causes of happiness." Then we generate great loving-kindness by thinking, "I myself will bring them happiness and its causes."

We visualize our body as a wish-granting jewel that can grant all the wishes of living beings. Then, as we breathe out, we give everything we have—our possessions, our family, our friends, and our body visualized as a wish-granting jewel—to every living being in the form of pure white light. We give all our good karma of the three times and all the happiness that results from it up to enlightenment. We also make offerings to all the enlightened beings. All the living beings receive everything that they want, including all the realizations of the path to enlightenment. After everyone has become enlightened in this way, we rejoice by thinking, "How wonderful it is that I have enlightened every single living being."

The physical breath we use in the tonglen meditation, entering and leaving our body, is the air we breathe all the time, a gross aspect of the wind energy that is the vehicle for the mind, that allows the mind to travel within the body. The two have different functions but they are one in essence, and so doing this practice, the wind energy becomes focused and our bodhichitta becomes stronger.

Integrating Tonglen with Daily Life

Tonglen also helps in daily life, encouraging us to actually get involved in taking other sentient beings' problems and suffering on ourselves and giving our happiness to others. For example, we can accept the responsibility for somebody else's mistake or decide not to sue somebody who has accused us of wrongdoing. Rather than becoming mad and spending hours arguing our innocence, we can take that blame on ourselves to protect that person from suffering and give them happiness. Tonglen is not just a meditation on the breath but also an active practice for our daily life.

We should do this meditation a few times in the morning and again in the evening and remember it during the rest of the day. This is especially important whenever we are plagued by an ongoing problem. Rather than being depressed and anxious, we can actually transform it into happiness by using tonglen to experience the problem in order to develop loving-kindness and compassion.

We crave peace and happiness and wish to have no suffering at all, but even the great peace of the arhats' nirvana seems like used toilet paper to a bodhisattva: something to be discarded immediately. Bodhisattvas pray to be reborn in hell so that they can be of benefit to all the hell beings. The texts say they feel unbelievably happy at the thought of rebirth in hell, like when a swan escapes the hot sun by going into a cool pond.

Of course, few of us are at that stage, but even if we have a headache and we take medicine for it, we should make our experience of the headache worthwhile by thinking, "I am experiencing this headache on behalf of all living beings. I am experiencing it on behalf of the numberless other beings who have created the cause to experience a headache now or in the future. May all their suffering be pacified. May they have the happiness that comes with the absence of this problem, and may they especially have ultimate happiness."

We can think in the same way about any problem we have. Before anxiety, fear, or any other negative emotion has the chance to arise, we should immediately think, "I'm experiencing this problem on behalf of all living beings." Then we should try to maintain this awareness. By dedicating for others, our experience becomes the path to free others from problems and bring them happiness, especially ultimate happiness.

An excellent technique for dealing with depression is to use it to generate the loving, compassionate thought of bodhichitta. We should think, "I am just one person, while others are numberless. How wonderful it would be if I, one person, could experience the depression of all living beings, as well as all their other sufferings, and allow them to have all happiness and peace, up to enlightenment." Whenever we feel ourselves sliding into depression, we should immediately think, "I am experiencing this depression on behalf of all other living beings." Thinking that the depression is not ours but that of all other living beings can be helpful. In this way the depression can become worthwhile.

This also applies to cancer or any other sickness. There are many examples of somebody recovering from a serious illness when taking and giving was done on their behalf. Depending on karma, sometimes the tonglen practitioner becomes sick in their place, sometimes not.

It's very important to help a sick person in that way when there is the chance; it can definitely help to do a mala of mantras every day while practicing tonglen for them. There are many times when doctors cannot help, when medicine is ineffectual or has serious side effects. Whether conventional medicine works or not has a lot to do with karma.

When sick, by taking all the suffering of others upon ourselves and giving them all our own happiness, we use the disease to generate the ultimate good heart of bodhichitta. This is the very heart of healing.

Rather than becoming obsessed and depressed with our illness, which creates more problems, we immediately think, "I have prayed to take on the problems of others and I have now received them. I will experience this illness on behalf of all living beings." Our illness is the illness of all living beings and since we have to experience it, we might as well use it to develop the ultimate good heart of bodhichitta. Seeing this as a wonderful opportunity to purify our negativities and create infinite merit, we suddenly feel incredibly happy. We feel unbelievably lucky to have this illness.

When Kirti Tsenshab Rinpoche was diagnosed with cancer, the doctor in Dharamsala said he was only 80 percent sure it was cancer and asked Rinpoche what he thought. Rinpoche replied he was so happy because the disease gave him an opportunity to practice taking all beings' suffering on himself and conquer the self-cherishing mind. He told others later that he had been practicing tonglen since he was a small child.

With bodhichitta, we experience a disease for other sentient beings, especially all those other sentient beings who are suffering from that same disease now and who will experience it in the future.

As I often say, our main goal in life is not to be healthy or to have a long life but rather to benefit other sentient beings. Whether we are healthy or unhealthy, rich or poor, praised or blamed, living or dying, our main aim is only to benefit others. If being healthy doesn't help us achieve this, it's useless; if being sick does, then it's very worthwhile. Happiness in life depends on having this attitude. In *The Jewel Lamp*, Khunu Lama Rinpoche said,

If one is in possession of bodhichitta
it is fine if one is sick, fine if one is dying,
fine if one is studying, and fine if one is meditating;
one seems to be fine no matter what one is doing.[128]

It's unrealistic to pray to destroy our self-cherishing in order to benefit others and at the same time pray never to have any problems. What we must practically do in our normal life is use whatever difficulties we have to ensure we develop on the path and work to lessen our self-concern. As Pabongka Dechen Nyingpo explained, if in the past we prayed to take others' sicknesses and sufferings on ourselves and now we are experiencing sickness or suffering, we should rejoice because we are succeeding in our prayers. We should feel as if we have just made a huge win in a lottery. Even if the problem increases, we shouldn't despair but feel extremely fortunate, thinking that if the problem stopped much earlier we would be denied the opportunity to continue to do so much purification and accumulate so much merit. Even if we were in a car crash, an earthquake, or a nuclear attack, where there is no chance of escape, we should feel this. Even if we are about to be born in hell, we should remember this.

We need to be bravehearted to do a tonglen practice, to willingly take on the suffering of all other sentient beings and give them all of our happiness. With the practice of giving we are not only wishing them to have happiness, but we are also taking the responsibility on ourselves to cause them to have all happiness. It's not that we wish them happiness and then nothing happens. We can't just offer them a kind word and then go ahead and live our life solely for ourselves. It's not like that at all. Loving-kindness is taking the responsibility on ourselves to cause them happiness.

We can even use the tonglen meditation at the time of death. Rather than rejecting death as something to fear and so miss an incredible opportunity to benefit ourselves and other living beings, we can use it to develop our mind on the path to enlightenment.

At the time of our death we should think, "I prayed in the past to take upon myself the suffering of death from other living beings; I am now experiencing my death on behalf of all the other living beings who are dying now and who will have to die in the future. How wonderful it would be for all of them to be free from the suffering of death and for me alone to experience it. Let them have this ultimate happiness."

Advanced meditators can transfer their consciousness to a pure land as they are dying by a practice called *powa*. But dying with such an altruistic wish is the best powa, the best way to transfer our consciousness to a buddha's pure land where there is no suffering of birth, old age, sickness, or death.

Doing tonglen practice might not immediately cure us of a terminal illness but it will definitely purify our mind and create infinite merit, causing us to complete the path and attain enlightenment. Then in future lives, if not this one, we will never have to experience any other disease again. Our life becomes most meaningful, most wonderful, the happiest life, with inner happiness, with great peace in our heart.

CONCLUSION: BECOMING
A SERVANT TO ALL BEINGS

WHEN WE HAVE attained bodhichitta, we can be whatever sentient beings need us to be. This is a wonderful wish we can have even now. Like Shantideva, we can pray,

> May I become an inexhaustible treasure
> for those who are poor and destitute;
> may I turn into all the things they could need
> and be placed close beside them.
> . . . .
> May I be a protector for those without one,
> a guide for all travelers on the way;
> may I be a bridge, a boat and a ship
> for all who wish to cross (the water).
>
> May I be an island for those who seek one
> and a lamp for those desiring light;
> may I be a bed for all who wish to rest
> and a slave for all who want a slave.
> . . . .
>
> And until they pass away from pain,
> may I be the source of life
> for all the realms of the varied beings
> that reach unto the ends of space.[129]

It's like our body can become a wish-granting jewel, giving them whatever they need. If they need food and water, we become that food and water; if they need a guide, we become that guide. We become their clothes to protect them from the cold, their shelter, their medicine, even the items in their bathroom: their soap, towel, and tissue paper. As Shantideva said, we pray to become the source of life for all the beings of the six realms.

Practicing Mahayana Buddhism, this should be our daily attitude; this is how we should lead our life, only for the service of others. With such an attitude, we will attain enlightenment extremely quickly.

A bodhisattva is a servant to all sentient beings. When I read these verses from Shantideva, I think of the incomparably kind Lama Yeshe, how everything Lama ever did was solely to benefit others. Holding the pure wish to serve others was why he was so successful in his life. From Lama's great bodhichitta the whole of the Foundation for the Preservation of the Mahayana Tradition (FPMT) grew, and now there are many, many centers and projects, all doing great benefit for sentient beings. However many people have transformed their minds through coming to a FPMT center, it is all due to the unbelievable kindness of Lama, to his vast vision and to the tireless work he did for us.

Lama Yeshe is an example of somebody who developed his mind until it became one of bodhichitta. Before Lama passed away in America, when his sickness manifested in Delhi, he said, "Even if the operation in America isn't successful, it doesn't matter, I don't mind. I won't be worried if the operation doesn't succeed because my life has been useful enough as a servant for other sentient beings." Of course, somebody such as Lama would never announce to the world that he was a bodhisattva, but this attitude shows that his whole life was totally dedicated to others, without even a shred of self-cherishing. Every second of his life was *only* for all sentient beings, and that is the definition of a bodhisattva.

With the foundation of the lamrim and a thorough study of bodhichitta through texts such as *A Guide to the Bodhisattva's Way of Life*, we can offer great service to others. I think working for a Dharma center is one of the best ways of doing this. Every day we meet sentient beings who need our help, and we have the opportunity to help them in a profound way. The center gives us the chance to benefit them and transform our mind very, very quickly. This is thought-transformation practice at a very practical level.

The bodhisattvas pray to become whatever sentient beings most need, such as a bridge or a boat to get them across the river or the medicine for their illness. Even if we aren't advanced enough to do such things, we can create the conditions for others to meet the great teachers; we can be a bridge in that way. We can help them secure their means of living so they then have the opportunity to listen to the Dharma. In that way, even if we don't have the ability to teach them the Dharma, we are helping to relieve them from both their material and Dharma poverty. We can help them transform their minds by giving them the opportunity to hear the teachings on bodhichitta, emptiness, and even Vajrayana. By doing so, we plant the seeds of enlightenment in their minds.

Reversing our habitual self-interest and serving others instead, in whatever way is most beneficial, is the best tonglen. If we don't sacrifice our own interests for others like this, there is always the danger of our negative mind increasing and our selfish concerns overwhelming us again. Therefore, giving our life in the service of other sentient beings is the best thing we can do. Since we have to separate from our body in any case, there is no point in cherishing this body at the expense of others.

From our side, if we don't practice the Dharma, that's it. Even if all the buddhas descend to teach the Dharma to us, even if all the great teachers such as Lama Tsongkhapa sit in front of us to guide us, as long as we don't practice we can never transform our mind from self-cherishing to cherishing others. Our attitude doesn't change; no compassion grows in our mind. Even if we live in a monastery or retreat in a cave for years, nothing changes.

On the other hand, if we work toward seeing ourselves as a servant to all other sentient beings, our life will become more and more meaningful. Then, when negative minds such as anger or spitefulness start to arise, we can easily avert them and compassion naturally arises in their place. In that way our entire life becomes incredibly happy, incredibly worthwhile. That doesn't mean we will never have problems, but we will be able to meet those problems with a totally different mind, one that allows us to transcend the petty concerns that would have drowned us before.

Sentient beings are most kind, most precious, most dear. All our past, present, and future happiness, including enlightenment, comes from *every* sentient being. We need to understand this deeply and also see how much they are suffering. They want happiness, but they always destroy the cause of happiness. They dislike suffering, but day and night they are always busy creating the cause of suffering. They are always running toward suffering. They destroy their merits because they don't know the Dharma. We *must* think, "I will free the numberless mother sentient beings from the oceans of samsaric suffering and bring them to the full enlightenment, the state of the omniscient mind, by myself alone. Therefore I will achieve enlightenment as quickly as possible." This is the kind of bodhichitta motivation we must have in our heart every second of our life.

APPENDICES:
BODHICHITTA MEDITATIONS

....

Just as the nectar called the philosopher's stone
turns iron into gold,
bodhichitta turns this unclean body
into the body of a buddha.

—KHUNU LAMA RINPOCHE,
THE JEWEL LAMP, VERSE 74

APPENDIX 1:
THE EQUANIMITY MEDITATION

....

This meditation comes from Lama Zopa's "Kopan Course No. 5,"
delivered at Kopan Monastery in Nepal, November 1973. https://www
.lamayeshe.com/article/chapter/kopan-course-no-5-index-page.

Do the visualization like this.

Think of a present friend, enemy, and stranger: three people discrimi-
nated by your mind. Visualize the person you don't like, who disturbs
you, in front of you on your left. Visualize the friend you are attached
to in front of you on your right.[130] Visualize the stranger in between
these two.

Then visualize, surrounding you, all the other infinite sentient beings:
your parents, the hell beings, the hungry ghosts, the animals, the
humans, the demigods, the gods, and the intermediate-state beings.
You should visualize all sentient beings in human form, because when
we lead them all in refuge prayers, it will be difficult to imagine bugs,
frogs, and so forth saying the prayers. Do whichever is most effective
for your mind; the whole point is to subdue your mind.

If you have difficulty finding a specific enemy, try thinking of somebody who gives you problems such as somebody who makes you angry
through rudeness, lying, or abusing you in some way. Perhaps somebody
has accused you of being foolish or jealous—something like that. For a
friend, it can be one of your parents, a relation, a person you are attached
to, or somebody who is attached to you. The stranger is somebody you
have neither attachment to nor aversion for.

If you don't have some specific person you are attached to, then try to have some feeling by visualizing that person giving you what you want. If you like getting presents, imagine them giving you a wonderful present; if you are attached to praise, imagine them praising you, and so forth. Imagine the friend giving you whatever makes you happy.

Then think of the feelings that arise when you look at these three people. When you look at the enemy, a feeling of dislike arises; when you look at the friend, a feeling of attachment arises; when you look at the stranger, a neutral feeling arises, neither dislike nor attachment.

When you have a clear visualization of these three beings among all other sentient beings and the feelings that arise because of these three, think like this: If you do something that the friend doesn't like or if they do something you don't like, they become your enemy. If you do something that the enemy likes or they do something you like, they become your friend. As these two have changed in the past according to the conditions, so they will change in the future. The friend is not the true friend; the enemy is not the true enemy. It is the same with the stranger. They are a stranger at the present, but according to changing conditions they can become either an enemy or a friend. The stranger has sometimes been a friend and sometimes an enemy in the past, and this will be the same in the future. Even the stranger is not a definite stranger.

Therefore there is no reason to react as if these three are permanent—to label one as "definite friend," one as "definite enemy," one as "definite stranger"—due to temporary conditions: what the friend does, what the enemy does, and what the stranger does. Think that in a little time all these things will change—"friend" will become "enemy," then "stranger," and so forth. Think of your parents and your partner, how your relationships with them have changed over your life and will continue changing. This is true of your friend. At the moment they have this status in your mind, but they have been continually changing and will continually change.

Think of this present friend, parents, and so forth—those you are currently attached to.

Think: "This friend has been my enemy numberless times in my previous lives. They have been my enemy by disturbing me in many different ways. Their being my enemy has no beginning; there is no time I can think before which they were not an enemy."

Think on this clearly and deeply, and check what feeling comes into your mind.

Think: "As my present enemy kills me, disturbs me, or harms me in some way, in the same way, this present friend has harmed me in my previous lives countless times."

Thinking back on the harm this person has done in numberless previous lives, check what effect it has on your mind, what feeling you have for them at this moment.

Think: "This friend I am now attached to will continually change in the future, will again become my enemy, continually harming me in my numberless future lives."

Thinking this, also check what effect it has on your mind, what feeling you have at this moment. If there is a lessening of attachment, your analysis has been accurate; if not, then you need to work on this aspect more.

Now, in the same way, check with the present enemy.

Think: "This enemy has been my friend numberless times in my previous lives. They made me happy by giving me things, by praising me, and so forth. Just as my present friend makes me happy, so has my present enemy countless times in numberless previous lives."

Imagine many, many previous lives where your current enemy has been your best friend and has been incredibly kind to you, and check what feeling comes to mind.

Think: "This enemy I now dislike will continually change in the future and will again become my friend, making me happy in my numberless future lives."

Thinking this, also check what effect it has on your mind, what feeling you have at this moment. If there is a lessening of dislike and anger, your analysis has been accurate; if not, then you need to work on this aspect more.

Now, in the same way, check with the present stranger.

Think: "At the present this person is a stranger, but they have been my friend and enemy in my previous lives, and they will be my friend and enemy in the future."

Imagine many past lives in which the stranger was your friend and many past lives in which they were your enemy. Then imagine many future lives in which the stranger becomes your friend and many in which they become your enemy.

Think: "The number of times this being has been a stranger is equal to the number they have been a friend and an enemy. They are a stranger now, but they have not been a stranger more than a friend or an enemy. Because my lives are countless, I can't say they have been a stranger more just because they are now."

Try to see how this person is equal in all ways to the two you currently label "friend" and "enemy." Check the feeling that comes to your mind. If the feeling is one of neither attachment, aversion, nor indifference, just neutrality, then feel the meditation is working.

Use the same analysis with the friend you have visualized.

Think: "The number of times this being has been a friend is equal to the number they have been an enemy and a stranger. They are a friend now, but they have not been a friend more than an enemy or a stranger. Because my lives are countless, I can't say they have been a friend more just because they are now."

Try to see how this person is equal in all ways to the two you currently label "enemy" and "stranger." Check the feeling that comes to your mind. If the feeling is one of neither attachment, aversion, nor indifference, just neutrality, then feel the meditation is working.

Use the same analysis with the enemy you have visualized.

Think: "The number of times this being has been an enemy is equal to the number they have been a friend and a stranger. They are an enemy now, but they have not been an enemy more than a friend or stranger. Because my lives are countless, I can't say they have been an enemy more just because they are now."

Try to see how this person is equal in all ways to the two you currently label "friend" and "stranger." Check the feeling that comes to your mind. If the feeling is one of neither attachment, aversion, nor indifference, just neutrality, then feel the meditation is working.

Just as you analyzed your feelings for these three beings, do the same with every other sentient being. Think that every sentient being has been a friend, an enemy, and a stranger countless times, and in that way try to have an equal feeling for all other sentient beings.

As you visualize like this, also visualize Guru Shakyamuni Buddha in front of you.

Then make this request from the heart: "It is not enough that I am born in the upper realms. Even if I am released from all samsaric suffering, it is not enough. All these sentient beings surrounding me have been my mother numberless times, and most of them are in incredible suffering, not having the wisdom to distinguish what is a positive action and what is a negative action. They always desire peace but always create negative karma. No matter how much they desire not to suffer, they purposely run toward it, destroying the cause of happiness. As I am the child of these mother sentient beings, so it is my responsibility to take care of them, to release them from suffering and lead them to everlasting happiness. To do that, may I completely purify all negativities, be released from samsara, and achieve the great enlightenment right now."

Then visualize light, representing Guru Shakyamuni Buddha's wisdom, coming from his holy body and absorbing into you and all other sentient beings and purifying all the delusions and mental defilements. Think that all the mental delusions and defilements belonging to you and all sentient beings are all purified. Even the subtle defilements are completely purified. Think that, from Guru Shakyamuni Buddha's holy body, billions of the Buddha's holy bodies come to above the head of every sentient being, then absorb into and become one with all the sentient beings. All sentient beings become Guru Shakyamuni Buddha, having achieved the two holy bodies, the dharmakaya and rupakaya.

Then the main Guru Shakyamuni Buddha comes to the top of your head, absorbs into you and becomes oneness. You also achieve the two holy bodies, the dharmakaya and rupakaya. All other sentient beings who became Guru Shakyamuni Buddha absorb into you from all the directions.

Training the mind in equanimity like this brings a result. Let's say you meditate like this in the morning session, and then after some time, maybe in the office or at a party somewhere, somebody you considered a friend criticizes you and another you considered an enemy helps you.

The situation you visualized is actually happening. Remembering the reasons that bring equanimity to the mind, that stop anger and attachment from arising, you naturally think that there is no point in getting angry at this enemy because they have given you so much help and benefit in past lives, just as there is no point in being attached to this friend. Both have been your helper in the past. In this way, no matter how abusive this person is or how kind that person is, your mind is not confused. The mind is free, abiding in equanimity.

APPENDIX 2: THE MAHAYANA EQUILIBRIUM MEDITATION

In The Wish-Fulfilling Golden Sun of the Mahayana Thought Training *(Kopan Monastery, Nepal, 1973), the source of this meditation, Rinpoche describes this meditation as more than the standard equanimity meditation because he has added a number of techniques for overcoming anger and developing patience.* https://www.lamayeshe.com/article /wish-fulfilling-golden-sun-mahayana-thought-training.

Think: "It is never enough to gain only liberation for myself. Attachment to personal peace, and striving solely for this, is both selfish and cruel."

Visualize that you are surrounded by all sentient beings, with your mother seated to your left and your father to your right. In front of you, visualize an enemy, someone who dislikes you or wishes you harm. Behind you, place your dearest friend, the person you are most attached to. To the side, visualize a stranger, somebody who arouses only neutral feelings.

Think: "There is no reason at all for me to be attached to and help my friend or to hate and harm my enemy.

"If I were to strive for only my own happiness and peace, there would be no reason for me to have been born human. Even as an animal, I could strive for this. The various animals have the same aim as many highly educated people—happiness of the self alone—and also create many negative actions, such as fighting and destroying enemies, cheating others with a political mind, and so forth, all in the pursuit of their own happiness. The only difference between such humans and animals is their shape.

"The main purpose of my having been born human is to strive for and achieve higher aims, to bring every sentient being to everlasting happiness. This is something no animal can ever do.

"Just as I wish to avoid suffering and find happiness, so too do all other sentient beings. Therefore all other sentient beings and I are equal, and there is no logical reason for me to care more about myself than others or to harm enemies or any other sentient being.

"For countless rebirths, with the self-cherishing mind, I have been discriminating other beings as 'friend,' 'enemy,' or 'stranger.' Chandrakirti said, 'Where there is the self-cherishing mind, there is the discrimination of other.' When partiality discriminates between self and other, attachment and hatred arise.

"All misfortune arises from acting under the influence of these negative minds. The self-cherishing mind causes attachment to self, which produces attachment to my own happiness. The entire range of negative minds arises from that.

"Anger is caused by greed and self-cherishing and makes me discriminate against whoever disturbs my happiness, hindering me in some way. This produces the enemy. In the same way, attachment creates the friend, somebody who helps me. Ignorance labels those who neither help nor hinder as strangers.

"Anger makes me hate and harm the enemy; attachment makes me cling to and help the friend; and ignorance makes me see the stranger as having a permanent self-nature. By acting under the influence of these negative minds, I lead myself into difficult and suffering situations.

They create danger and suffering for myself and others and bring no peace.

"Since beginningless time the two negative actions of helping out of attachment and harming out of anger have thrown me into samsaric suffering, making it impossible for me to achieve the perfect peace of liberation and enlightenment.

"Negative actions leave negative imprints on the consciousness; these ripen into endless experiences of suffering. If I continue to behave in this way, I will experience the same suffering over and over again for eons and will receive neither realizations nor enlightenment itself.

"The three objects of friend, enemy, and stranger are false and have been labeled incorrectly for extremely temporary reasons. The current friend, enemy, and stranger have not always been friend, enemy, and stranger in my countless previous lives. Even the enemy of last year can become my friend this year and yesterday's friend become my enemy today. It can all change within an hour.

"A text says, 'If you try for a moment to befriend an enemy, he will become your friend. The opposite occurs if you treat a friend as an enemy. Therefore, the wise, understanding the impermanent nature of temporary relationships, are never attached to them, nor to food, clothing, or reputation.'

"The Buddha said, 'In another life, the father becomes the son; the mother, the wife; the enemy, a friend. It always changes. In cyclic existence, nothing is certain.' Therefore there is no reason to be attached to friends or to hate enemies.

"If the ignorant concept of true existence were true, the three designations of 'friend,' 'enemy,' and 'stranger' should have existed from countless previous lives and should continue to exist through the present to beyond enlightenment. This makes complete nonsense of the concept of enlightenment, since the Buddha's sublime enlightened mind is completely free of the delusions and imprints that create such distinctions.

"Out of his compassion, the Buddha taught the equanimity meditation so that I, too, might become free of delusions, imprints, and ignorant discrimination. The concepts of 'friend,' 'enemy,' and 'stranger' are false because they and their basis are totally illusory. There is no truly existing other, just as there is no truly existing I.

"My problems are created not by the enemy but by me. In my previous lives, I harmed others through ignorance and the results of this return in this life, causing me hardship and suffering.

"The Buddha said, 'In previous lives, I have killed all of you before and you have all slaughtered me. Why should we now be attached to each other?'

"Chandrakirti said, 'It is foolish and ignorant to retaliate to an enemy's attack with spite in hopes of ending it, as the retaliation itself only brings more suffering.' Therefore there is no reason to retaliate.

"The enemy is the object of my practice of patience, which helps me overcome my anger. I should not hate this enemy who brings peace into my mind.

"The enemy is infinitely more precious than any material possession. They are the source of all my past, present, and future happiness. I should never hate the enemy but instead give up any possession for their peace.

"An enemy is my greatest need, the source of all beings' enlightenment, including my own. The enemy is my most precious possession. For their peace I can give up myself.

"From now on I must never hate or harm the enemy or any other being.

"The enemy harming me mentally and physically is under the control of their negative mind. There is no reason to get angry or to retaliate by harming them. They are like the stick that someone uses to beat another. It is not their fault; just as the pain I experience from a beating is not the fault of the stick.

"If I had clear wisdom I would see that harming others out of hatred is harming myself out of hatred. Obviously I should not harm others.

"All sentient beings, including the enemy, are the object of the buddhas' compassion. The numberless buddhas hold the enemy and all other beings dear to their hearts. Therefore, harming another, even slightly, is like harming the infinite buddhas.

"The Buddha always considers all sentient beings, including enemies, to be more important than himself. Mindlessly harming another being for my own benefit is the act of a mind of stone.

"The enemy and all other sentient beings have been my mother countless times. The infinite buddhas with their holy body, speech, and mind serve all beings, enemies included. Therefore I must never give harm to any other being.

"Not harming my worst enemy—my own ignorance—and destroying an outer enemy instead is like killing a friend by mistaking them for an enemy. I should not harm the outer enemy but the inner one, the actual cause of all my suffering.

"Because of realizations based on the equanimity meditation, no bodhisattva would ever see another sentient being as an enemy, even if they all rose up against them.

"The enemy is merely a concept created by my hatred, just as friends and strangers are concepts created by my attachment and ignorance. I should not believe the distorted perceptions of my negative minds.

"If I investigate with my wisdom, I will never find my attachment's friend or my hatred's enemy anywhere, neither inside nor outside their body. Wisdom tells me that these are merely names.

"For all these reasons, I can now clearly see how foolish and nonsensical I have been over beginningless lifetimes.

"If I could realize this equanimity meditation, it would be my most priceless possession. Equanimity brings peace to me and numberless beings through all my future lives."

APPENDIX 3: THE SEVEN POINTS OF CAUSE AND EFFECT MEDITATION

....

This meditation is a combination of one in The Wish-Fulfilling Golden Sun *and one in "Kopan Course No. 5."*

1. RECOGNIZING THAT ALL SENTIENT BEINGS HAVE BEEN OUR MOTHER

That all sentient beings have been our mother can be proved by logical reasoning and shown by scriptural authority, with quotes such as from Nagarjuna's *Friendly Letter*, which says,

> A heap of all the bones each being has left
> would reach to Meru's top or even higher.
> To count one's mother's lineage with pills
> the size of berries, the earth would not suffice.[131]

Think: "Because the mind is beginningless, samsaric transmigration is beginningless, and my previous lives are numberless. But due to different individual karma, my present mother was not my mother in all previous lives. For instance, when this mother was an elephant, I was an ant, born from a mother ant; when I was a yak, she was a flea; and so on.

"However, the mother of my present human life has been my human mother numberless times. She has also been my mother countless times when we were both animals: as turkeys, hens, cows, ants, and so forth.

"Of all the realms of samsara, there is none in which I was never born. I have been born in every single place throughout the entire extension of space. Innumerable times I have taken each and every physical form in existence, even the most ugly and miserable of all."

Think of all the different species there are in the world—animals, birds, fish, insects, and so forth—and think that each being of each species has been your mother countless times.

Visualize your mother sitting on your left, your father on your right, your enemy in front of you, and your friend behind, and then visualize all other sentient beings surrounding you.

Think: "They have all been my mother, and they are all trapped in samsara, suffering terribly without any means of escape. Just as I would do anything to free this life's mother from any suffering, so I must do whatever I can to free all these beings, my mothers from previous lives."

Even though all sentient beings have been your mother, because of your ignorance you have forgotten this, only remembering this present life's mother because you are still in this same body she gave to you. Make the determination that you will train yourself to see no difference between your present life's mother and the mothers from all your previous lives. They are all equally precious.

Think: "The time when sentient beings began to be my mother does not exist. Such a time is not the object of even the omniscient minds of the enlightened beings, so it cannot be that of the limited minds of ordinary beings. What is true, as above, for my present mother is also true for all other sentient beings."

2. RECALLING THE KINDNESS OF THOSE BEINGS

Even worldly people are grateful for the kindness of their mother, which extends from conception until death.

Think: "My mother has been kind to me in four ways: giving me this body, protecting me from life's dangers, leading me in the path of the world, and bearing many hardships and accumulating negative karma on my behalf.

"Firstly, she has been incredibly kind by giving me this physical body with its eight freedoms and ten richnesses. My mother's kindness is responsible for all the opportunities I have, enabling me to make use of my physical body and lead the sort of life that I do.

"From the time of my conception she has been worried and concerned about me. When I was in the womb she worried day and night, not moving as freely as before and always taking more care of me than of herself, because of the great love and compassion she had for her baby. She took much care in eating—renouncing desirable food and eating only that which would not give me harm, avoiding foods that were too hot and too cold, and so forth. If she hadn't taken care of me when I was in the womb, I wouldn't have been born alive.

"At the time of my birth, she bore extreme suffering, feeling as if her body were about to split apart and fearing that her life was in danger. If my mother hadn't wanted to bear the suffering of childbirth, I wouldn't have been born.

"If she hadn't fed me well, I wouldn't have enjoyed the various functions of my physical body, such as using my eyes to see the most beautiful objects, my ears to hear the most beautiful sounds, my nose to smell the sweetest perfumes, my tongue to enjoy the most delicious tastes.

"Secondly, my mother has been incredibly kind by protecting me from life's dangers. She always took good care of me, feeding me properly, protecting me from many dangers. When I was a baby, without any sense of disgust, she always kept me clean of kaka, pee-pee, snot, and so forth. She always tried to keep me warm and protected, and she gave me the best clothes and food that she could. She would also keep the best part of her own food and other enjoyments for me.

"Thirdly, she led me in the path of the world, making me study so that I could have a comfortable life and be respected. Because of her kindness I have become successful working with my body, speech, and mind, and being skillful and creative with my hands. All this depends on my mother's kindness.

"Fourthly, my mother bore so many hardships and accumulated negative karma to ensure I had everything I wanted. She told lies to give me a good reputation and to hide my faults and bad behavior. To protect me from danger she fought or did anything possible to help, taking more care of me than of herself.

"She chose to go hungry rather than let me be hungry, be sick herself rather than let me become sick. If she had a choice, she would have chosen to die rather than let me die. And this is nowhere near the extent of her kindness.

"In all, she took great care of my life with much suffering, creating bad karma by making other beings suffer so that I would be happy.

"Moreover, because my present mother has been my mother in countless human lives, she has been infinitely kind to me since time without beginning.

"In *Friendly Letter*, Nagarjuna said,

> Know that every being has drunk more milk
> than all the four great oceans could contain,
> and still, by emulating common folk,
> they'll circle, drinking ever more and more.[132]

"If all the milk I have ever received from my mother could be collected, it would fill infinite space, and I could continue to drink it in future lives. Similarly, the food received from her is as infinite as space, as is all my past kaka and pee-pee, the result of that food. So too is the infinite, immense ocean of tears she shed out of worry for me, and the numberless bodies she sacrificed to protect my life.

"Besides the kindnesses she gave me as a human, there is the kindness she gave as all different beings.

"I have received exactly the same amount of benefits from each sentient being. Therefore, as my present mother has been infinitely kind to me, so has every other sentient being.

"There has not been one sentient being that I have not called out 'Mummy' to with tears in my eyes, that I have not taken refuge in, that I have not been completely dependent on for every aspect of my life. There is not one sentient being who has not benefited me in this way, even the beings I now call 'enemy.' They have all been unimaginably kind to me infinite times."

3. RESOLVING TO REPAY THAT KINDNESS

Think: "Attaining bodhichitta depends on having great compassion and great love, which comes from the unselfish love that sees only beauty in others. This can easily be achieved by considering sentient beings as my mother and remembering their kindness to me. This is done because, of the two parents, living beings generally cherish their mother more than their father.

"Even worldly people feel the responsibility of repaying help received from their mother or from other people, even if this help is in small, insignificant ways. For instance, this help may be in satisfying their desires; by giving invitations to parties, food, or cups of tea; or by saying one or two sweet words, pleasing to their ears. Also, even deeply ignorant animals such as dogs help their master in return for kindness received, so why can't I do the same?

"Yet repaying mother sentient beings in their worldly needs is not enough, nor is it the best way, because it can't destroy their suffering or its cause.

"I must repay the kindness of all the mother sentient beings who have been extremely kind to me numberless times in my past lives. The way to truly repay them is by freeing them from all the suffering, so that they are able to attain the sublime bliss, the highest among all the happiness, enlightenment."

4. DEVELOPING LOVING-KINDNESS

Think: "I will generate loving-kindness by remembering the kindness of all sentient beings. All these kind mother sentient beings, even if they have temporary happiness, are devoid of ultimate happiness. However much they wish for happiness, in practice what they do is run to destroy the cause of happiness by feeling emotions such as anger and attachment. Almost all of my kind mother sentient beings are ignorant of the cause of happiness, and even if some know its cause, they lack the means to practice it. Despite only ever wanting happiness, even in one day, in one hour, in one minute, what they accumulate as much as possible is the cause of suffering.

"Therefore I will cause all these kind mother sentient beings to have all the happiness and the cause of happiness. I will make this determination and generate great loving-kindness by remembering that enemy, friend, stranger, and all sentient beings are equal in wanting happiness and wanting to avoid suffering, and all are equal in having shown me unimaginable kindness over infinite lives."

5. DEVELOPING COMPASSION

Think: "Whether or not sentient beings know the cause of suffering, they are unable to abandon it and therefore continuously experience suffering. Even those who do not suffer the suffering of suffering or the suffering of change experience pervasive compounding suffering, the suffering of samsara. I will cause all mother sentient beings to be free from all the suffering and causes of suffering, all the obscurations."

Having this determination is the way of generating great compassion.

Think: "If I generate compassion for all sentient beings, they will all receive happiness from me; if I don't generate compassion for all sentient beings, they won't. Therefore I am responsible for bringing happiness and peace to all sentient beings.

"Nothing is more important than developing compassion. Compassion is more important than my friends, wealth, or education. It is the source of all happiness for myself and for all society.

"Compassion is more important than having friends because even if I have many friends, without compassion there is no happiness, peace, or satisfaction in my life. Compassion is more important than wealth because no matter how much wealth I have, it does not bring satisfaction or happiness in the heart. Compassion is more important than education because no matter how well educated I am, no matter how much knowledge I have, if I don't have compassion there can never be satisfaction, peace, or happiness in this life. Without it there is no meaning in life.

"Compassion is the source of all happiness for myself and for society. Without compassion and virtuous karma, there can be no happiness in my family, in my society, in my country, or in the world. The good heart of loving-kindness and compassion is a very important source of success and the happiness of satisfaction and enjoyment of life."

6. ATTAINING THE SPECIAL ATTITUDE

Think: "Wishing all sentient beings to have happiness and be free from sufferings, I will do this work by myself alone. I will take all the responsibility to free each sentient being, including my enemies, from all suffering and help them obtain all happiness. I will take the whole responsibility on my own shoulders.

"Starting with my family and friends around me, I will take full responsibility to free them from all suffering and bring them all happiness up to enlightenment. Then I will take full responsibility for all the sentient beings in my area, my country, in the world, and in all the universes, freeing them all from suffering, including my enemies, and bringing them all to full enlightenment by myself alone.

"My kind mother sentient beings are unaware of the causes of happiness and suffering and are blinded by delusions, and so they only ever create the cause of suffering, like a blind person stumbling toward a cliff. In that way they are so pitiful. I have met a virtuous teacher, especially a Mahayana virtuous teacher, and so I can help them if I want. They have been so kind that, of course, I want to do anything I can to repay that kindness, therefore I will take the responsibility to lead them to happiness. Like a son or daughter will do whatever is necessary to help a sick mother, this is completely my responsibility.

"What sentient beings want is the highest happiness—enlightenment—and in order to lead them to enlightenment I must reveal the path. In order to do that I need to understand every single mind, every single method and means. The only possible way to do this is attaining enlightenment myself. There is no other solution to perfectly guide sentient beings.

"To practice the path, to attain enlightenment for the sake of all sentient beings, even if I have to suffer in the hell realm for as many eons as there are drops in the ocean, then I can do it, I can bear the suffering. That sentient beings must remain in samsara for even one minute, even a second, is so unbearable for me, like so many eons of suffering. Therefore I need to achieve enlightenment, quicker and quicker, which means entering the lightning-fast Vajrayana path."

7. BODHICHITTA

Think: "Having passed though the six steps from recognizing that all beings have been my mother to special attitude, I will then attain bodhichitta, the mind that seeks enlightenment for the sake of all sentient beings.

Bodhichitta is the thought to benefit every single sentient being, without exception, without excluding one single hell being, one single hungry ghost, one single animal, one single human being, one single demigod, one single god, one single intermediate-state being. It's the thought to benefit every being on the ground, in the ground, in the seas, in the air—every ant on every mountain, every fish in every ocean, every bird and insect in every field, every single sentient being in all the six realms. How wonderful I have the potential to attain this peerless mind."

APPENDIX 4: A TONGLEN MEDITATION

This meditation comes from The Wish-Fulfilling Golden Sun.

MOTIVATION

All sentient beings should be living in perfect happiness and its cause right now, but it is extremely difficult for them to achieve this from their side alone.

As we look at kind mother sentient beings, they appear lost, their wisdom eye blinded by the cataract of ignorance. Crazy with delusion, unconscious, they are always stepping over the very fearful precipice into the three lower realms.

All mother sentient beings are hungry for happiness and yet are completely ignorant of its causes; all mother sentient beings do not want even the slightest suffering and yet they create only its causes. They do not know of the peerless happiness of enlightenment or even the perfect happiness of liberation.

Lacking a virtuous teacher to lead them to those perfect goals, they commit many negative actions of the three doors of body, speech, and mind, and so are constantly being reborn in the lower realms.

But we have attained the perfect human rebirth with the possibilities of practicing the Dharma and fully developing method and wisdom, and having met the guru who can lead us to enlightenment, we are able to recognize what is to be practiced and what is to be avoided.

Therefore, for all these reasons we should develop great compassion for all mother sentient beings and take the responsibility on ourselves of leading them all to destroy the causes of suffering and attain the causes of perfect happiness. To do that, we offer all our happiness, including enlightenment, and all our belongings to all mother sentient beings and, in turn, take all their suffering and problems.

The practice of *taking* makes the practice of compassion practical and successful. The practice of *giving* makes the practice of love practical and successful.

Before starting this practice, great compassion should be meditated on deeply by thinking with feeling how good it would be if all mother sentient beings were completely released from suffering and by seeing all the different sufferings they are experiencing.

Also, great love should be deeply meditated on with strong, heartfelt feeling by thinking that all sentient beings should have great happiness, by visualizing giving them all the greatest happiness, including enlightenment, and rejoicing that we are able to do that. The main purpose of this practice is to control and destroy the self-cherishing mind.

The Actual Practice

As you slowly breathe in, imagine that you take all the suffering and causes of suffering of other living beings in through your nostrils in the form of black smoke.

If you have an illness or some other problem, focus first on all the numberless other beings with that same problem, then think of all the other problems experienced by living beings as well as their causes. As you slowly breathe in the black smoke, like plucking a thorn from their flesh, you immediately free all the numberless living beings from all their suffering.

The black smoke comes in through your nostrils and absorbs into the self-cherishing mind in your heart, completely destroying it. At the same time, the false I that ignorance holds to be truly existent also becomes completely empty, as it is empty in reality.

Meditate for as long as possible on this emptiness, the ultimate nature of the I. This becomes powerful purification. Each time you take upon yourself the suffering of other beings, you collect skies of merit, skies of good karma, purifying all obstacles to the development of your mind. It also purifies the cause not only of disease but of all other problems as well.

To do the meditation more elaborately, you can take from others—again, in the form of black smoke—all the undesirable environments that they experience. For example, imagine that you are breathing in the red-hot burning ground of the hot hells, the icy mountains of the cold hells, the inhospitable environments of the hungry ghosts and animals, and the dirty places of human beings. The black smoke comes in through your nostrils and down to your heart, where it absorbs into your self-cherishing mind and completely destroys it. Even the object that your self-cherishing treasures, the real I that appears to exist from its own side, becomes completely empty.

Your meditation should not stop with ordinary beings. You can also take all the subtle obscurations from the arhats and higher bodhisattvas in the same way. There is nothing to take from the gurus and buddhas; all you can do is make offerings to them.

Next, do the *giving* part. Generate loving-kindness by thinking that even though living beings want happiness, they lack it because they are ignorant of its causes or unable to create them. Even if they achieve some temporary happiness, they still lack the ultimate happiness of full enlightenment.

Think, "How wonderful it would be if all living beings had happiness and the causes of happiness." Then generate great loving-kindness by thinking, "I myself will bring them happiness and its causes."

Visualize your body as a wish-granting jewel that can grant all the wishes of living beings. Then, as you breath out, give everything you have to every living being in the form of pure white light. Give all your good karma of the three times and all the happiness that results from it up to enlightenment, your possessions, your family, your friends, and your body visualized as a wish-granting jewel. Also make offerings to all the enlightened beings.

All the living beings receive everything that they want, including all the realizations of the path to enlightenment. Those who want a friend find a good friend; those who want a job find a satisfying job; those who want a doctor find a qualified doctor; those who want medicine find excellent medicine; those who want a guru find a perfect guru. For those with incurable diseases, you become the medicine that cures them.

By visualizing this extensive practice of generosity, you incidentally create the cause of your own wealth and success in this life and in future lives. Being generous to others creates the cause of your own success, and with that success you can then benefit others even more. In addition to these temporary benefits, you will receive the ultimate benefit of enlightenment.

Since animals mainly need protection, visualize protecting them from being attacked by other animals and giving them food, shelter, and whatever else they need. They receive everything they want, and everything they receive becomes the cause for them to actualize the path and become enlightened.

In a similar way, give the worldly gods everything they need, such as protective armor. They also then all become enlightened. Give the arhats and bodhisattvas whatever realizations they need to complete the path to enlightenment.

As with the taking part, the next aspect of the meditation is to transform their environment. When you do the practice of giving to all the hell beings, visualize completely transforming their environment into a beautiful, blissful pure land, with perfect enjoyments and no suffering at all. For instance, all the red-hot iron houses, which are one with fire, become jewel palaces and mandalas. All the hell beings receive everything they want and then become enlightened.

Do the same for the hungry ghosts. Visualize transforming their environment into a pure realm and give them thousands of different foods that all taste like nectar. The hungry ghosts receive everything they need, but the ultimate point is that they all become enlightened.

In this way you can visualize the environment of the various beings transformed into a pure land free from all suffering, where the trees are wish-granting trees and the bird songs are mantras, where every sound is the sound of the Dharma, where the beings continuously receive the teachings from the deity. This is an unbelievable practice because it manifests the result right now.

It is even more beneficial to visualize *yourself* as a pure land. You *yourself* transform into the pure land, into all the needs of others, rather than manifesting them as external objects. You become everything for them: their food as nectar, their environment as a pure land, and so forth. How you benefit them is unimaginable, with incalculable benefits, like the lights of a great city we see from a plane as we are coming in to land. To give even one sentient being whatever they need is incredible, so thinking of transforming yourself into everything that every being needs is utterly unimaginable.

After everyone has become enlightened in this way, rejoice by thinking, "How wonderful it is that I have enlightened every single living being."

The Dedication of Merits

The merits created by the tonglen practice in the past, present, and future should be dedicated to the hell beings, becoming the enjoyments they need to cut off their ignorance and suffering. Similarly, such merits should be dedicated to the hungry ghosts, the animals, the humans, the demigods, and the gods.

The merits should be dedicated to the arhats and bodhisattvas in order for them to attain the highest realizations and so they become one with the Buddha, and to the gurus that their holy wishes be immediately realized. The merits appear as all kinds of different offerings for the enjoyment of gurus, bodhisattvas, and buddhas.

The final dedication of merits should be to prevent all hindrances to the teachings of the buddhas, so that they exist until the end of samsara.

APPENDIX 5: A MEDITATION ON UNIVERSAL RESPONSIBILITY

Lama Zopa gave this meditation at the Kopan course No. 36, Kopan Monastery, Nepal, November 2003.

When we attain the special attitude, the sixth of the seven points of cause and effect, we take on the responsibility for every sentient being, to lead them from all suffering and to every happiness, including enlightenment. We need to meditate on this universal responsibility over and over.

Think: "I have full responsibility for all the numberless hell beings, to free them from the most unbearable of all sufferings, the sufferings of the hell realm, and to lead them to all the happiness up to enlightenment."

Feel this way.

Think: "I have full responsibility for all the numberless hungry ghosts, to free them from the most unbearable sufferings of the hungry ghost realm and to lead them to all the happiness up to enlightenment."

Feel this way.

Think: "I have full responsibility for all the numberless animals, to free them from all the most unimaginable sufferings of the animal realm and to lead them to all the happiness up to enlightenment."

Feel this way.

Think: "I have full responsibility to free the numberless human beings from the oceans of problems and to lead them to all the happiness up to enlightenment."

Feel this way.

As it is mentioned in the teachings, we should include all the problems that we have gone through and those of our own friends and family members and people we know. We should contemplate the suffering we see around us: all the human beings' problems that we see every day on television, all the problems that we see in newspapers, all the global problems, the country's problems, the individual people's problems, the problems within relationships. We should contemplate all these problems and their causes—karma and delusion—and the three types of suffering: the suffering of suffering, the suffering of change, and pervasive compounding suffering.

There is so much we can achieve. Happiness is not just temporary samsaric pleasures—the pleasure of sleeping, the pleasure of eating, the pleasure of sex, the pleasure of singing, the pleasure of having wealth, the pleasure of being famous, and so forth. What worldly beings think of as happiness, due to their lack of wisdom, is nothing more than temporary pleasure and is actually only suffering.

Therefore our job is to free all beings from each of the three types of suffering.

Think: "I have full responsibility for the numberless demigods, to free them from oceans of their sufferings and to lead them to all the happiness up to enlightenment."

Feel this way.

Think: "I have full responsibility for the numberless gods, to free them from oceans of their sufferings, all their hallucinations, all their igno-rance, all their desires, which continuously create the cause of samsara and of being again reborn in the lower realms. I must do this and lead them to all the happiness up to enlightenment."

Feel this way.

Think: "I have full responsibility for the numberless intermediate-state beings, to free them from their most terrifying karmic appearances, the violence of the four elements, and all those unbelievable fears, and to lead them to all the happiness up to enlightenment."

Feel this way.

In conclusion, think: "Therefore, whether the other person practices compassion or not, first I myself must practice compassion. No matter how others treat me, I must only practice compassion to them; the change must come from my side.

"Therefore, to be able to offer all this service of leading sentient beings to all the happiness up to enlightenment, I need to attain all the realiza-tions of the lamrim path of the higher capable being. To do that, I need to actualize the graduated path of the middle capable being, and for that I need to actualize the graduated path of the lower capable being, starting from the perfect human rebirth.

"The root of the path is guru devotion, correctly devoting to the virtu-ous friend. Then I should live my life solely for others, offering service to others, obtaining happiness for the numberless other sentient beings."

GLOSSARY

Abhidharma (*Chö ngönpa*). One of the Three Baskets (*Tripitaka*) of the Buddhist canon, the others being the Vinaya and the Sutra; the systematized philosophical and psychological analysis of existence that is the basis of the Buddhist systems of tenets and mind training.

aggregates (*skandha*). The psychophysical constituents that make up a sentient being: form, feeling, discriminative awareness, compositional factors, and consciousness. Beings of the desire and form realms have all five, whereas beings in the formless realm no longer have the aggregate of form.

arhat (*drachompa*). Literally, "foe destroyer." A person who has destroyed his or her inner enemy, the delusions, and attained liberation from cyclic existence.

arya (*phakpa*). Literally, "noble." One who has realized the wisdom of emptiness.

Asanga, Arya (c. 300–370). The fourth-century Indian master who received directly from Maitreya Buddha the extensive, or method, lineage of Shakyamuni Buddha's teachings. Said to have founded the Cittamatra school of Buddhist philosophy. He is one of six great Indian scholars, known as the Six Ornaments.

aspirational bodhichitta (*mönsem jangchup sem*). Also called *wishing* or *aspiring bodhichitta*; the spontaneous, uncontrived mind that wishes to attain full enlightenment for the benefit of all sentient beings. *See also* bodhichitta; engaging bodhichitta.

Atisha Dipamkara Shrijnana (982–1054?). The renowned Indian master who went to Tibet in 1042 to help in the revival of Buddhism and established the Kadam tradition. His text *Lamp for the Path to Enlightenment* (*Bodhipathapradipa*) was the first lamrim text.

attachment. A disturbing thought that exaggerates the positive qualities of an object and wishes to possess it; one of the six root delusions.

Avalokiteshvara (Chenrezig). The buddha of compassion. A male meditational deity embodying the compassion of all the buddhas. The Dalai Lamas are said to be emanations of this deity.

bhumi. Ground, or level, as in the ten bodhisattva levels. *See* ten grounds or stages.

Bodhgaya. The small town in the state of Bihar in North India where Shakyamuni Buddha became enlightened.

bodhichitta (jangchup sem). A principal consciousness that combines the two factors of wishing to free all beings from suffering and wishing to attain enlightenment because of that; the spontaneous altruistic mind of enlightenment can be either aspirational or engaging.

bodhisattva (jangchup sempa). One who possesses bodhichitta.

bodhisattva vows. The vows taken when one enters the bodhisattva path.

Bodhisattvayana. The Bodhisattva Vehicle, another name for Paramitayana or Sutrayana; the nontantric Mahayana path.

Brahma. The Hindu god of creation, one of the principal three deities with Vishnu and Shiva.

buddha, a (sanggye). A fully enlightened being. One who has totally eliminated (*sang*) all obscurations veiling the mind and has fully developed (*gye*) all good qualities to perfection. See *also* enlightenment.

buddha nature. The clear light nature of mind possessed by all sentient beings; the potential for all sentient beings to become enlightened by removing the two obscurations to liberation and to omniscience.

Buxa Duar. A small town in West Bengal in eastern India where most of the Tibetan monks who escaped to India in 1959 were accommodated.

calm abiding (shamatha; shiné). A state of concentration in which the mind is able to abide steadily, without effort and for as long as desired, on an object of meditation. There are nine stages in its development.

capable being (lower, middle, or higher). See graduated path of the three capable beings.

causative phenomena. Things that come about in dependence upon causes and conditions; includes all objects experienced by the senses as well as the mind itself; impermanent phenomena.

chakra (*tsankhor*). One of five energy wheels or focal points of energy along the central channel (*sushumna* or *avadhuti, tsa uma*) upon which one's concentration is directed, especially during the completion stage of highest yoga tantra. The main chakras are the crown, throat, heart, navel, and secret place (the sex organ). In some systems, the first, at the brow, and the last, at the secret place, are omitted.

Chandragomin. A famous seventh-century Indian lay practitioner who challenged Chandrakirti to a debate that lasted many years. His writings include *Twenty Verses on the Bodhisattva Vows* (*Bodhisattvasamvaravimshaka*) and *Letter to a Disciple* (*Shishyalekha*).

Chandrakirti (c. 600–650). The Indian Buddhist philosopher who wrote commentaries on Nagarjuna's philosophy. His best-known work is *A Guide to the Middle Way* (*Madhyamakavatara*).

changeable mental factors (*anyathabhava-chaitta*). One of the six groups of mental factors; these four factors—sleep, contrition, investigation, and analysis—can be virtuous, nonvirtuous, or neutral, depending on the other factors involved. *See also* mental factors.

charya tantra. The second of four classes of tantra, also called *performance tantra* because it emphasizes rituals and recitation. *See also* four classes of tantra; kriya tantra; yoga tantra; highest yoga tantra.

Chekawa Yeshe Dorje, Geshe (1101–75). The Kadampa geshe who was inspired by Geshe Langri Tangpa's *Eight Verses on Mind Training* and later composed the famous thought-transformation text *Seven-Point Mind Training.*

Chenrezig. See Avalokiteshvara.

clear light (*ösel*). Very subtle mind. This subtlest state of mind occurs naturally at death and through successful tantric practice and is used by practitioners to realize emptiness. *See also* six yogas of Naropa.

common siddhi. See eight common siddhis.

compositional factors (*samskara*). Also called *conditioning factors*; the fourth of the five aggregates, consisting of forty-nine of the fifty-one mental factors (excluding feeling and cognition) that compound the result—that is, they are *compounding* as opposed to compounded phenomena, which refers to the result itself.

conventional bodhichitta (*kundzop jangchup sem*). The altruistic mind of enlightenment; a mental primary consciousness holding the two aspirations of wishing to benefit all sentient beings and wishing to attain enlightenment in order to do this. *See also* ultimate bodhichitta.

cyclic existence (*samsara*; *khorwa*). The six realms of conditioned existence: three lower—hell being (*naraka*), hungry ghost (*preta*), and animal (*tiryanc*); and three upper—human (*manushya*), demigod (*asura*), and god (*deva* or *sura*). It is the beginningless, recurring cycle of death and rebirth under the control of karma and delusion and fraught with suffering. It also refers to the contaminated aggregates of a sentient being.

dakini (*khandroma*). Literally, a "female sky-goer." A female being who helps arouse blissful energy in a qualified tantric practitioner.

Dalai Lama (b. 1935). Gyalwa Tenzin Gyatso. Revered spiritual leader of the Tibetan people and tireless worker for world peace; winner of the Nobel Peace Prize in 1989; a guru of Lama Zopa Rinpoche.

delusion (*klesha*, *nyönmong*). An obscuration covering the essentially pure nature of the mind, causing suffering and dissatisfaction; the main delusion is ignorance, and all the others come from this. *See also* root delusions; secondary delusions; three poisons.

demigod (*asura*, *lhamayin*). A being in the god realms who enjoys greater comfort and pleasure than human beings but who suffers from jealousy and quarreling. *See also* six realms; cyclic existence.

dependent arising. Also called *dependent origination*. The way that the self and phenomena exist conventionally as relative and interdependent. They come into existence in dependence upon causes and conditions; their parts; and most subtly, the mind imputing, or labeling, them. *See also* twelve links of dependent origination.

desire realm. One of the three realms of samsara, comprising the hell beings (*naraka*), hungry ghosts (*preta*), animals (*tiryanc*), humans (*manushya*), demigods (*asuras*), and the six lower classes of gods (*devas* or *asuras*); beings in this realm are preoccupied with desire for objects of the six senses. *See also* form realm; formless realm.

Dharamsala. A village in northwestern India, in Himachal Pradesh. The residence of His Holiness the Dalai Lama and the Tibetan government in exile.

dharmakaya (*chöku*). The truth body of a buddha (the other "body" being the form body, or rupakaya); the blissful omniscient mind of a buddha, the result of the wisdom side of the path. It can be divided into the wisdom body (*jnanakaya*; *ye she nyi ku*) and the nature body (*svabhavikakaya*; *ngo wo nyi ku*). *See also* rupakaya.

disturbing thoughts. See delusion.

disturbing-thought obscurations (*kleshavarana, nyöndrip*). Also known as *gross obscurations*, these are the less subtle of the two types of obscurations, the ones that block liberation. *See also* obscurations to knowledge; two obscurations.

Drepung Monastery. The largest of the three major Geluk monasteries, founded near Lhasa by one of Lama Tsongkhapa's disciples. Now reestablished in exile in South India.

Dromtönpa (*Dromtöm Gyalwai Jungne*) (1005–64). Kadampa master and one of Atisha's three main disciples, the other two being Khutön Tsöndrü Yungdrung and Ngok Lekpé Sherab (collectively known as "the trio Khu, Ngok, and Drom").

effortful (or contrived) bodhichitta. The wish to achieve enlightenment for all sentient beings that arises through reasoning, as opposed to aspirational bodhichitta, which is uncontrived. *See also* bodhichitta; effortless bodhichitta.

effortless bodhichitta. The spontaneous, uncontrived wish to achieve full enlightenment for the benefit of all sentient beings, without needing reasoning, like a mother's concern for a beloved child. *See also* bodhichitta; effortful bodhichitta.

eight common siddhis (*sadharanasiddhi*; *thunmong gi ngödrup*). Mundane attainments, usually listed as the sword of invincibility; the eye potion enabling one to see the gods; swift footedness (the ability to cover great distance extremely quickly); invisibility; the art of extracting the essence (rejuvenation); becoming a sky-traveler (the ability to fly); the ability to make medicinal (invisibility) pills; and the power of perceiving treasures under the earth, as opposed to the supreme siddhi (enlightenment). *See also* siddhi.

eight freedoms. The eight states from which a perfect human rebirth is free: being born as a hell being, hungry ghost, animal, long-life god, or barbarian, or in a dark age when no buddha has descended, holding wrong views, and being born with defective mental or physical faculties. *See also* ten richnesses.

eight Mahayana precepts. One-day vows to abandon killing; stealing; lying; sexual contact; taking intoxicants; sitting on high seats or beds; eating at the wrong time; and singing, dancing, and wearing perfumes and jewelry.

eight worldly dharmas. The worldly concerns that generally motivate the actions of ordinary beings: being happy when given gifts and unhappy when not given them; wanting to be happy and not wanting to be unhappy; wanting praise and not wanting criticism; wanting a good reputation and not wanting a bad reputation.

emptiness (*shunyata*; *tongpanyi*). The absence, or lack, of true existence. Ultimately every phenomenon is empty of existing truly or from its own side or independently.

engaging bodhichitta (*jugsem jangchup sem*). The altruistic mind of enlightenment that actively engages in the six perfections and the four means of drawing sentient beings to the Dharma after the bodhisattva vows have been taken. *See also* aspirational bodhichitta; bodhichitta; four means of drawing disciples to the Dharma; six perfections.

enlightenment (*bodhi*; *jangchup*). Full awakening; buddhahood; omniscience. The ultimate goal of a Mahayana Buddhist, attained when all limitations have been removed from the mind and one's positive potential has been completely and perfectly realized. It is a state characterized by infinite compassion, wisdom, and skill.

equalizing and exchanging self and others. The second of two methods used in Tibetan Buddhism to develop bodhichitta. The other method is the *seven points of cause and effect.*

equanimity. The absence of the usual discrimination of sentient beings into friend, enemy, or stranger, deriving from the realization that all sentient beings are equal in wanting happiness and not wanting suffering and that since beginningless time all beings have been all things to each other. An impartial mind that serves as the basis for the development of great love, great compassion, and bodhichitta.

five aggregates. See aggregates.

five paths. The paths along which beings progress to liberation and enlightenment: the path of merit, the path of preparation, the path of seeing, the path of meditation, and the path of no more learning.

five powers. The five forces to be practiced both in this life and at the time of death: the power of motivation, the power of acquaintance, the power of the white seed (developing positive qualities), the power of destruction (self-cherishing), and the power of prayer.

form realm (rupadhatu; zukkyi kham). The second of samsara's three realms, with seventeen classes of gods. *See also* desire realm; formless realm.

formless realm (arupyadhatu; zukmé kyi kham). The highest of samsara's three realms, with four classes of gods involved in formless meditations: limitless sky, limitless consciousness, nothingness, and neither existence nor nonexistence (also called *tip of samsara*). *See also* desire realm; form realm.

four classes of tantra. The division of tantra into *kriya* (action), *charya* (performance), yoga, and highest yoga tantra (*anuttara yoga tantra*; also sometimes referred to as *maha-anuttara yoga tantra*).

four immeasurables (apramana). Also known as *the four immeasurable thoughts* or the *four sublime attitudes (brahmavihara)*, these are four states of mind or aspirations: loving-kindness (*maitri; jampa*), compassion (*karuna; nyingjé*), sympathetic joy (*mudita; gaba*), and equanimity (*upeksha; tang nyom*). They are usually expressed in the prayer—may all sentient beings have happiness and its causes, be free from suffering and its causes, be inseparable from sorrowless bliss, and abide in equanimity—or longer variations of the same.

four kindnesses of the mother. The second of the seven points of cause and effect technique for developing bodhichitta, remembering the kindness of the mother can include how the mother has been kind in four ways: the kindness of giving her body, the kindness of protecting our life from danger, the kindness of bearing hardship, and the kindness of leading us in the ways of the world. The lineage of this came to Lama Zopa Rinpoche from Khunu Lama Tenzin Gyaltsen Rinpoche. *See also* seven points of cause and effect.

four means of drawing disciples to the Dharma. The second of two sets of practices of the bodhisattva (the other is the *six perfections*): giving, speaking kind words, teaching to the level of the student, and practicing what you teach.

four noble truths. The subject of Buddha's first turning of the wheel of Dharma: the truths of suffering, the origin of suffering, the cessation of suffering, and the path leading to the cessation of suffering as seen by an arya.

four unknowing minds. The four unknowing minds are the four types of very subtle ignorance that arhats and higher bodhisattvas still have that a buddha does not, due to the subtle imprints of delusions not yet fully eliminated. They are the inability to see the secret actions of a buddha, the inability to see the subtle karma of sentient beings, the inability to see things that happened an incredible length of time ago, and the inability to see an incredible distance.

four ways of clinging. If you cling to this life, you are not a Dharma practitioner; if you cling to future lives' samsara, your mind is not in renunciation; if you cling to cherishing the I, that is not bodhichitta; if you cling to the I, that is not the right view.

Ganden Monastery. The first of the three great Geluk monastic universities near Lhasa, founded in 1409 by Lama Tsongkhapa. It was badly damaged in the 1960s and has now been reestablished in exile in South India.

Geluk. One of the four main traditions of Tibetan Buddhism, it was founded by Lama Tsongkhapa in the early fifteenth century and has been propagated by such illustrious masters as the successive Dalai Lamas and Panchen Lamas.

Gen. Literally, "elder." A title of respect.

geshe. Literally, "a spiritual friend." The title conferred on those who have completed extensive studies and examinations at Geluk monastic universities. The highest level of geshe is the *lharampa.*

gönpa. Usually refers to the main meditation hall, or temple, within a monastery.

graduated path (lamrim). A presentation of Shakyamuni Buddha's teachings in a form suitable for the step-by-step training of a disciple. The lamrim was first formulated by the great Indian teacher Atisha when he came to Tibet in 1042. *See also* three principal aspects of the path; Atisha.

graduated path of the three capable beings. Also known as the *three scopes* or *three levels of practice*, the three levels of the lower, middle, and higher capable being, based on the motivations of trying to attain a better future rebirth, liberation, and enlightenment. *See also* higher capable being; middle capable being; lower capable being.

great compassion (mahakaruna; nyingjé chenpo). The compassion that includes not only the wish for all sentient beings to be free from suffering and its causes but the heartfelt determination to accomplish this on one's own. *See also* immeasurable compassion.

guru devotion. The sutra or tantra practice of seeing the guru as a buddha, then devoting oneself to him or her with thought and action.

Guru Puja (Lama Chöpa). A special highest yoga tantra practice composed by Panchen Losang Chökyi Gyaltsen. *See also* highest yoga tantra.

happy transmigratory being. A samsaric being in the realms of gods (*devas* or *suras*), demigods (*asuras*), or humans (*manushyas*).

Heaven of Thirty-Three. The highest of the god-realm abodes in Buddhist cosmology; it is atop Mount Meru and ruled by Indra.

hell (narak). The samsaric realm with the greatest suffering. There are eight hot hells, eight cold hells, and four neighboring hells. *See also* six realms; cyclic existence.

heresy (*logta*). Also called *mistaken wrong views*, one of the five afflicted views that are part of the root afflictions. A deluded intelligence that rejects the existence of something that exists, such as karma, reincarnation, the Three Jewels, and so forth, and ascribes existence to that which is nonexistent. It is also the holding of incorrect views about the guru.

Heruka Chakrasamvara. Male meditational deity from the mother tantra class of highest yoga tantra. He is the principal deity connected with the Heruka Vajrasattva practice.

higher capable being. The highest of the three levels of practice or scopes, it has the goal of full enlightenment. *See also* graduated path of the three capable beings; lower capable being; middle capable being.

highest yoga tantra (*anuttara yoga tantra*). The fourth and supreme division of tantric practice, sometimes called *maha-anuttara yoga tantra*. It consists of the generation and completion stages. Through this practice one can attain full enlightenment within one lifetime. *See also* four classes of tantra; kriya tantra; charya tantra; yoga tantra.

Hinayana. Literally, "Small, or Lesser, Vehicle." One of the two general divisions of Buddhism. Hinayana practitioners' motivation for following the Dharma path is principally their intense wish for personal liberation from conditioned existence, or samsara. Two types of Hinayana practitioner are identified: hearers and solitary realizers. *See also* shravaka; pratyekabuddha; individual liberation.

hungry ghost (*preta*). The hungry ghost realm is one of the three lower realms of cyclic existence, where the main suffering is hunger and thirst. *See also* six realms; cyclic existence.

ignorance (*avidya*; *marigpa*). Literally, "not seeing" that which exists or the way in which things exist. There are basically two kinds: ignorance of karma and ignorance of ultimate truth. The fundamental delusion from which all others spring. The first of the twelve links of dependent origination. *See also* twelve links of dependent origination.

immeasurable compassion. The wish for all sentient beings to be free from all suffering and its causes. *See also* great compassion.

impermanence (mitakpa). The gross and subtle levels of the transience of phenomena. The moment things and events come into existence, their disintegration has already begun.

imprint (pagcha). The seed, or potential, left on the mind by positive or negative actions of body, speech, and mind.

individual liberation. The liberation achieved by the hearer (*shravaka*) or the solitary realizer (*pratyekabuddha*) within the Hinayana tradition, as compared with enlightenment achieved by a practitioner of the Mahayana tradition.

inherent (or intrinsic) existence. What phenomena are empty of; the object of negation or refutation. To ignorance, phenomena appear to exist independently, in and of themselves, to exist inherently.

initiation. Transmission received from a tantric master allowing a disciple to engage in the practices of a particular meditational deity. It is also referred to as an *empowerment* and can be given as a full empowerment (*wang*) or a permission to practice (*jenang*).

inner fire. See tummo.

intermediate state (bardo). The state between death and rebirth.

Jampa Wangdu, Geshe (d. 1984). An ascetic meditator who was a close friend of Lama Yeshe and a guru of Lama Zopa Rinpoche.

Jataka Tales. The volumes of stories, mostly in the Pali canon but also within the Sanskrit and Tibetan texts, that relate to the lives of Shakyamuni Buddha before he became enlightened. The tales generally hold strong moral lessons.

Kadam. The order of Tibetan Buddhism founded in the eleventh century by Atisha, Dromtönpa, and their followers, the Kadampa geshes; the forerunner of the Geluk school, whose members are sometimes called the New Kadampas. *See also* Atisha; Dromtönpa.

Kadampa geshe. A practitioner of Kadam lineage. Kadampa geshes are renowned for their practice of thought transformation.

Kagyü. The order of Tibetan Buddhism founded in the eleventh century by Marpa, Milarepa, Gampopa, and their followers. One of the four main schools of Tibetan Buddhism. *See also* Geluk; Nyingma; Sakya.

Kamalashila (740–95). The great Indian scholar from Nalanda Monastery who accompanied Shantarakshita to Tibet to try to revitalize Buddhism there. He is noted for his three texts called *Stages of Meditation* (*Bhavanakrama*).

Kangyur. Literally, "translation of the (Buddha's) word." The part of the Tibetan canon that contains the sutras and tantras. It contains 108 volumes. *See also* Tengyur.

Khunu Lama Tenzin Gyaltsen (1894–1977). Also known as *Negi Lama* and *Khunu Rinpoche*, he was an Indian scholar of Sanskrit and Tibetan and a great master and teacher of the Rimé (nonsectarian) tradition of Tibetan Buddhism. He famously gave teachings to His Holiness the Dalai Lama on Shantideva's *Guide* and was also a guru of Lama Zopa Rinpoche. He composed a well-known text, *The Jewel Lamp: A Praise of Bodhichitta*, translated into English as *Vast as the Heavens, Deep as the Sea.*

Kirti Tsenshab Rinpoche (1926–2006). A highly attained and learned ascetic yogi who lived in Dharamsala, India, and who was one of Lama Zopa Rinpoche's gurus.

Kopan Monastery. The monastery near Boudhanath in the Kathmandu Valley, Nepal, founded by Lama Yeshe and Lama Zopa Rinpoche.

kriya tantra. The first of four classes of tantra, also called *action tantra* because it emphasizes external activities such as prayers, mudras, and so forth. *See also* four classes of tantra; charya tantra; yoga tantra, highest yoga tantra.

kundalini. Literally, "coiled." The system of energy channels (*nadi*) and centers (*chakra*) within the human body. *See also* chakra.

lamrim. The graduated path. A presentation of Shakyamuni Buddha's teachings in a form suitable for the step-by-step training of a disciple. *See also* Atisha; three principal aspects of the path.

Lamrim Chenmo (*The Great Treatise on the Stages of the Path to Enlightenment*). Lama Tsongkhapa's most important work, a commentary on Atisha's *Lamp for the Path to Enlightenment*, the fundamental lamrim text.

Langri Tangpa (1054–1123). Dorje Senge. Author of the famous *Eight Verses on Mind Training*.

Lawudo. A small area in the Solu Khumbu region of Nepal about three hours' walk west from Namche Bazaar just above Mende. Site of the cave where the Lawudo Lama meditated for more than twenty years and now the Lawudo Retreat Center. Lama Zopa Rinpoche is the reincarnation of the Lawudo Lama.

liberation (*nirvana* or *moksha*). The state of complete freedom from samsara; the goal of a practitioner seeking his or her own escape from suffering. "Lower nirvana" is used to refer to this state of self-liberation, while "higher nirvana" refers to the supreme attainment of the full enlightenment of buddhahood. Natural nirvana is the fundamentally pure nature of reality, where all things and events are devoid of any inherent, intrinsic, or independent reality.

lineage lama. A spiritual teacher who is in the line of direct guru-disciple transmission of teachings, from the Buddha to the teachers of the present day.

Ling Rinpoche (1903–83). The late senior tutor to His Holiness the Fourteenth Dalai Lama; the ninety-seventh Ganden Tripa; a guru of Lama Zopa Rinpoche. His reincarnation now teaches in Asia and the rest of the world.

loving-kindness (*maitri*; *yiong jampa*). In the context of the seven points of cause and effect, the wish for all beings to have happiness and its causes, with the added dimension of *yiong* ("beautiful" or "affectionate"); often translated as "affectionate loving-kindness." Rinpoche suggests this is the "loving-kindness of seeing others in beauty." *See also* seven points of cause and effect.

lower capable being. The first of the three levels of practice or scopes, the lower capable being has the goal of a better future existence. *See also* graduated path of the three capable beings; higher capable being; middle capable being.

lower realms. The three realms of cyclic existence with the most suffering: the hell being (*naraka*), hungry ghost (*preta*), and animal (*tiryanc*) realms. *See also* six realms; cyclic existence.

Madhyamaka (*umapa*). The Middle Way school of Buddhist philosophy; a system of analysis founded by Nagarjuna, based on the *Prajnaparamita*, or perfection of wisdom, sutras of Shakyamuni Buddha, and considered to be the supreme presentation of the wisdom of emptiness. This view holds that all phenomena are dependent originations and thereby avoids the mistaken extremes of self-existence and nonexistence, or eternalism and nihilism. It has two divisions, Svatantrika and Prasangika. With Cittamatra, one of the two Mahayana schools of philosophy.

Mahayana. Literally, "Great Vehicle." It is one of the two general divisions of Buddhism. Mahayana practitioners' motivation for following the Dharma path is principally their intense wish for all mother sentient beings to be liberated from conditioned existence, or samsara, and to attain the full enlightenment of buddhahood. The Mahayana has two divisions, Paramitayana (Sutrayana) and Vajrayana (a.k.a. Tantrayana or Mantrayana).

main mind. See principal consciousness.

Maitreya (*Jampa*). After Shakyamuni Buddha, the next (fifth) of the thousand buddhas of this fortunate eon to descend to turn the wheel of Dharma. Presently residing in the pure land of Tushita (Ganden). Recipient of the method lineage of Shakyamuni Buddha's teachings, which, in a mystical transmission, he passed on to Asanga.

mala. A rosary of beads for counting mantras.

mandala (*khyilkhor*). A circular diagram symbolic of the entire universe. The abode of a meditational deity.

Manjushri (*Jampalyang*). The bodhisattva (or buddha) of wisdom. Recipient of the wisdom lineage of Shakyamuni Buddha's teachings, which he passed on to Nagarjuna.

mantra. Literally, "mind protection." Mantras are Sanskrit syllables— usually recited in conjunction with the practice of a particular meditational deity—and embody the qualities of the deity with which they are associated.

Mara. Personification of the delusions that distract us from Dharma practice; what Shakyamuni Buddha overcame under the bodhi tree as he strove for enlightenment.

maras. The four external and internal hindrances or obstacles to our spiritual progress. They are the mara of the (contaminated) aggregates, the mara of delusions, the mara of the Lord of Death, and the mara of the deva's son (the demon of desire and temptation).

Marpa (1012–96). Founder of the Kagyü tradition of Tibetan Buddhism. He was a renowned tantric master and translator, a disciple of Naropa, and the guru of Milarepa.

meditation (*gom*). Familiarization of the mind with a virtuous object. There are two types: single-pointed (*jok gom*), also called *stabilizing*, *placement*, or *fixed*; and analytic or insight meditation (*che gom*). *See also* single-pointed concentration.

mental factors (*chaitasika dharma*; *semlay jungwa chö*). Literally, "arising from the mind," as defined by Vasubandhu, a secondary aspect of the mind that apprehends a particular quality of the object that the main mind is perceiving. There are traditionally fifty-one mental factors divided into six groups: five omnipresent factors, five object-determining factors, eleven virtuous factors, six root afflictions, twenty secondary afflictions, and four changeable factors.

merit. Positive imprints left on the mind by virtuous, or Dharma, actions. The principal cause of happiness. The merit of virtue, when coupled with the merit of wisdom, eventually results in rupakaya. *See also* two merits.

middle capable being. The second of the three levels of practice or scopes, the middle capable being has the goal of liberation from suffering. *See also* graduated path of the three capable beings; higher capable being; lower capable being.

Milarepa (1040–1123). Tibet's great yogi, who achieved enlightenment in his lifetime under the tutelage of his guru, Marpa, who was a contemporary of Atisha. One of the founding fathers of the Kagyü school.

mind (*citta, sem*). Synonymous with *consciousness* and *sentience*. Defined as that which is "clear and knowing"; a formless entity that has the ability to perceive objects. Mind is divided into six principal consciousnesses and fifty-one mental factors. *See also* mental factors; principal consciousness.

mind training (*lojong*). *See* thought transformation.

Mount Meru. The mythical center of the universe in Buddhist cosmology.

Nagarjuna (c. 150–250). The Indian philosopher and tantric adept who propounded the Madhyamaka philosophy of emptiness. He is one of six great Indian scholars, known as the Six Ornaments.

nagas. Snakelike beings of the animal realm who live in or near bodies of water; commonly associated with fertility of the land but can also function as protectors of religion.

Nalanda. A Mahayana Buddhist monastic university founded in the fifth century in North India, not far from Bodhgaya, which served as a major source of the Buddhist teachings that spread to Tibet.

Naropa (1016–1100). The Indian mahasiddha, a disciple of Tilopa and guru of Marpa and Maitripa, who transmitted many tantric lineages, including that of the renowned *six yogas of Naropa*.

Nyingma. The Old Translation school of Tibetan Buddhism, which traces its teachings back to the time of Padmasambhava, the eighth-century Indian tantric master invited to Tibet by King Trisong Detsen to clear away hindrances to the establishment of Buddhism in Tibet. The first of the four main schools of Tibetan Buddhism. *See also* Geluk; Kagyü; Sakya.

nyungné. A two-day Thousand-Armed Chenrezig retreat that involves fasting, prostrations, and silence.

object-determining mental factors (*vishayapratiniyama-chaitta*; *semjung yülngé*). One of the six groups of mental factors, the factor that enhances the experience of the object in some way. There are five: aspiration, belief, mindfulness, stabilization, and wisdom. *See also* mental factors.

obscurations to knowledge (*jneyavarana*; *shedrip*). One of the two obscurations, the more subtle ones that block enlightenment; also known as *subtle obscurations*, *obscurations to enlightenment*, and *cognitive obscurations*. *See also* disturbing-thought obscurations; two obscurations.

om mani padme hum. The *mani*; the mantra of Chenrezig, buddha of compassion.

omnipresent mental factors (*sarvatraga-chaitta*; *semjung kündro*). One of the six groups of mental factors, the factor that must be present for a mind to apprehend an object. There are five: feeling, discrimination, intention, mental engagement, and contact. *See also* mental factors.

Pabongka Dechen Nyingpo (1871–1941). An influential and charismatic lama of the Geluk order, Pabongka Rinpoche was the root guru of His Holiness the Dalai Lama's senior and junior tutors. He also gave the teachings compiled in *Liberation in the Palm of Your Hand*.

Panchen Losang Chökyi Gyaltsen (1570–1662). The first Panchen Lama, who composed *Guru Puja* and *Path to Bliss Leading to Omniscience*, a famous lamrim text; a tutor of the Fifth Dalai Lama. *See also* Guru Puja.

pandit. Scholar; learned person.

paramita. *See* six perfections.

Paramitayana. Literally, "Perfection Vehicle." The Bodhisattva Vehicle; a section of the Mahayana sutra teachings; one of the two forms of Mahayana, the other being Vajrayana. Also called *Bodhisattvayana* or *Sutrayana*.

parinirvana. The final nirvana the Buddha attained when he passed away in Kushinagar.

penetrative insight (*vipashyana*). The deep analysis of an object, usually emptiness, that conjoins with calm abiding (*shamatha*) to gain the direct realization.

perfect human rebirth. The rare human state, qualified by eight freedoms and ten richnesses, which is the ideal condition for practicing the Dharma and attaining enlightenment. *See also* eight freedoms; ten richnesses.

perfections (*paramita*). *See* six perfections.

performance tantra (charya tantra). See charya tantra.

pervasive compounding suffering. The most subtle of the three types of suffering, it refers to the nature of the five aggregates, which are contaminated by karma and delusions. *See also* aggregates; three types of suffering.

Potowa, Geshe (1031–1105). Also known as *Potowa Rinchen Sel,* he entered Reting Monastery in 1058 and became its abbot for a short time; one of the three great disciples of Dromtönpa, patriarch of the Kadampa lineage. *See also* Dromtönpa.

powa. The practice whereby the consciousness is forcibly ejected from the body into a pure land just before the moment of death.

Prasangika Madhyamaka (Uma thalgyurpa). The Middle Way Consequence school, a subschool of the Middle Way school of Buddhist philosophy. *See also* Madhyamaka; Svatantrika Madhyamaka.

pratyekabuddha. A solitary realizer; a Hinayana practitioner who strives for nirvana in solitude, without relying on a teacher. *See also* shravaka.

principal consciousness (vijnana; namshé). Synonymous with *main mind* or *primary mind* or *consciousness,* one of the two divisions of mind, the other being mental factors; that which is clear and knowing and which perceives its object directly, without any conceptual overlay. There are six main minds, one for each sensory base (eye, ear, and so forth) and the mental main mind, which can be either perceptual or conceptual. *See also* mental factors.

puja. Literally, "offering"; a religious ceremony, usually used to describe an offering ceremony such as the Offering to the Spiritual Master (*Guru Puja*).

pure land. A pure land of a buddha is a place where there is no suffering. In some but not all pure lands, after taking birth, the practitioner receives teachings directly from the buddha of that pure land, allowing them to actualize the rest of the path and then become enlightened.

purification. The eradication from the mind of negative imprints left by past nonvirtuous actions, which would otherwise ripen into suffering. The most effective methods of purification employ the four opponent powers, the powers of the object, regret, resolve, and the remedy.

realization. A valid mind that holds a stable, correct understanding of a Dharma subject, such as emptiness, that effects a deep change within the continuum of the person. The effortless experience resulting from study and meditation supported by guru devotion and ripened by purification and merit-building practices.

refuge. The door to the Dharma path. Having taken refuge from the heart, we become an inner being or Buddhist. There are three levels of refuge—Hinayana, Mahayana, and Vajrayana—and two or three causes necessary for taking refuge: fearing the sufferings of samsara in general and lower realms in particular; faith that Buddha, Dharma, and Sangha have the qualities and power to lead us to happiness, liberation, and enlightenment; and (for Mahayana refuge) compassion for all sentient beings.

relative bodhichitta. See conventional bodhichitta.

renunciation. The state of mind of not having the slightest attraction to samsaric pleasures for even a second and having the strong wish for liberation. The first of the three principal aspects of the path to enlightenment. *See also* bodhichitta; emptiness.

rinpoche. Literally, "precious one." Epithet for an incarnate lama, that is, one who has intentionally taken rebirth in a human form to benefit sentient beings on the path to enlightenment.

root delusions. One of the six groups of mental factors, these are the deluded or nonvirtuous minds that subsequently lead to the secondary afflictions. There are six: desire, anger, pride, ignorance, afflicted doubt, and afflicted view. *See also* mental factors.

rupakaya (zukku). The form body of a fully enlightened being; the result of the complete and perfect accumulation of merit. It has two aspects: *sambhogakaya* (enjoyment body), in which the enlightened mind appears to benefit highly realized bodhisattvas; and *nirmanakaya* (emanation body), in which the enlightened mind appears to benefit ordinary beings. *See also* dharmakaya.

sadhana. Method of accomplishment; the step-by-step instructions for practicing the meditations related to a particular meditational deity.

Sakya. One of the four main schools of Tibetan Buddhism, it was founded in the province of Tsang in 1073 by Khön Könchok Gyalpo (1034–1102), the main disciple of Drogmi Lotsawa. *See also* Geluk; Kagyü; Nyingma.

samsara (khorwa). Cyclic existence; the six realms of conditioned existence, three lower—hell being (*naraka*), hungry ghost (*preta*), and animal (*tiryanc*)—and three upper—human (*manushya*), demigod (*asura*), and god (*deva* or *sura*). The beginningless, recurring cycle of death and rebirth under the control of karma and delusion, fraught with suffering. Also refers to the contaminated aggregates of a sentient being.

Sangha (gendun). Spiritual community; the third of the Three Jewels of Refuge. In Tibetan *gen dun* literally means "intending (*dun*) to virtue (*gen*)." Absolute Sangha are those who have directly realized emptiness; relative Sangha refers to a group of at least four fully ordained monks or nuns.

secondary delusions. One of the six groups of mental factors, these refer to the deluded or nonvirtuous minds that arise in dependence on the root delusions, such as attachment, anger, and so forth. There are twenty: belligerence, resentment, concealment, spite, jealousy, miserliness, deceit, dissimulation, haughtiness, harmfulness, nonshame (shamelessness), nonembarrassment (inconsideration), lethargy, excitement, nonfaith (faithlessness), laziness, nonconscientiousness, forgetfulness, nonintrospection (nonalertness), and distraction. *See also* mental factors.

self-cherishing. The self-centered attitude of considering your own happiness to be more important than that of others; the main obstacle to the realization of bodhichitta.

sentient being. An unenlightened being; any being whose mind is not completely free from gross and subtle ignorance.

Sera Monastery. One of the three great Geluk monasteries near Lhasa; founded in the early fifteenth century by Jamchen Chöjé, a disciple of Lama Tsongkhapa; now also established in exile in South India. It has two colleges, Sera Je, with which Lama Zopa Rinpoche is connected, and Sera Mey.

Serlingpa. A renowned tenth-century Sumatran master. Atisha traveled to Sumatra and for twelve years received teachings on thought transformation (*lojong*) and bodhichitta from him.

seven points of cause and effect. One of the two techniques within Mahayana Buddhism for developing bodhichitta. There are six causes: recognizing that all beings have been our mother, recalling the kindness of those beings, resolving to repay that kindness, loving-kindness, great compassion, and special attitude. These lead to the one result: bodhichitta.

shamatha. See calm abiding.

Shantideva (685–763). The Indian Buddhist philosopher and bodhisattva who propounded the Prasangika Madhyamaka view. He wrote the quintessential Mahayana text, *A Guide to the Bodhisattva's Way of Life* (*Bodhicaryavatara*).

Shariputra. One of the two principal disciples of the Buddha, with Maudgalyayana.

shravaka. A hearer; a Hinayana practitioner who strives for nirvana on the basis of listening to teachings from a teacher. *See also* pratyekabuddha.

siddhi. A realization or attainment, either common or supreme. Common siddhis refer to psychic powers acquired as a byproduct of the spiritual path; supreme siddhi refers to great liberation or enlightenment. *See also* eight common siddhis.

single-pointed concentration (*samadhi*). A state of deep meditative absorption; single-pointed concentration on the actual nature of things, free from discursive thought and dualistic conceptions.

six perfections (*paramita*). The practices of a bodhisattva. On the basis of bodhichitta, a bodhisattva practices the six perfections: generosity, morality, patience, enthusiastic perseverance, concentration, and wisdom. *See also* Paramitayana.

six realms. The general way that Buddhism divides the whole of cyclic existence, with three suffering realms (hell, hungry ghost, and animal) and three fortunate realms (human, demigod, and god). *See also* cyclic existence.

six yogas of Naropa. Six advanced tantric practices devised by the great Indian pandit Naropa (1016–1100): the yoga of inner fire (*tummo*), of illusory body (*gyulu*), of clear light (*ösel*), of the dream state (*milam*), of the intermediate state (*bardo*), and of the transference of consciousness (*powa*).

solitary realizer. See pratyekabuddha.

special attitude. The sixth of the seven points of cause and effect technique for developing bodhichitta, where the practitioner takes on the responsibility to lead all sentient beings to enlightenment by themselves. This is the final step before actually attaining bodhichitta. *See also* seven points of cause and effect.

spirits. Beings not usually visible to ordinary people; they can belong to the hungry ghost or god realms, and they can be beneficent as well as harmful.

stupa. Buddhist reliquary object ranging in size from huge to a few inches in height and representing the enlightened mind.

subtle obscurations (*shedrip*). *See* obscurations to knowledge.

suffering of change. What is normally regarded as pleasure, which because of its transitory nature sooner or later turns into suffering. *See also* three types of suffering.

suffering of suffering. Also called the *suffering of pain*, the commonly recognized suffering experiences of pain, discomfort, and unhappiness. *See also* three types of suffering.

sutra. A discourse of the Buddha recognized as a canonical text.

Sutra. One of the Three Baskets of the Buddha's teachings. *See also* Abhidharma; Vinaya.

Sutrayana. The Sutra Vehicle, another name for Bodhisattvayana or Paramitayana; the nontantric path that encompasses both Hinayana practices such as the thirty-seven wings of enlightenment and Mahayana bodhisattva practices such as the six perfections. Because the two accumulations of merit and wisdom—the respective causes of the rupakaya and the dharmakaya—are gathered in this vehicle, it is also called the *Causal Vehicle.*

Svatantrika Madhyamaka (Uma rangyü). The Middle Way Autonomous school, a subschool of the Middle Way school of Buddhist philosophy. *See also* Madhyamaka; Prasangika Madhyamaka.

taking and giving (tonglen). The meditation practice of generating bodhichitta by taking on the suffering of others and giving them our happiness.

tantra. The secret teachings of the Buddha; a scriptural text and the teachings and practices it contains. Also called *Vajrayana* or *Mantrayana.*

Tara (Drölma). A female meditational deity who embodies the enlightened activity of all the buddhas; often referred to as the mother of the buddhas of the past, present, and future. The *Praises to the Twenty-One Taras* prayer is usually recited before debate sessions at Tibetan Buddhist monasteries.

ten grounds or stages (bhumi). The ten stages a bodhisattva progresses through once reaching the path of seeing: the first level being there, the second to seventh during the path of meditation, and the eighth to tenth during the path of no more learning.

ten nonvirtuous actions. General actions to be avoided so as not to create negative karma. Three of body (killing, stealing, and sexual misconduct); four of speech (lying, speaking harshly, slandering, and gossiping); and three of mind (covetousness, ill will, and wrong views).

ten richnesses. Along with the eight freedoms, the defining features of the perfect human rebirth: being born as a human being; in a Dharma country and with perfect mental and physical faculties; not having committed any of the five immediate negativities; having faith in the Buddha's teachings; when a buddha has descended; when the teachings have been revealed; when the complete teachings still exist; when there are still followers of the teachings; and having the necessary conditions to practice the Dharma, such as the kindness of others. *See also* eight freedoms.

Tengyur. Literally, "translation of the commentaries." Part of the

Tibetan canon that contains the Indian pandits' commentaries on the Buddha's teachings. It contains about 225 volumes (depending on the edition).

Thirty-Five Buddhas. Also called *Thirty-Five Confession Buddhas.* Used in the practice of confessing and purifying negative karmas, the group of thirty-five buddhas visualized while reciting the *Sutra of the Three Heaps* and performing prostrations.

Thokmé Sangpo (1295–1371). Also known as *Gyalsä Ngulchu Thokmé.* A great master of the Nyingma and Sakya traditions and author of *Thirty-Seven Practices of a Bodhisattva* and a famous commentary on Shantideva's *A Guide to the Bodhisattva's Way of Life.*

thought transformation (*lojong*). Also known as *mind training* or *mind transformation.* A powerful approach to the development of bodhichitta, in which the mind is trained to use all situations, both happy and unhappy, as a means to destroy self-cherishing and self-grasping.

Three Baskets (*Tripitaka*). The three divisions of the Dharma: Vinaya, Sutra, and Abhidharma.

Three Jewels (*Triratna, Könchok Sum*). Also called the *Triple Gem* or the *Three Rare Sublime Ones*; the objects of Buddhist refuge: the Buddha, Dharma, and Sangha. Lama Zopa Rinpoche prefers "Three Rare Sublime Ones" as a more direct translation of *Könchok Sum.*

three poisons. Attachment, anger, and ignorance.

three principal aspects of the path. The three main divisions of the lamrim: renunciation, bodhichitta, and the right view (of emptiness).

Three Rare Sublime Ones. See Three Jewels.

three types of suffering. The suffering of suffering, the suffering of change, and pervasive compounding suffering.

tonglen. See taking and giving.

torma. An offering cake used in tantric rituals. In Tibet, tormas were usually made of tsampa, but other edibles such as biscuits will suffice.

transmigratory beings. Sentient beings who pass from one realm to another, taking rebirth within cyclic existence.

Tripitaka. See Three Baskets.

true existence. The type of concrete, real existence from its own side that everything appears to possess; in fact, everything is empty of true existence.

truth body. See dharmakaya.

tsampa. Roasted barley flour; a Tibetan staple food.

Tsongkhapa, Lama Je (1357–1419). Founder of the Geluk tradition of Tibetan Buddhism and revitalizer of many sutra and tantra lineages and the monastic tradition in Tibet. *See also* Lamrim Chenmo.

tummo. Inner fire, the energy residing at the navel chakra, aroused during the completion stage of highest yoga tantra and used to bring the energy winds into the central channel. It is also called *inner* or *psychic heat. See also* six yogas of Naropa.

Tushita (Ganden). The Joyous Land. The pure land of the thousand buddhas of this eon, where the future buddha, Maitreya, and Lama Tsongkhapa reside.

twelve deeds of the Buddha. The deeds that Guru Shakyamuni Buddha and all buddhas perform. They are descending from Tushita Heaven, entering the mother's womb, birth, studying arts and handicrafts, enjoying life in the palace, renunciation, undertaking ascetic practices, going to Bodhgaya, defeating the negative forces (Mara), attaining enlightenment, turning the wheel of Dharma, and entering parinirvana.

twelve links of dependent origination (*dvadashanga-pratityasamutpada*; *tendrel yenlak chunyi*). Also called the *twelve dependent-related limbs* or *branches*; the twelve steps in the evolution of cyclic existence: ignorance, karmic formation, consciousness, name and form, sensory fields, contact, feelings, attachment, grasping, becoming (existence), birth, and aging and death. This is Shakyamuni Buddha's explanation of how karma and delusion bind sentient beings to samsara, causing them to be reborn into suffering again and again; depicted pictorially in the Tibetan Wheel of Life.

two bodhichittas. Conventional bodhichitta, wishing to attain enlightenment in order to free all sentient beings from suffering, and ultimate bodhichitta, the realization of emptiness within a bodhi-sattva's mental continuum. *See also* conventional bodhichitta; ulti-mate bodhichitta.

two merits. Also called the *two accumulations* or *two types of merit*: the merit of virtue (also called the *merit of fortune* or the *collection of merit*), which develops the method side of the path by practicing generosity and so forth; and the merit of (transcendental) wisdom (also called the *collection of wisdom*), which develops the wisdom side of the path by meditation on emptiness and so forth.

two obscurations (*dvi-avarana*; *drip nyi*). Deluded mental states that block the attainment of liberation and enlightenment. They are the grosser kind, called disturbing-thought obscurations or obscurations to liberation (*kleshavarana*, *nyöndrip*); and the subtle obscurations, the imprints left when those are purified, called obscurations to knowledge or obscurations to enlightenment (*jneyavarana*, *shedrip*).

two truths (*satyadvaya*; *denpa nyi*). The two ways of relating to phe-nomena: conventional or all-obscuring truth (*samvritisatya*; *kundzop denpa*), which is the truth to a worldly mind; and ultimate truth (*paramarthasatya*; *döndam denpa*), the truth to a mind engaged in ultimate analysis.

ultimate bodhichitta (*dondam jangchup sem*). The nondual transcenden-tal realization of emptiness within a bodhisattva's mental contin-uum. *See also* two bodhichittas; conventional bodhichitta.

vajra (*dorjé*). Literally, "adamantine"; the four- or five-spoke implement used in tantric practice.

Vajrasattva (*Dorjé Sempa*). Male meditational deity symbolizing the inherent purity of all buddhas. A major tantric purification practice for removing obstacles created by negative karma and the breaking of vows.

Vajrayana. Another name for *tantra*; the Adamantine Vehicle; the sec-ond of the two Mahayana paths. It is also called *Tantrayana* or *Man-trayana*. This is the quickest vehicle of Buddhism, as it allows certain practitioners to attain enlightenment within a single lifetime.

view of the changeable aggregates. One of the five extreme views where we see our constantly changing aggregates as permanent and uncaused. Also called the *reifying view of the perishable aggregates.*

Vinaya. The Buddha's teachings on ethical discipline (morality), monastic conduct, and so forth; one of the Three Baskets. *See also* Abhidharma; Sutra.

virtuous mental factors. One of the six groups of mental factors, the factor that turns the overall apprehension of the object from its opposite, nondesire from desire, and so forth. There are eleven: faith, shame, embarrassment, nondesire, nonhatred, nonignorance, effort, pliancy, conscientiousness, equanimity, and nonharmfulness. *See also* mental factors.

vows. Precepts taken on the basis of refuge at all levels of Buddhist practice. *Pratimoksha* precepts (vows of individual liberation) are the main vows in the Hinayana tradition and are taken by monks, nuns, and laypeople; they are the basis of all other vows. Bodhisattva and tantric precepts are the main vows in the Mahayana tradition. *See also* Vinaya.

Wheel of Life. The depiction of cyclic existence, showing the six realms cycling around the hub of ignorance, greed, and hatred symbolized by a pig, a rooster, and a snake, with the twelve links of dependent origination as the outer rim, all in the jaws and claws of Yama, the Lord of Death. *See also* the six realms; twelves links of dependent origination.

wisdom. Different levels of insight into the nature of reality. There are, for example, the three wisdoms of hearing, contemplation, and meditation. Ultimately, there is the wisdom of realizing emptiness, which frees beings from cyclic existence and eventually brings them to enlightenment. The complete and perfect accumulation of wisdom results in dharmakaya.

wish-granting jewel. Also called *wish-fulfilling jewel.* A jewel that brings its possessor everything that he or she desires.

wishing bodhichitta. *See* aspirational bodhichitta.

worldly concern. *See* eight worldly dharmas.

wrong view. Any mistaken or deluded understanding, as opposed to deluded minds such as the three poisons, that leads to suffering. In Buddhism there are various ways of defining wrong views. The most common is as the last of the ten nonvirtues, heresy (*logta*), but it can also be either all five of the afflicted views among the unwholesome mental factors—the view of the transitory aggregates, extreme views, views of superiority of belief, the views of superiority of morality and discipline, and mistaken or wrong views—or the last one alone.

yama. A guardian of the hell realm.

Yama. The Lord of Death, seen on the Wheel of Life.

Yamantaka. Also known as *Vajra Bhairava* and *Dorjé Jigje.* A male meditational deity from the father tantra class of highest yoga tantra.

Yeshe, Lama (1935–84). Born and educated in Tibet, he fled to India, where he met his chief disciple, Lama Zopa Rinpoche. They began teaching Westerners at Kopan Monastery in 1969 and founded the Foundation for the Preservation of the Mahayana Tradition (FPMT) in 1975.

yoga. Literally, "to yoke." The spiritual discipline to which one yokes oneself in order to achieve enlightenment.

yoga tantra. The third of four classes of Buddhist tantra, with an increased emphasis on internal activities compared with the previous two tantras. *See also* four classes of tantra; kriya tantra; charya tantra; and highest yoga tantra.

NOTES

....

1. Shantideva 1.11, as translated in Batchelor 1979, 3.
2. Rinpoche often refers to the historical Buddha as Guru Shakyamuni Buddha, placing "Guru" before his name to remind us of the inseparability of our own guru and the Buddha.
3. These are the six realms of existence of this, the desire realm: the realms of the hell beings (*naraka*), the hungry ghosts (*preta*), the animals (*tiryanc*), the human beings (*manushya*), the demigods (*asura*), and the gods (*deva* or *sura*).
4. The different types of mental factors are the omnipresent mental factors, the object-determining mental factors, the virtuous mental factors, the root delusions, the secondary delusions, and the variable mental factors. See Tsering 2006, 21–94, and Rabten 1978, 99–162.
5. Tsongkhapa (1357–1419) was the founder of the Geluk tradition of Tibetan Buddhism.
6. The Buddhadharma can be divided into two: the Hinayana, or Lesser Vehicle, teachings, which are aimed at individual liberation; and the Mahayana, or Great Vehicle, teachings, which are aimed at attaining enlightenment. The Mahayana can be subdivided further into Mahayana Paramitayana, or Bodhisattva Vehicle, and Mahayana Vajrayana, or Tantric Vehicle.
7. There are two levels of obscurations or hindrances that block our spiritual development: the gross disturbing-thought obscurations (*kleshavarana, nyöndrip*) that prevent liberation from samsara; and obscurations to enlightenment (*jneyavarana, shedrip*), the subtle hindrances that prevent omniscience.
8. The ten nonvirtues are general actions to be avoided so as not to create negative karma: three of body (killing, stealing, sexual misconduct), four of speech (lying, speaking harshly, slandering, and gossiping), and three of mind (covetousness, ill will, and wrong views).
9. Khunu Lama Tenzin Gyaltsen (1894–1977), also known as Negi Lama and Khunu Rinpoche, was an Indian scholar of Sanskrit and Tibetan and a great master and teacher of the Rimé (nonsectarian) tradition of Tibetan Buddhism. He famously gave teachings to His Holiness the Dalai Lama on Shantideva's *Guide to the Bodhisattva's Way of Life*. He was also a guru of Lama Zopa Rinpoche. His wonderful text *The Jewel Lamp: A Praise of Bodhichitta* is translated into English as *Vast as the Heavens, Deep as the Sea*.
10. Khunu Lama 21, as translated in Sparham 1999, 31.
11. Shantideva, *Guide to the Bodhisattva's Way of Life* 1.21–22.
12. Shantideva 3.29–30.
13. Shantideva 1.7.
14. Abhisamayalamkara, one of the five main texts studied in the great Geluk monasteries along with Gunaprabha's *Vinaya Sutra*, Chandrakirti's *Entering the Middle*

Way (*Madhyamakavatara*), Vasubandhu's *Treasury of Knowledge* (*Abhidharma-kosha*), and Dharmakirti's *A Commentary on Dignaga's Compendium of Valid Cognition* (*Pramanavarttika*).

15. *Kadam* refers to the order of Tibetan Buddhism, the forerunner of the Geluk school, founded in the eleventh century by Atisha, Dromtönpa, and their followers, the Kadampa geshes. Kadampa geshes are renowned for their practice of thought transformation.

16. *Dvadashanga-pratityasamutpada, tendrel yenlak chunyi.* Also called the twelve dependent-related limbs or branches, these are the twelve steps in the evolution of cyclic existence: ignorance, karmic formation, consciousness, name and form, sensory fields, contact, feelings, attachment, grasping, becoming (existence), birth, and aging and death. This is Shakyamuni Buddha's explanation of how delusion and karma bind sentient beings to samsara, causing them to be reborn into suffering again and again.

17. See Gyaltchok and Gyalsten 2006, 517, for the root text, and the same text, 521–66, for commentaries on the four clingings.

18. The worldly concerns that generally motivate the actions of ordinary beings. See Rinpoche's *How to Practice Dharma* (Zopa 2012).

19. Taken from *Essential Buddhist Prayers*, Vol. 1. 2011 (FPMT), 95.

20. A rosary of beads for counting mantras.

21. The step-by-step instructions for practicing meditation on a particular deity.

22. There are three realms of existence: the *desire realm* (*kamadhatu, döpé kham*), which is six realms including the human realm, where beings are controlled by desire for the objects of the six senses; the *form realm* (*rupadhatu, zukkyi kham*), which is achieved through great concentration; and the *formless realm* (*arupyadhatu, zukkyi pä kham*), which is achieved through concentration so strong that the beings there have transcended a physical body.

23. Taken from *Essential Buddhist Prayers*, Vol. 1. 2011 (FPMT), 94.

24. Buddhism explains that there are five aggregates (*skandha*), five psychophysical constituents that make up a sentient being: form, feeling, discriminative awareness, compositional factors, and consciousness.

25. Shantideva 1.6.

26. The intermediate state, or *bardo*, is the state between death and the next rebirth.

27. Taken from *Essential Buddhist Prayers*, Vol. 1. 2011 (FPMT), 98.

28. Shantideva 5.17.

29. See Pabongka, as translated in Richards 1991, 127.

30. Shantideva 5.18.

31. Shantideva 5.19.

32. Translated by Thupten Jinpa in Gyaltchok and Gyalsten 2006, 276. *Eight Verses on Mind Training* is the seminal mind training (*lojong*) text written by Langri Tangpa (1054–1123), an important Kadampa geshe.

33. The *eight freedoms* are freedom from being born as a hell being, as a hungry ghost, as an animal, as a long-life god, in a dark age when no buddha has descended, as a barbarian, as a fool, or as a heretic. The *ten richnesses* are being born as a human being, in a Dharma country, with perfect mental and physical faculties, free from the five immediate negativities, with devotion to the Buddha's teachings, when a

buddha has descended, when the teachings have been revealed, when the complete teachings still exist, when there are still followers of the teachings, and having the necessary conditions to practice Dharma, such as the kindness of others. See Rinpoche's *The Perfect Human Rebirth* (Zopa 2013).

34. Shantideva 3.28.

35. Milarepa (1040–1123) was Tibet's great yogi who achieved enlightenment in his lifetime under the tutelage of his guru, Marpa, who was a contemporary of Atisha. He was one of the founders of the Kagyü school.

36. Shantideva 1.4.

37. According to Buddhist cosmology, there are four world systems clustered around Mount Meru, one for each cardinal point. Ours is the southern continent, Jambudvipa (Rose-apple Land, Dzambuling), the others being Godaniya (Cattle Gift Land, Balangchö) in the west, Kuru (Unpleasant Sound, Draminyen) in the north, and Videha (Tall Body Land, Lüphakpo) in the east. These continents appear in the mandala offering and are part of the symbolic representation of the entire universe.

38. *Chakras* are energy wheels along the central channel upon which the concentration is directed, especially during the completion stage of highest yoga tantra. The main chakras are the crown, throat, heart, navel, and secret place (the sex organ).

39. Although in Tibetan Buddhist teachings Tushita (Ganden) usually refers to the Tushita pure land—the "Joyous Land," the pure land where the thousand buddhas of this fortunate eon, including Lama Tsongkhapa and Maitreya, abide—in this instance it refers to the Tushita god realm, situated around Mount Meru with many other god realms, including the Heaven of Thirty-Three, the highest of the god realm abodes in Buddhist cosmology, atop Mount Meru and ruled by Indra.

40. Shantideva 4.18–20. The footnote in Batchelor 1987 for verse 20 quotes the sutra reference: "O monks, suppose that this great earth were to become an ocean upon which a single yoke were being tossed about by the wind and thus being moved from here to there. If under that ocean there were a blind turtle, do you think it would be easy for it to insert its head into that yoke when it rises to the surface only once every hundred years?" "No, Lord, it would not," replied the monks. The Lord then said, "In a similar fashion, O monks, it is extremely hard to obtain the human state."

41. See Rinpoche's full explanation of the symbolism of this analogy in *The Perfect Human Rebirth* (Zopa 2013), 104–6.

42. Shantideva 4.24–25.

43. Shantideva 1.5.

44. Shantideva 4.17.

45. Shantideva 1.23–24.

46. Khunu Lama vv. 338–39.

47. Gyatso 1990, 54.

48. Shantideva 2.54–56.

49. Tsongkhapa vv. 21–22, as translated in Jinpa 2007, 3.

50. Roasted barley flour; the staple food of Tibet.

51. Six advanced tantric practices devised by the great Indian pandit Naropa (1016–1100); they are the yoga of inner fire (*tummo*), illusory body (*gyulu*), clear light

(*ösel*), the dream state (*milam*), the intermediate state (*bardo*), and the transference of consciousness (*powa*).

52. Shantideva 1.9.

53. Khunu Lama v. 129.

54. Pabongka, as translated in Richards 1991, 500.

55. Quoted in Pabongka, as translated in Richards 1991, 507; as translated in Tharchin and Engle 2001, this is attributed to the Kashyapa chapter.

56. *Sugata* is an epithet for a buddha; literally, "one gone (*gata*) to bliss (*su*)."

57. Shantideva 1.32–33.

58. Shantideva 1.27.

59. The fourth-century Indian master who received teachings directly from Maitreya Buddha.

60. Atisha vv. 15–17, as translated in Sonam 1997, 150.

61. Khunu Lama v. 10.

62. Nagarjuna 1.20–21, as translated in Hopkins 1998, 96.

63. Khunu Lama v. 42.

64. Khunu Lama v. 41.

65. Shantideva 1.14.

66. Shantideva 1.10.

67. Khunu Lama v. 286.

68. Khunu Lama v. 26.

69. A *puja*, literally "offering," is a religious ceremony, usually used to describe an offering ceremony such as the Offering to the Spiritual Master.

70. Shantideva 1.8.

71. Khunu Lama v. 325.

72. The bodhisattva's path; another term for Paramitayana, the nontantric aspect of the Mahayana.

73. The sixth-century CE Indian Buddhist philosopher who wrote commentaries on Nagarjuna's philosophy. His best-known work is *A Guide to the Middle Way*.

74. Khunu Lama v. 298.

75. From *Visualizing Yourself as the Deity*, www.lamayeshe.com/article/e-letter-no-35-february-2006, taken from the February 2006 LYWA newsletter, from an edited transcript of Lama Yeshe's teaching at Manjushri Institute, July 1977. Accessed 08/01/2018.

76. *Flower Garland Sutra*, as translated in Cleary, 288.

77. Serlingpa was a renowned tenth-century Sumatran master. Atisha traveled to Sumatra and for twelve years received teachings on thought transformation (*lojong*) and bodhichitta from him.

78. Chekawa Yeshe Dorje (1101–75). His *Seven-Point Mind Training* was inspired by Langri Tangpa's *Eight Verses on Mind Training*. Thupten Jinpa's translation of *Seven-Point Mind Training* is available here: www.wisdompubs.org/landing/seven-point-mind-training. See also Gyaltchok and Gyalsten 2006, 83, for the root text, and 87–132 for commentaries. See also Rabten and Dhargyey 1977.

79. Shantideva 1.15.

80. Shantideva 1.17.

81. *Guru Puja* v. 97.

82. Translated by Thupten Jinpa in Gyaltchok and Gyalsten 2006, 276.

83. This is verse 4: "When I encounter beings of unpleasant character / and those oppressed by intense negative karma and suffering, / as though finding a treasure of precious jewels, / I will train myself to cherish them, for they are so rarely found."

84. Translated by Thupten Jinpa in Gyaltchok and Gyalsten 2006, 276.

85. Khunu Lama v. 72.

86. Khunu Lama v. 31.

87. See also Pabongka, as translated in Richards 1991, 401.

88. Nagarjuna v. 68.

89. Sangpo v. 10, as translated by Ruth Sonam 1997. See also Sonam 1997.

90. Chandragomin v. 99, as translated in Hahn 1999, 117.

91. In Pabongka, as translated in Richards 1991, 529–30. Pabongka Rinpoche differentiates "love" (*maitri, jampa*) and "love through the force of attraction" (*yiong jampa*). Geshe Sopa calls *yiong jampa* "affectionate love" (Sopa 2008, 85). I have been unable to find a Sanskrit equivalent of the Tibetan *yiong jampa*.

92. Nagarjuna vv. 283–85, as translated in Hopkins 1998, 130–31.

93. Chandrakirti 1.1–2, as translated in Padmakara Translation Group, 2002, 59.

94. Vows to abandon killing; stealing; lying; sexual contact; taking intoxicants; sitting on high seats or beds; eating at the wrong time; and singing, dancing, and wearing perfumes and jewelry for one day.

95. Namtösé, Vaishravana in Sanskrit, is one of the Four Great Kings, the protectors of the Buddha's Vinaya.

96. *Guru Puja* v. 89.

97. Quoted in Pabongka, as translated in Richards 1991, 247. This is commonly attributed to a quote in Prajnavarman's *Commentary to the Collection of Uplifting Sayings*, although this is not verified. (See Pabongka, as translated in Tharchin and Engle 1990, 11n11.)

98. Shantideva 8.131.

99. Related to this, but with more points, Lama Zopa Rinpoche has taught what he calls the Mahayana Equilibrium Meditation, which is included in this book. See appendix 2, "The Mahayana Equilibrium Meditation."

100. Shantideva 5.80.

101. Shantideva 6.112–13.

102. *Guru Puja* v. 92.

103. Sangpo vv. 15–16, as translated by Ruth Sonam 1997

104. I have been unable to find a reference for this quote, however, it closely resembles the sutra *In Praise of Worshipping Sentient Beings* (*Sattvaradhanastava*) put into verse by Nagarjuna, as translated in Jnana and Devi: "(4) Benefit to beings, even for a moment, is the worship of me / for it pleases the mind of the worshiped. / With a harmful nature, or causing injury to others, / even the finest offerings do not become the worship of me. . . . (6) The highest benefit to beings itself is the supreme worship to me. / Harming sentient beings is the worst harm to me. / Since my happiness and suffering is same as that of beings, / in what way is the one causing harm to beings my disciple?"

105. *Guru Puja* v. 90.
106. Shantideva 4.30–31
107. Paraphrase of Shantideva 5.7–8.
108. *Guru Puja* v. 91.
109. The four elements of earth, fire, water, and wind represent the elemental aspects of our body: its form, its heat, its liquidity—the blood, mucus, and so forth—and its winds, which move within the body.
110. Shantideva 8.129–30.
111. Shantideva 8.134.
112. Shantideva 8.135.
113. Shantideva 8.136.
114. Chekawa, as translated by Thupten Jinpa in Gyaltchok and Gyalsten 2006, 83.
115. Shantideva 6.42.
116. Translated by Thupten Jinpa in Gyaltchok and Gyalsten 2006, 276.
117. Shantideva 8.172.
118. Khunu Lama v. 162.
119. *Guru Puja* v. 94.
120. The eight common or mundane siddhis (*asadharanasiddhi, tünmong gingödrub*) are attainments of psychic power acquired as byproducts of the spiritual path, including invisibility, the ability to fly or travel great distances extremely quickly, and so forth. Four of the five forms of clairvoyance—divine hearing, knowing others' thoughts, remembering past lives, knowing the various rebirths of sentient beings—fall into common siddhis and so are not considered helpful in developing toward enlightenment; the fifth clairvoyance—knowledge of the exhaustion of contaminations—can only be known by arhats and buddhas.
121. Sangpo v.11, as translated by Ruth Sonam 1997.
122. Shantideva 6.14.
123. Shantideva 8.95, 99. This section is written as a debate between the self-cherishing mind and the selfless one, hence the question posed in the second verse.
124. Shantideva 8.111–12.
125. Shantideva 5.109.
126. Chekawa, as translated by Thupten Jinpa in Gyaltchok and Gyalsten 2006, 83.
127. For the actual meditation, see appendix 4, "A Tonglen Meditation."
128. Khunu Lama v. 296.
129. Shantideva 3.10, 18–19, 22.
130. Some texts state that the friend should be in front of you and the enemy behind. In *The Wish-Fulfilling Golden Sun* (Zopa 1973), Rinpoche suggests another configuration: all sentient beings surrounding you, with your mother seated to your left and your father to your right. In front of you, an enemy; behind you, your dearest friend; to the side, a stranger. Rinpoche often advises to visualize it in whichever way is most effective for you. See the meditation that follows in the text.
131. Nagarjuna v. 68.
132. Nagarjuna v. 67.

BIBLIOGRAPHY

Sutras (listed by English title)

Flower Garland Sutra (*Avatamsakasutra*; *Mdo phal po che*). Published as *The Flower Ornament Scripture: A Translation of the Avatamsaka Sutra*, 1984, 1986, 1987, 1989, 1993. Translated by Thomas Cleary. Boston: Shambhala Publications.

Heart of Wisdom Sutra (*Prajnaparamitahrdayasutra*; *Shes rab kyi pha rol tu phyin pa'i snying po'i mdo*). Foundation for the Preservation of the Mahayana Tradition. Accessed 07/31/2018. https://fpmt.org /education/teachings/sutras/heart-sutra.

King of Samadhi Sutra (*Samadhirajasutra*; *Ting nge 'dzin gyi rgyal po'i mdo*). 1994. Commentary by Thrangu Rinpoche. Translated by Erik Schmidt. Hong Kong: Rangjung Yeshe Publications.

Sutra of Golden Light. The King of the Glorious Sutras Called the Exalted Supreme Golden Light (*Arya Suvarnaprabhasottamasutrendrarajanamamahayanasutra*; *'Phags pa gser 'od dam pa mdo sde'i dbang po'i rgyal po zhes bya ba theg pa chen po'i mdo*). 2010. Portland, OR: FPMT. Accessed 07/31/2018. https://fpmt.org/education/teachings /sutras/golden-light-sutra.

Indian and Tibetan Works

Asanga, and Maitreya. 1992. *Ornament of Clear Realization* (*Abhisamayalankara*; *Mngon par rtogs pa'i rgyan*). Published as *Abhisamayalankara Prajnaparamita Upadesa Sastra: The Work of Bodhisattva Maitreya*. Edited by Theodore Stcherbatsky and Eugene Obermiller. New Delhi: Sri Satguru.

————. 2005. *The Adornment of the Mahayana Sutras* (*Mahayanasutra-lankara*; *Mdo sde rgyan*). Published as *Universal Vehicle Discourse Literature.* Translated by Lozang Jamspal, Robert Thurman, and American Institute of Buddhist Studies. New York: American Institute of Buddhist Studies.

Atisha. 1997. *Lamp for the Path to Enlightenment* (*Bodhipathapradipa*; *Byang chub lam gyi sgron ma*). Published as *Atisha's Lamp for the Path to Enlightenment.* Commentary by Geshe Sonam Rinchen. Translated and edited by Ruth Sonam. Ithaca, NY: Snow Lion Publications.

Chandragomin, and Matricheta. 1999. *Letter to a Great King* (*Maha-rajakanishkalekha*; *Rgyal po chen po ka nis ka la springs pa'i spring yig*) by Matricheta and *Letter to a Disciple* (*Shishyalekha; Slob ma la springs pa'i spring yig*) by Chandragomin. Published as *Invitation to Enlightenment.* Translated by Michael Hahn. Berkeley, CA: Dharma Publishing.

Chandrakirti. 2004. *A Guide to the Middle Way* (*Madhyamakavatara*; *Dbu ma la 'jug pa'i tshig le'ur byas pa*). Published as *Introduction to the Middle Way, Chandrakirti's Madhyamakavatara.* Translated by Padmakara Translation Group. Boston: Shambhala Publications. Also published as *Introduction to the Middle Way: Chandrakirti's Madhyamakavatara with Commentary by Dzongsar Jamyang Khyentse Rinpoche.* 1996, 2002. Edited by Alex Trisoglio. Translated by Jakob Leschly. Dordogne, France: Khyentse Foundation.

Chekawa Yeshe Dorje. 2006. *Seven-Point Mind Training* (*Blo sbyong don bdun ma*). In *Mind Training: The Great Collection*, translated by Thupten Jinpa, 83–85. Boston: Wisdom Publications.

Chökyi Gyaltsen, Panchen Losang, and Jamphäl Lhundrub. 2011. *Guru Puja* (*Lama Chöpa Jorchö*). Compiled and edited by Lama Zopa Rinpoche. Portland, OR: FPMT.

Dharmakirti. 2000. *A Commentary on Dignaga's Compendium of Valid Cognition* (*Pramanavarttika*; *Tshad ma rnam 'grel*). Published as *Dharmakirti's Pramanavarttika.* Translated by Tom J. F. Tillemans. Vienna: Verlag Der Osterriechischen.

Dharmarakshita. 2006. *The Wheel of Sharp Weapons* (*Blo sbyong mtshon cha 'khor lo*). In *Mind Training: The Great Collection*, translated by Thupten Jinpa, 133–53. Boston: Wisdom Publications.

Khunu Lama Tenzin Gyaltsen. 1999. *The Jewel Lamp: A Praise of Bodhichitta* (*Byang chub sems kyi bstod pa rin chen sgron ma*). Published as *Vast as the Heavens, Deep as the Sea*. Translated by Gareth Sparham. Boston: Wisdom Publications.

Gyaltchok, Shonu, and Konchok Gyaltsen, comps. 2006. *Mind Training: The Great Collection* (*Theg pa chen po blo sbyong brgya rtsa*). Translated and edited by Thupten Jinpa. Boston: Wisdom Publications.

Nagarjuna. 1995a. *The Fundamental Wisdom of the Middle Way* (*Mulamadhyamakakarika*; *Dbu ma rtsa ba'i tshig le'ur byas pa shes rab ces bya ba*). Published as *The Fundamental Wisdom of the Middle Way: Nagarjuna's Mulamadhyamakakarika*. Translated by Jay L. Garfield. New York: Oxford University Press.

———. 1995b. 2005. *Friendly Letter* (*Suhrillekha*; *Bshes pa'i spring yig*). With a commentary by Kangyur Rinpoche. Translated by Padmakara Translation Group. Ithaca, NY: Snow Lion Publications. Also published as *Nagarjuna's Letter*. 1979. Translated by Geshe Lobsang Tharchin and Artemus B. Engle. Dharamsala, India: Library of Tibetan Works and Archives.

———. 1998. *Precious Garland of Advice for the King* (*Rajaparikatharatnavali*; *Rgyal po la gtam bya ba rin po che'i phreng ba*). Published as *Nagarjuna's Precious Garland: Buddhist Advice for Living and Liberation*. Translated by Jeffrey Hopkins. Ithaca, NY: Snow Lion Publications.

———. n.d. *In Praise of Worshipping Sentient Beings* (*Sattvaradhanastava*; *Sems can mgu bar bya ba'i bstod pa*). Translated by Prabodha Jnana and Abhaya Devi. Way of Bodhi. Accessed 08/01/2018. https://www.wayofbodhi.org/in-praise-of-worshipping-sentient-beings.

Pabongka Rinpoche. 1991. *Liberation in the Palm of Your Hand* (*Rnam grol lag bcangs*). Translated by Michael Richards. Boston: Wisdom Publications. Also published in three parts as: *Liberation in Our Hands: Part One—The Preliminaries*, 1990; *Liberation in Our Hands:*

Part Two—The Fundamentals, 1994; *Liberation in Our Hands: Part Three—The Ultimate Goals*, 2001.Translated by Geshe Lobsang Tharchin and Artemus B. Engle. Howell, NJ: Mahayana Sutra and Tantra Press.

Sangpo, Thokmé. 1997. *Thirty-Seven Practices of the Bodhisattva* (*Rgyal sras lag len so bdun ma*). Commentary by Geshe Sonam Rinchen. Edited and translated by Ruth Sonam. Boston: Snow Lion Publications.

Shantideva. 1987. *A Guide to the Bodhisattva's Way of Life* (*Bodhisattvacaryavatara*; *Byang chub sems dpa'i spyod pa la 'jug pa*). Translated by Stephen Batchelor. Dharamsala, India: Library of Tibetan Works and Archive.

Tangpa, Langri. 2000. *Eight Verses on Mind Training* (*Blo sbyong tshigs rkang brgyad ma*). Published as *Transforming the Mind: Eight Verses on Generating Compassion and Transforming Your Life*. By His Holiness the Dalai Lama. New York: Thorsons.

Tayang, Lama Losang. 1984. *Hundred and Eight Verses in Praise of Great Compassion* (*Snying rje chen po la bstod pa'i tshigs bcad brgya rtsa brgyad pa*). Published as *Precious Crystal Rosary*. Translated by José Ignacio Cabezón. Mysore, India: Mysore Printing and Publishing House.

Tsongkhapa, Je. 2000. *Hymns of Experience of the Steps on the Path* (*Lam rim nyams mgur*). Published as *Songs of Spiritual Experience: Condensed Points of the Stages of the Path*. Translated by Geshe Thubten Jinpa. Accessed 08/22/2018. http://www.tibetanclassics.org/html-assets/Songs%20of%20Experience.pdf.

———. 2000, 2002, 2004. *The Great Treatise on the Path to Enlightenment* (*Lam rim chen mo*). 3 vols. Translated by the Lamrim Chenmo Translation Committee. Ithaca, NY: Snow Lion Publications.

Vasubandhu. 1991. *Treasury of Knowledge* (*Abhidharmakoshabhashya*, *Chos mngon pa'i mdzod kyi bshad pa*). Translated by Louis de le Vallée Poussin and Leo M. Pruden. Berkeley, CA: Asian Humanities Press.

English-Language Texts

FPMT (Foundation for the Preservation of the Mahayana Tradition). 2006, 2008, 2011. *Essential Buddhist Prayers: An FPMT Prayer Book, Volume 1, Basic Prayers and Practices.* Portland, OR: FPMT.

Gyatso, Tenzin, His Holiness the Fourteenth Dalai Lama. 1990. *My Tibet.* London: Thames and Hudson.

Lati Rinbochay. 1980. *Mind in Tibetan Buddhism.* Translated by Elizabeth Napper. Ithaca, NY: Snow Lion Publications.

Rabten, Geshe. 1978. *The Mind and Its Functions.* Le Mont Pèlerin, Switzerland: Editions Rabten Choeling.

Rabten, Geshe, and Geshe Ngawang Dhargyey. 1977. *Advice from a Spiritual Friend.* Boston: Wisdom Publications.

Sopa, Geshe Lhundub. 2004, 2005, 2008, 2016, 2017. *Steps on the Path to Enlightenment.* 5 vols. Boston: Wisdom Publications.

Tsering, Geshe Tashi. 2005. *The Four Noble Truths.* Boston: Wisdom Publications.

———. 2006. *Buddhist Psychology.* Boston: Wisdom Publications.

Zopa, Lama Thubten. 1973. *The Wish-Fulfilling Golden Sun of the Mahayana Thought Training.* Boston: Lama Yeshe Wisdom Archive. Accessed 08/01/2018. https://www.lamayeshe.com/article/wish-fulfilling-golden-sun-mahayana-thought-training. For the original edition see also https://fpmt.org/wp-content/uploads/education/teachings/texts/prayers-practices/wishfulfilling_golden_sun_c5.pdf. Accessed 08/01/2018.

———. 2001a. *The Door to Satisfaction: The Heart Advice of a Tibetan Buddhist Master.* Boston: Wisdom Publications.

———. 2001b. *Transforming Problems into Happiness.* Boston: Wisdom Publications.

———. 2008. *Heart Advice for Death and Dying.* Portland, OR: FPMT.

———. 2012. *How to Practice Dharma: Teachings on the Eight Worldly Dharmas.* Boston: Lama Yeshe Wisdom Archive.

———. 2013. *The Perfect Human Rebirth: Freedom and Richness on the Path to Enlightenment.* Boston: Lama Yeshe Wisdom Archive.

Zopa, Lama Thubten, and Kathleen McDonald. 2010. *Wholesome Fear: Transforming Your Anxiety about Impermanence and Death.* Boston: Wisdom Publications.

INDEX

ABOUT THE AUTHOR

....

LAMA ZOPA RINPOCHE is one of the most internationally renowned masters of Tibetan Buddhism, working and teaching ceaselessly on almost every continent.

He is the spiritual director and cofounder of the Foundation for the Preservation of the Mahayana Tradition (FPMT), an international network of Buddhist projects, including monasteries in six countries and meditation centers in more than thirty; health and nutrition clinics, and clinics specializing in the treatment of leprosy and polio; as well as hospices, schools, publishing activities, and prison outreach projects worldwide.

Lama Zopa Rinpoche is the author of numerous books, including *The Four Noble Truths*, *Transforming Problems into Happiness*, *How to Enjoy Death*, *Ultimate Healing*, *The Door to Satisfaction*, *How to Be Happy*, *Wholesome Fear*, *Wisdom Energy*, and *Dear Lama Zopa*, all from Wisdom Publications.

ABOUT THE EDITOR

GORDON MCDOUGALL was director of Cham Tse Ling, the FPMT's Hong Kong center, for two years in the 1980s and worked for Jamyang Buddhist Centre in London from 2000 to 2007. He helped develop the Foundation of Buddhist Thought study program and administered it for seven years. Since 2008 he has been editing Lama Zopa Rinpoche's lamrim teachings for Lama Yeshe Wisdom Archive's FPMT Lineage series.

WHAT TO READ NEXT
FROM WISDOM PUBLICATIONS

....

How to Be Happy
Lama Zopa Rinpoche

"Rinpoche works with determination and great sincerity in the service of Buddha's teachings and sentient beings."—His Holiness the Dalai Lama

Ultimate Healing
The Power of Compassion
Lama Zopa Rinpoche

"This truly is an awesome book."—Lillian Too

Transforming Problems into Happiness
Foreword by His Holiness the Dalai Lama
Lama Zopa Rinpoche

"A masterfully brief statement of Buddhist teachings on the nature of humanity and human suffering. . . This book should be read as the words of a wise, loving parent."—*Utne Reader*

How to Enjoy Death
Preparing to Meet Life's Final Challenge without Fear
Lama Zopa Rinpoche

A beautifully crafted limited edition!

Introduction to Tantra
Lama Thubten Yeshe
Edited by Jonathan Landaw
Foreword by Philip Glass

"The best introductory work on Tibetan Buddhist tantra available today."—Janet Gyatso, Harvard University

Bliss of Inner Fire
Heart Practice of the Six Yogas of Naropa
Lama Thubten Yeshe
Foreword by Lama Zopa Rinpoche

"An impressive contribution to the growing body of Buddhist literature for an English-reading audience."—*The Midwest Book Review*

Becoming Vajrasattva
The Tantric Path of Purification
Lama Thubten Yeshe
Foreword by Lama Zopa Rinpoche

"Lama Yeshe was capable of translating Tibetan Buddhist thought not only through language, but by his presence, gestures, and way of life."—Gelek Rimpoche, author of *Good Life, Good Death*

The Four Noble Truths
A Guide to Everyday Life
Lama Zopa Rinpoche

The Buddha's profound teachings on the four noble truths are illuminated by a Tibetan master simply and directly, so that readers gain an immediate and personal understanding of the causes and conditions that give rise to suffering as well as the spiritual life as the path to liberation.

About Wisdom Publications

Wisdom Publications is the leading publisher of classic and contemporary Buddhist books and practical works on mindfulness. To learn more about us or to explore our other books, please visit our website at wisdompubs .org or contact us at the address below.

Wisdom Publications
199 Elm Street
Somerville, MA 02144 USA

We are a 501(c)(3) organization, and donations in support of our mission are tax deductible.

Wisdom Publications is affiliated with the Foundation for the Preservation of the Mahayana Tradition (FPMT).